AF477382

INDIA THROUGH AMERICAN EYES
100 YEARS AGO

India Through American Eyes 100 Years Ago

edited by

PRAN NEVILE

PRIMUS BOOKS
An imprint of Ratna Sagar P. Ltd.
Virat Bhavan
Mukherjee Nagar Commercial Complex
Delhi 110 009

Offices at
CHENNAI LUCKNOW
AGRA AHMEDABAD BANGALORE COIMBATORE DEHRADUN GUWAHATI HYDERABAD
JAIPUR KANPUR KOCHI KOLKATA MADURAI MUMBAI PATNA RANCHI VARANASI

First published 2014

ISBN: 978-93-80607-56-6

Published by Primus Books

Laser typeset by Digigrafics
Gulmohar Park, New Delhi 110 049

Printed and bound in India by Replika Press Pvt. Ltd.

To the Memory of

SAVITRI

My wife
friend
and
companion
for over 66 years

Contents

Preface

It WAS IN 1993 WHILE RESEARCHING in the US Library of Congress for my book *Nautch Girls of India* that I stumbled upon a fascinating eyewitness account of a nautch performance at Bombay by an American writer Lily Strickland Anderson, published in the August 1925 issue of *ASIA: The American Magazine on the Orient.* I was struck by the tone and tenor of the account and the writer's eloquent appreciation of Indian dance and music. This persuaded me to study American writings on India beginning from the twentieth century, the traveller's accounts, and the observations and impressions of American soldiers in India during World War II. In the course of my research, I discovered in the bound volumes of *ASIA*, several feature articles on subjects covering political, economic, religious, social and cultural scene in India both from historical and current perspectives. The authors included Asia experts, politicians, scholars in Asian studies, eminent journalists and artists.

ASIA: The American Magazine on the Orient, the official journal of the American Asiatic Association was founded in 1901, renamed as *Asia and the Americas* in 1942 and was closed down in 1946. The purpose of the Association was 'to contribute to a satisfactory adjustment of relations between Asiatic counties and the rest of the world by removal of sources of misunderstanding and the dissipation of ignorant prejudices; and to cooperate with all other agencies, religious, educational and philanthropic designed to remove existing obstacles to the peaceful progress of these countries'. *ASIA* was probably the first international magazine to publish a special 'Indian Number' as early as 1923 with a fascinating American focus on India, then still a British colony. The leading contributor in this issue was the former British Secretary of State for India E.S. Montague, famous for the Montague-Chelmsford Reforms, 1919. He wrote about 'self-government for India'. The other notable writer was the renowned India expert of the time Gertrude Emerson, Associate Editor of *ASIA*, who met Mahatma Gandhi and recorded her observations on his personality and his strategies of non-violent non-cooperation for freedom movement. Her scholarly piece 'This is India' in the same issue highlights the antiquity of Indian civilization, her philosophic thought toward an identification of the self with spiritual forces and her quest for knowledge of the supreme truth.

In the course of my exploration in the Library of the Congress, I also discovered a vast collection of photographs of practically all major historic monuments and also those depicting scenes of principal Indian cities with a bewildering diversity of people at the turn of the twentieth century. The fabulous collection of F.G. Carpenter, the noted American author and traveller underlined India's overwhelming beauty, its sheer richness and diversity. Forgotten for nearly 50 years, I was the first to discover and study this pictorial treasure in the US Library, a deed duly acknowledged by the editor of *SPAN*, published by the American Embassy, New Delhi.

It was a difficult task to make a selection out of this wealth of published material on India culled from *ASIA*. The subjects covered are educative and informative, for both the general reader and scholar engaged in studies on India. As editor, I invite you to join me in this brief sojourn to the past and share with me the experience of observing an American focus on India.

New Delhi PRAN NEVILE

Monuments of Historic India

Johnston & Hoffmann

In 326 BC when Alexander the Great crossed the Indus in his brief invasion of the Punjab, India was still a chaotic land in which many unstable, ambitious states were struggling for supremacy. Magadha (the modern Bihar) soon afterwards gained the ascendency, and under the Maurya or Peacock dynasty built up the first Indian empire. The third and greatest of the Maurya monarchs, Asoka (273–232 BC) has left us a remarkable record of his times carved in elaborate rock and pillar edicts throughout his vast domain, from the north-west frontier of the Punjab to Mysore and from the Bay of Bengal to the Arabian Sea. Stricken with remorse for the suffering caused by his single war, waged against the Kalingas, Asoka became an ardent Buddhist and devoted the remainder of his long reign to the active promulgation of the faith. He accomplished for Buddhism what Constantine later did for Christianity. Thousands of converts to Buddhism were made throughout the empire; and missions invested with royal prestige were despatched to neighbouring states. The Great Stupa at Sanchi is one of a group of Buddhist memorials near Bhilsa which still bear witness to the religious devotion of the age of Asoka and to the exquisite art attained by Indian builders in that early period.

**ASIA*, March 1923—An eight page insert of photographs.

Johnston & Hoffmann

During the chaotic centuries that followed upon the disintegration of the Maurya empire, Buddhism continued to play a leading part in Indian history, sometimes under the active championship of devout Buddhist monarchs like Kanishka, sometimes under the protection of kings who, like the Guptas or the tolerant Harsha, were primarily worshippers of the old Hindu gods. Meantime zealous Buddhist missionaries had carried the faith into Ceylon, Burma, China and other distant lands. In the process of expansion and adaptation to meet the needs of great multitudes of converts at home and abroad, the early Hinayana Buddhism had developed into the more popular Mahayana form. In India, notably, Buddhist art kept pace with the growth of the faith. An extraordinary series of paintings showing the gradual development of Buddhist art from a time shortly after Asoka's reign to about AD *600 has been preserved in the 29 rocky caves of Ajanta. The nineteenth, the Chaitya chapel here shown, was hewn out about* AD *500 by the Mahayana sect. During this very period when Buddhism was spreading so rapidly abroad, it exhibited signs of gradual but unmistakable decay in India, and by 800 it was practically extinct. Medieval and modern Hinduism, which dates from that time, is the joint product of early Buddhism and the Vedic faith.*

Johnston & Hoffmann

In the fifth and sixth centuries the Huns and kindred races swept down from the north into India, bringing confusion in their wake. Even the rigid caste system of the ancient Vedas was undermined. There followed what is known as the Rajput period (650–1200). Rajputs, or 'king's sons', unheard of in earlier times, suddenly began to play a conspicuous part in the history of north and west India. Not a race, but a social group or caste of aristocratic rank and warlike habits descended mainly from foreign invaders, the Rajputs seem to have been accepted by the influential Brahmans as representing the Kshatriyas or warriors of the old Vedic legends. From 800 to 850 they succeeded in gaining control of practically every throne from the Indus to Berar, and in the centuries that followed, these Rajput chieftains vied with each other in their ardent support of the arts of civilization. The Temple Gateway of Amber, the ancient capital of the Rajput state, Jaipur, is a typical example of the delicate and fantastic workmanship of this medieval Hindu period. When the Mahommedans invaded India in the last quarter of the twelfth century, the Rajputs struggled in desperate opposition until finally, defeated by Mahommed Ghori, they were forced to migrate in a body to the hills and deserts now known as Rajputana, where they set up a Rajput state. Later, under the far-sighted policy of the Mogul Emperor, Akbar, the Rajput chiefs once again rose to power and became stalwart supporters of the empire.

Johnston & Hoffmann

Asoka's masterful attempt to make of India a permanent Buddhist state was doomed to ultimate failure. Long before the dawn of recorded history, Brahmanism, with its elaborate system of the four castes—Brahmans or priests, Kshatriyas or nobles, Vaisyas or peasants, and Sudras or 'hewers of wood'—had won its way throughout India, and its sway was difficult to shake. For centuries the two religions existed side by side. After Asoka's death the huge Magadha empire disintegrated. Sungas, Kanvas, Saka satraps, Kushans—dynasty rose against dynasty. Finally in the golden age of the Guptas (AD 320–620) Magadha regained much of its early glory, but with a new trend; for, though tolerant of Buddhism, the Guptas as a family showed a marked preference for the worship of Vishnu. Buddhism was already on the wane in this period, which saw the beginnings of a brilliant renaissance of Hindu art. The best extant architecture of this Hindu period is to be found in outlying states comparatively free from the Mahommedan ravages of a later age. Thus in Orissa, on the Bay of Bengal, in the holy city of Bhuvaneswar with its hundreds of temples nestled among rocky hills, is the great Sivaite temple, built by the Kesari, or Lion, dynasty (474–1132), perhaps the finest specimen of a purely Hindu temple existing in India today.

Johnston & Hoffmann

As the result of continuous aggressive warfare at the beginning of his reign, Akbar, greatest of the Moguls (1556–1605), speedily became undisputed ruler of a larger portion of India than had ever before acknowledged the sway of any one man. Akbar was, in addition, a brilliant civil administrator, wisely conciliating the Rajput chiefs and enlisting their active support. Always broadly tolerant of the diverse religious elements within his domain, he at length renounced Mahommedanism in favour of an eclectic 'Divine Faith' of his own invention, which became the state religion. Akbar's reign is also famous for its architecture, characterized by magnificence and a happy blending of Hindu and Mahommedan styles. The Gate of Victory gives a hint of the marvels of the ancient deserted capital of Fatehpur Sikri, which Akbar built and occupied with all the splendour and opulence of his court from 1570 to 1585, when he became dissatisfied with it and quitted it forever.

The Mogul empire attained its greatest glory during the reign of Shah Jahan, the grandson of Akbar. His court was beyond doubt the most magnificent that India has ever seen. Throughout the great territory over which he ruled the authority of the empire was never seriously questioned, and in spite of petty wars, long years were devoted to the constructive arts of peace and prosperity. Shah Jahan possessed a genuine love for architecture and erected many splendid forts and temples, of which by far the best known is the exquisite Taj Mahal at Agra. The Taj, which has often been called the most perfect building in existence, was completed in 1653 as a memorial shrine for the remains of the Emperor's wife, Mumtaz Mahal. The latter part of Shah Jahan's reign was marked by the first activity of the Mahrattas of the Deccan, destined to play a prominent part in the history of the ensuing century. His last years were troubled also by the rebellion of his son, Aurangzeb, by whom he was imprisoned in 1658, for the remainder of his life. But Aurangzeb, the last of the great Moguls, was only partially successful in maintaining the glory of the empire, and after his death the ancient power of the Mogul emperors rapidly collapsed. Already, too, new invaders were sailing in from the south, seeking gain and presaging the long period of British control.

Johnston & Hoffmann

Delhi, famous as the seat of the great Mogul court at the height of its magnificence, boasts a comparatively brief but brilliant history, associated chiefly with the rise and fall of Mahommedan civilization in India. In 1206, after the first quarter-century of Mahommedan invasions had gained a foothold for Islam in India, Kutb-ud-din, founder of the slave dynasty, proclaimed himself sultan of Delhi, and thereafter the city assumed considerable importance as headquarters and base for further Mahommedan conquests. It was not, however, until 1648, when Shah Jahan moved his court from Agra, that Delhi became the official capital of the Mogul empire. Shah Jahan was the builder of the great wall and imperial palace, now known as the 'Fort', pictured above, the famous Peacock Throne and innumerable other storied splendors. Since 1912 Delhi has been the official capital of the Government of India, and British barracks now stand in the midst of the forts and temples of the old Mogul empire.

Johnston & Hoffmann

The Sikhs were originally a peaceful, reformed sect of Hindus, following the teachings of their leader, Nanak of Lahore, who preached the unreality of caste distinctions. In 1577, Akbar, the Mogul emperor, ceded to Ram Das, their fourth 'guru', or religious leader, the ground for the city of Amritsar, which became the sacred headquarters of the sect. Ram Das himself built the famous Golden Temple on an island in the midst of the great Holy Tank or Pool of Immortality from which the city derives its name. Two centuries later it was rebuilt on the same spot after the destruction wrought by the invading Ahmad Shah Durani. Under the later gurus the 'Khalsa', or Sikh brotherhood, was established on a distinctly political and military basis in bitter opposition to the Mahommedans then in power, and from this time on Sikh history becomes a record of warlike activity. In the middle of the eighteenth century the Sikhs, under their leader, Ranjit Singh, finally won supremacy over the Punjab; and Lahore then became the centre of their power, Amritsar remaining the religious centre. Later the Sikhs invaded British territory and as a result were twice conquered. In 1849, at the close of the Second Sikh War, the Punjab was finally annexed to British India. Riots at Amritsar and other cities in the Punjab and the recent struggle between zealous modern reformers of the Sikh 'gurdwaras', or shrines, and the British government testify that the Sikhs retain their distinctly religious and warlike character to the present day.

Introduction

Pran Nevile

AFTER VISITING INDIA IN 1896, Mark Twain, the celebrated American literary figure wrote: 'So far as I am able to judge, nothing has been left undone, either by man or nature, to make India the most extraordinary country that the sun visits on his round. Perhaps it will be simplest to throw away the tags and generalize her with one all-comprehensive name, as the "Land of Wonders"—India is the only foreign land I ever daydream about or deeply long to see again.'

Fifty years later, an American soldier John W. Wohlfarth, after his brief tenure in India, was so much captivated by the country and its people that he recorded in his diary: 'The world needs India intact! Tear down Roman ruins if you will, level Cyclopean walls, build bridges with stones of gothic abbeys and feudal fortresses but lay no hand on the glory and grandeur of India.'

India and America were linked right from 1492 when Christopher Columbus discovered America in his search for a sea route to India. The wealth and riches of India as reported by Marco Polo, the Italian globetrotter of thirteenth century, had fired the aspirations of many adventurers and explorers to visit India. A pioneer adventurer in the age of sailing ships, Columbus was incidentally responsible for causing confusion by calling the natives of America as Indians. Columbus thought that he had landed on the eastern shores of India. On his return to Spain, Columbus was showered with grand praise and honour for his discovery of a sea route to India. Columbus' later voyages did nothing to disillusion the great explorer and until his dying day he never realized that he had discovered a new world and continued to insist that the lands discovered by him were an extension of Asian mainland. He had brought with him six local inhabitants as slaves and called them 'Indians' hence the name stuck and generations of original inhabitants of America, due to Columbus' error, are termed as 'American Indians'. Other explorers soon disproved the theory that Columbus had reached India. In 1497, just five years later, the Portuguese explorer Vasco da Gama embarked on another voyage and found the new sea route to India.

Early Impressions

During the first half of the eighteenth century both America and India shared a common colonial master, i.e. Great Britain. During this colonial period the Americans had little knowledge of India and its people with their rich old civilization and culture. Some contact had started through English soldiers and seamen who had lived both in America and India. Americans were fed with stories of the East India Company's exploits, their highly profitable trade, and fabulous wealth amassed by Company officials through private trade and other means, be they fair or foul. This had tempted some American youths to go to India via London, the headquarters of the Company. Elehu Yale, born in Boston (1649–1723), had moved to England with his family. Through contacts, Yale managed to join the East India Company at Calcutta as a writer in 1671. Clever and resourceful, Yale rose through the ranks to attain the position of Governor of Madras. He amassed a vast fortune and earned the status of a British Nabob and merchant prince. On his return to England he settled down in his country house which was proclaimed as 'one of the seven wonders of Wales'. It is after him that Yale University in New Haven is named on account of his generous donations. Yale's connection with India contributed in its own way in stimulating American interest in knowledge of India. There was a fascinating account published in the *Virginia Gazette* about a Mughal Emissary's visit to Governor Yale. The Emissary was reported as 'of majestic Form and the Magnificance of his Pearls and Diamonds is beyond description'. This was a picture of India that was enshrined in American minds for nearly two centuries.

Even with the scarcity of information on India, there were some intellectuals who strove hard to learn about the teachings and beliefs of the Hindus. Charles Thompson (1729–1824) a member of the cultured Philadelphia Society along with Benjamin Franklin shared their pursuit of knowledge of Hinduism. In the face of this paucity of information about Indian culture and heritage, there was wide publicity about East India Company's dubious activities and its exploitation of Indians as recorded by the *Virginia Gazette* in 1767: 'It is said that the great riches acquired in the East Indies are not obtained by mere trade, but chiefly by rapine, and plundering of the poor innocent natives.' In later years as American relations with the mother country became more and more strained, American newspapers were more forthcoming in criticizing Britain and were sympathetic towards Indians.

Apart from sharing the common heritage of British colonialism, it is a little known fact that the history of the two countries, America and India, is also joined by an Englishman, Lord Cornwallis. His defeat by American forces at Yorktown paved the way to American Independence while his coming to India as Governor General in 1786, ostensibly bound by Pitt's India Act led to a brazen defiance of the policy to refrain from warfare. This defiance set Britain on a new path of forceful conquest that would ultimately lead to the establishment of the Raj in India.

During the colonial period, American knowledge of India was fed by some casual news reports published in local newspapers like the *Virginia Gazette* received from the English press. Apart from some reports of the East India Company, the Indians did not figure as being of any great interest. It was only after American Independence that we observe the emergence of a desire to learn about the countries of the Orient. India was usually depicted as a land of Maharajas with their harems and marble palaces, faqirs, snake charmers, tigers, and elephants, where famines and hurricanes brought great human suffering. There were also some fascinating reports of enormous opulence and the glamourous lifestyles of the Indian ruling nawabs and Rajas. One such report about a nawab's wife, which was published in 1743 described her glittering costume, her elaborate sophisticated make-up, and her exotic jewellery studded with diamonds and pearls, which adorned her body from head to toe. There was also mention of the lavish hospitality where refreshments were served on gold plates and guests were entertained with 60 dishes. This picture of luxury must have confounded the readers of colonial America.

Commercial Relations

During the colonial period Indian goods like cotton and silk textiles, spices, indigo, saltpetre, sugar, etc., had reached American markets indirectly through re-exports from London—the destination of the East India Company's exports from India. Direct trade with India started only after American Independence when the Indian Ocean was opened to American vessels. The first American ship to reach India was the *S.S. United States* in December 1785. The ship carried a mixed cargo of lead, copper, iron, tobacco, twine, and cordage. The entry of American ships into Indian waters was facilitated by navigational charts published in Britain and Europe as well as by crew members with past experience of working in British ships. During the first decade of Indo-US trade, the British, though reluctant to allow any competition from American newcomers, tolerated them since

American ships could be useful in handling the private trade of East India Company employees. By 1789, there were 40 American ships trading in Asian waters and the British got concerned about American competition, even though they brought much needed silver dollars with them.

In the famous Joy Treaty of 1794, American ships were permitted to trade only at British controlled ports and they were to return directly to the US without carrying any cargo for Europe. They were also excluded from the 'country trade' in India. Some American shippers however chose to defy these restrictions and continued to engage in trade between ports in the Indian Ocean. Indo-US trade continued to thrive through the early years of the nineteenth century. During the European wars of 1793–1815, American neutrality promoted the global expansion of its merchant navy and Indian trade was an important element of American commercial expansion. During this period, American merchants used the services of Indian commercial agents in Calcutta and Bombay to operate in the local markets which fetched greater profits than dealing through British mercantile houses. By the turn of the nineteenth century, a large variety of Indian hand-woven cotton and silk piece goods were much in demand as such materials could not be found anywhere else. Indian cotton and silk textiles with a variety of patterns and colours were extremely popular for making dresses. The quality ranged from coarse cloth to fine muslins. Kashmiri woollen shawls, soft and warm, were also in demand for the rich. These highly valued trade goods fostered a high regard for India and generated a wider interest in learning more about its history and culture. American traders brought back a variety of curios and handicrafts along with the staple cargo. The most spectacular import from India was an elephant in 1797 which was sold for the princely sum of $10,000. However, the buyers made it a profitable venture by taking it on tour around leading American cities and charging 25 cents per head for viewing it.

In 1799, wealthy American merchants and captains of ships joined hands to set up the Salem East India Marine Society which built a museum to display a variety of curios and other unusual objects never seen before in America. These included traditional weapons, musical instruments, hookahs, and even a silver-trimmed palanquin to show the mode of travelling in India. Other notable exhibits included prints and lithographs based on paintings by British and Indian artists depicting Indian scenes, its landscape and monuments, native people and their colourful costumes, British lifestyle, and pictures of events of imperial interest.

With the end of war in Europe in 1815, there was a decline in Indo-US trade due to various factors, which included the new competition of British private merchants who were permitted to enter the India trade by the 1813 East India Company Charter. There were other factors too which led to the drop in Indo-US trade exchanges. With the cessation of hostilities and the introduction of peace, the Americans were deprived of their special position as neutrals in war.

Wartime had brought about notable developments in transportation and manufacturing sectors. New York emerged as a leading port and centre of foreign trade, thereby affecting the fortunes of Boston merchant specialists in the India trade. The 1820s and 1830s presented a notable change in trade patterns: the growth of American industrial production and introduction of high tariffs on the import of manufacturers. It hit the Indian textiles and other manufactured goods markets, replacing them with raw materials—indigo saltpetre, and hides. This new trend in trade was part of a global shift which saw the rapid industrialization of America and Europe. The demand for other raw materials including shellac, gum, copal, and camphor increased with the expansion of American industry. American merchants continued to find more to import from India than to export, with the balance of trade in favour of India. It was in this period that a most unlikely export cargo to India appeared: American ice. This memorable phenomenon in the history of Indo-US trade thus deserves special mention.

American Ice to India

The introduction of American ice in 1833 brought great jubilation and feasting in Calcutta. It replaced mountain ice, brought down at heavy cost and inconvenience, and other native ice which would be produced in ice pits during winter nights and preserved for the summer, entailing colossal wastage. After over twenty years of experimenting in the early nineteenth century, an American entrepreneur named Fredrick Tudor succeeded in transporting ice from a cold to a hot climate. The ice blocks were cut from frozen ponds rented near Boston and stored in an ice house before loading them on board a ship which had an in-built ice house.

The first shipment of American ice arrived in Calcutta in September 1833 by the *S.S. Tussany*, after a four-month voyage around the Cape. Wrapped in felt and pine sawdust, two-thirds of the ice cargo in solid form was received with great excitement, so much so that Governor General Lord Bentinck presented an inscribed silver-gilt cup to the ship's captain, William C. Rogers, for having successfully landed the first shipment of American ice in India. This encouraged the exporter Fredrick Tudor to make ice shipments to Bombay and Madras also. Ice houses were soon constructed in all three ports to store the precious ice cargo and preserve it against heat. There was a growing demand for this crystal-clear ice among the local European population and wealthy Indians. Selling at four *annas* a *seer* (half the price of native ice), it became popular with everyone who could afford it. Tudor in turn made a fortune through this ice trade for over thirty years, until the technology of making ice was introduced in India.

Trade Revival

Bilateral trade languished for two decades after 1820. However, in the late 1840s it witnessed a revival with the changing composition of trade. In addition to the traditional Indian exports of hides and skins, indigo, and saltpetre, two new products were added to the list. These were linseed from which oil was extracted for the growing paint and varnish industry, as well as jute products such as yarn, twine, cloth, and gunny bags to meet increasing demand for packaging material for commodities. While these new items notably increased the volume of Indian exports, there was a further decline in the exports of cotton and silk textiles. By the mid-nineteenth century, the structure of American exports to India also changed as half of its volume consisted of cotton textiles, jeans and drills, and all kinds of twilled cottons, the same class of fabrics of common usage which were once the staple import from India. Thereafter other types of business relationships developed in the late nineteenth century and early twentieth century. The biggest and most remarkable American business involvement in India was Tata Iron & Steel Company, which was, in its time, the largest steel plant in Asia. A fascinating account of the building of the $70 million plant in India by the American engineer Charles Page Perin pays glorious tribute to Jamsetji Nusservangi Tata for his initiative and determination to found the greatest of modern industries, i.e. a steel plant in India. At first Tata received very little encouragement from the British government in London, but he was promised help in his project in the United States where he went in 1902. The transformation of a jungle area into a city such as Jamshedpur, the home of the steel mill, is described as a phenomenon almost without parallel. At the same time Perin, after his first meeting with J.N. Tata, hailed him as the 'ablest commercial genius India has ever produced'.

American businessmen began visiting India in greater numbers from the early twentieth century. They found a market for their various industrial products and novelties. The invention of gramophones and cylinder records by Thomas Alva Edison in 1877 marked the dawn of a new era in the world of music. Considering the great potential in India, the American Gramophone Company set up its Office in Calcutta in 1901 and within a year or so, its leading technical expert F.W. Gaisburg landed in Calcutta with his recording team. He travelled all over India and recorded over 600 titles. Most of the artists were well known professional dancing girls and singers who were given special training by American experts for gramophone recordings of three minute duration. The American company, with its trademark featuring an image of a dog listening to a gramophone horn with 'His Master's Voice', enjoyed a virtual monopoly in India during the twentieth century.

Another noteworthy invention was the stereograph: a double photograph of the same subject presenting a 3D solid image when seen through a binocular viewer of stereography. Many American photographers had begun visiting India from the late nineteenth century and took photographs and stereo pictures of the country's landscape and people for their boxed sets featuring different aspects of Indian historical and geographical studies for worldwide distribution. The life of stereography however, was less than a century and it practically vanished from the scene after 1930 with the advent of cinema, radio, and TV. The US Library of Congress is perhaps the only repository of a vast collection of stereographs of India covering not only the magnificent sights and sounds of the country at large but also the picturesque façade of Empire, which included the majestic Delhi Durbars of 1903 and 1911 with all their regal splendour and the dazzling pageantry of the Indian Maharajas and princes.

After the First World War, the American motor car industry grew into one of the leading industries of the country, witnessing the notable expansion and introduction of new technology. British motor cars had monopolized the Indian market on account of Imperial Preference in the import tariffs. The American car makers, despite higher tariffs, succeeded in marketing their more attractive models in India. It was also aggressive American salesmanship that helped them in promoting their sales and also their modern set up of after-sales service. We come across a fascinating account of the 'Tactics of Motor Car Selling in India' by an American sales executive who found the Indian ruling Maharajas and Princes to be the most promising buyers; the motor car had succeeded the elephant as the emblem of supreme dignity. Some of them would order all nickel parts gilded and others asked for silver-plated car bodies. The Maharaja of Mysore was said to have the finest collection of motor cars and a splendid garage for their upkeep. It was also reported that on the occasion of the marriage of Raja Hari Singh, the heir apparent to the throne, H.H. the Maharaja of Jammu & Kashmir, gave an order for 50 cars for his high ranking guests.

Official Contacts

The United States took steps to have direct official contacts with India soon after gaining Independence. It was in November 1792 that President George Washington appointed Benjamin Joy as American Consul at Calcutta 'and other parts and places on the coast of India and Asia'. The need to have a consul emanated from the growing commercial relations between India and America. The East India Company had, in 1788, accorded the most-favoured nation treatment to the commerce of the United States. This encouraged an increasing number of American ships to sail to India.

The British authorities at Calcutta refused to grant Joy consular recognition. He was told that the Governor General, 'having no instructions from England, does not think himself at liberty to admit you to the Public Charter of a Consul entitled to privileges, but you may reside here as a Commercial Agent, subject to the Civil and Criminal Jurisdiction of this country'. Joy functioned as a commercial agent. He informed the State Department about his appointment of William Abbot whom he described as the 'Secretary to the Nabob of Arcot' to be United States Consular Agent at Madras. Joy himself left Calcutta in 1795 due to ill health and sent his resignation after reaching Boston in January 1796.

American trade with India was disrupted by the European war in 1812, but later, in 1813, the East India Company's monopoly was abolished by the British authorities and trade with India was thrown open to both British and foreign merchants. Then, by virtue of a convention concluded between the US and British Government, it was formally agreed that vessels of the United States should be admitted to Bombay, Calcutta, Madras, and Prince of Wales Island, and that American citizens could henceforth enjoy 'free trade between the said settlements and the United States in all articles of which the importation and exportation, respectively to and from the said territories shall not be entirely prohibited'.

In 1838, American consular relations were re-established not in Calcutta but in Bombay with appointment of Philemon Parker who took charge in August 1839. However, as only five or six American ships docked at Bombay in a year, and as he was reluctantly allowed only to act as Commercial Agent and not as Consul, he left Bombay and informed the State Department that he had authorized an American resident, E.A. Webster to act as Vice Commercial Agent of the United States. He was however discharged for misconduct and left Bombay in 1842. It was only a decade later that the first American, Edward Ely, was duly acknowledged by the British authorities as Consul and took charge at Bombay in May 1852. At that time American trade was confined to port of Bombay, with 15 American ships entering the port in a year. Ely died while still serving as Consul in January 1858 and after that there was no American representation until 1890 when an American, Henry Ballantine, took over as Consul, followed by Henry J. Sommer Jr who, in 1894, had a brief tenure before being succeeded by his Vice Consul Samuel Comfort. But this time a line of steamships had been established between New York and India to dock at Bombay and Calcutta thus facilitating direct shipment of goods both ways without any trans-shipment.

In 1899 William T. Fee was appointed Consul at Bombay on a regular annual salary of $2,000. With the introduction of steamship service, American businessmen, academicians, and tourists began visiting India. Fee was quite active in promoting wider contact between America and India, despite British indifference and even opposition. Fee served as Chairman of the American-Indian Famine Relief Committee and arranged a shipment of 5,000 tons of American corn for the famine sufferers in India. In 1901, he was also instrumental in the shipping to America of choice mango grafts for the purpose of cultivation.

There was no regular American representation in Calcutta until the 1840s when Jones Richards was appointed in 1843. Then, in the late 1860s an American Consulate General was established in Calcutta. The Consular Agency in Madras was set up in 1867. However, it was only after the establishment of an orderly American Foreign Service in 1924 that regular officials were appointed at Calcutta and Bombay.

During the Second World War, a reciprocal exchange of representatives was agreed to between the US government and the British government, in consultation with the Government of India. Thomas M. Wilson, a foreign service officer, was the first to be appointed as Commissioner of the USA to India with the rank of minister in July 1941. In December 1942, he was succeeded by William Phillips who, as Personal Representative of the President, held the rank of ambassador and he was succeeded by George R. Merrel who later became charge d' affairs of the American Embassy in India in November 1946. India was represented in the USA by an Agent General to the British Embassy in Washington, Sir Girja Shankar Bajpai, who followed suit and took over as charge d' affairs of the Indian Embassy in Washington on 8 November 1946.

American Missionaries

The first American missionaries, mostly of Protestant denomination, arrived in India in 1810. They did not follow trade or the flag and had no political connection but were attracted to India in the hope of spreading the gospel. They did not meet with much success and their reports on India after their return were mostly negative and dominated by descriptions of poverty and repulsive religious practices. This adversely influenced the American public opinion of India. According to an eminent Indologist, W. Norman Brown, many missionaries were ardently evangelistic yet at the same time, were untrained in the study of religion as a science, uninformed on either their own or Indian religions, and unappreciative generally of the civilizations existing in India. Such persons were inclined to picture America's superior economic culture as attributable to superior religion and morality, thus confusing the material and spiritual. Their numbers steadily increased so that by the turn of the twentieth century, they numbered 1025, increasing by 1922 to 2,478 missionaries.

Some of these missionaries engaged themselves in setting up educational institutions, medical facilities, hospitals, etc., and were widely appreciated for their commendable work. Their contribution in promoting women's education in India was indeed most praiseworthy. The famous IT college in Lucknow and the Women's Christian College in Madras owe their existence to their pioneering initiative in this field. In the same way, the medical missionaries were instrumental in founding the Christian Medical Hospital and College in Vellore; one of the best of its kind in Asia. A noteworthy achievement of the missionaries was the establishment of the Youngmen's Christian Association (founded in London in 1844) which was generously supported by Americans. A large number of American secretaries of the associations took charge of those branches whose membership was mostly Indian. The first American Secretary was David McConaughy who organized the Madras YMCA in 1890. The movement spread rapidly and by 1891, when the first national convention was held, there were 35 associations. A notable aspect of American missionary work was the principle of non-discrimination between the Indian and American clergy.

The YMCA engages itself in manifold activities. Its programme includes sports, physical education, formal and informal training, hostel facilities, seminar, and lectures on different disciplines. These activities are designed to meet the needs of the upcoming younger generation. The YMCAs also run special training schools for disabled, deaf, and mute children. It is no wonder that YMCAs have emerged as popular centres for many people in all major cities and towns of the country.

The Young Women's Christian Association, founded in England in 1855, was also established in India. It was intended to look after the welfare of young women by providing them with residential and holiday homes as well as informal education and vocational training.

American Indologists

The first American Indologist to study Indian religion and philosophy in-depth was Ralph Waldo Emerson (1803–82). He read *Bhagwad Gita* and *Vishnu Purana* translated by European and English scholars. He was influenced by the writings of Sir William Jones (1746–94), the renowned translator of Sanskrit literature and founder of the Asiatic Society of Bengal in 1784. He developed a lively interest in India and its civilization and culture. Emerson's writings on Hindu scriptures (including *Upanishads*) represent the maturity of his understanding of some of the fundamental concepts of Hinduism. He was enamoured with the subject of illusion (*maya*) and wrote that he 'found men victims of illusions in all parts of life. Children, youths, adults, and old men are all led by one bauble or another. Yogindra, the goddess of illusion is stronger than the Titans, stronger than Apollo'.

Henry David Thoreau (1817–62) was another eminent scholar who was equally fascinated by Hindu thought and philosophy, and was also influenced by the writings of Sir William Jones and especially his translation of *The Laws of Manu*. He wrote eloquently about its eternal value as 'it addresses what is deepest and most abiding in man'. He was swayed by the message of *Bhagwad Gita* and hailed it as the best of Hindu scriptures for its pure intellectuality and the fact that its sanity and sublimity had impressed the minds of soldiers and merchants alike. He was indeed the most well-read scholar of Indian literature of his time. He himself lived an austere life and died very young. Thoreau was in fact admired and even accepted by Mahatma Gandhi as the teacher who inspired him to perfect the weapon of 'Civil Disobedience'.

The American Oriental Society was founded in 1842. Yale University was the first to introduce the teaching of Sanskrit in 1841 and was followed by John Hopkins University in 1876, Harvard and Colombia in 1880, Chicago in 1892, and Pennsylvania in 1904. This served as a groundwork for the multidisciplinary South Asian Studies that came about in the twentieth century.

A reverse religious flow had begun with the inflow of the writings of Raja Rammohun Roy, the great Indian religious reformer. He was said to be the first Indian to influence American thinkers. His interpretation of Christianity coincided with the ideas and tenets of Unitarianism. His brand of Hinduism aroused interest among American intellectuals on the Orient as it provided them with a positive view of Indian civilization, which could counteract the negative descriptions of Hindu religion and society by some of the missionaries.

India is the only country that has offered America alternative religious experiences for more than a hundred years. The first person to make a direct impact on the common American was Swami Vivekananda a disciple of Sri Ramakrishna. His address at the World Parliament of Religions held in Chicago in 1893 left the audience spellbound and he was acknowledged to be one of the Parliament's outstanding personalities. Vivekananda founded the first American Vedanta Society in New York city.

After the First World War, there was an increasing American interest in knowing more about India. During the 1920s and 1930s, American academic work was carried on by scholar missionaries working in India in missionary educational institutions. They numbered less than a hundred out of some thousands of American missionaries in India. Some American scholars—humanists and social scientists—did make trips to India during this interwar period for study and research of Indian religions, literature, philosophy, and history. The most eminent among them was Professor W. Norman Brown who carried on with his teaching and research in India in 1922–4, 1927–9, and 1934–5. Another was John Clark Archer, a professor of comparative religion at Yale who undertook research on Sikh history in 1937 at Khalsa College, Amritsar. In 1939 the anthropologist Dorothy Spencer made a study of Munda tribes of Chota Nagpur. The US Library of Congress also became interested in Sanskrit literature and deputed its Sanskrit scholar Horace Poleman to India for a year (1939–40) to collect Sanskrit manuscripts.

In a way, the work of these scholars laid the foundations for the present-day study of South Asia in American Universities and generated interest for enlarging the established classical studies field to more contemporary subjects. At this time, only two academic organizations—the Archaeological Institute of America (AIA) and the American Oriental Society (AOS)—were interested in providing assistance to American scholars for doing research in India. Credit must go to Norman Brown again for ardently pursuing his aim of setting up an American research centre in India. His plan was interrupted by the Second World War but he continued with zeal and determination to promote further US study and research of all aspects of India. After Indian Independence in 1947, Brown succeeded in procuring sufficient funds to establish a full-fledged programme of South Asian Studies at the University of Pennsylvania in 1948.

In the decades following Indian Independence, thousands of Americans have come to India for study, research, and work under numerous programmes and several agencies in different fields. After the availability of 'PL480' funds in 1961 the American Institute of Indian Studies was established. During its lifetime of over 50 years, and with headquarters now in Gurgaon and several regional centres, it has become the 'apex of the pyramid of South Asian Studies in the US'.

American Travellers

One of the earliest American travellers to India was Bayard Taylor who came here in 1853 as a correspondent of the *New York Tribune*. His fascinating account of his travels by horse-cart and palanquin from Bombay to Calcutta, and of the landscape, monuments, and people of India was indeed highly interesting and popular with American readers. Taylor gives graphic accounts of the beauty and landscape of the Bombay of the 1850s. He was both amused and surprised by his first ride in a palanquin carried on the shoulders of four men. At that time, one could travel from one end of India to another by palanquin but he preferred the horse-drawn *Dak* buggy and travelled extensively, visiting Indore, Delhi, Meerut, Agra, Mussoori, Cawnpore, Lucknow, Allahabad, Benaras, and Calcutta. His absorbing account about these places and his meetings with local Indians and British residents in India is highly informative and of great historical value. He admires the Parsee entrepreneurs of Bombay for their business skills and was struck by their remarkable achievements in ship building. He makes a special mention of H.M. Wadya the famous ship builders who built several ships for the British Navy for more than half a century. The first of these, the *Mindon*, had been in service for nearly fifty years and her condition testified to the excellence of her construction. On New Year's Day in 1853, Taylor was entertained by his Parsee hosts, the Wadya family to a fabulous nautch party attended by some Englishmen, Americans (with the exception of missionaries), and local Indian elite. He describes how he was greeted with bunches of fragrant roses and sprinkling of rose-water from silver vases. Though not much impressed by the dance of nautch girls, he was exceedingly pleased by some of the songs sung by them. Taylor visited a number of magnificent forts, palaces and temples but he was most enchanted by the Taj, which he eloquently describes with the following words:

> The Taj truly is, as I have already said, a poem. It is not only a pure architectural type, but also a creation which satisfies the imagination, because its characteristic is Beauty. Did you ever build a Castle in the Air? Here is one, brought down to earth, and fixed for the wonder of ages; yet so light it seems, so airy, and, when seen from a distance, so like a fabric of mist and sunbeams, with its great dome soaring up, a silvery bubble, about to burst in the sun, that, even after you have touched it, and climbed to its summit, you almost doubt its reality.

He was particularly critical of British imperial arrogance and the disgusting manner in which Indians were treated, irrespective of their rank and position. In concluding remarks on his Indian tour he wrote: 'I have never made a more interesting, or instructive journey or visited a country better worthy of thorough and conscientious study. The historical problem which it presents is yet distant from its solution and it is one which no member of the Anglo-Saxon race can contemplate with indifference.'

Another notable visitor was Revd William Butler who wrote *The Land of the Veda* in 1871. His approach was that of a missionary in that he denigrated Hindu religious practices and lamented the sad plight of Indian women, without comprehending the true position and objective study of the Hindu way of life and its enlightened philosophy. Then he writes about his study of Indian *fakirs*, their knowledge and activities. He makes an interesting observation about the effect of soft music at the Taj Mahal. While quoting some observer, he writes that 'a flute played gently in the vault below where the remains of the emperor and his consort repose, produces a sound, which is perhaps the finest to be heard as if it were from heaven and breathed by angels'.

The most distinguished visitor to land here was the American literary luminary Mark Twain in 1896 who toured India for three months lecturing and collecting information for his book *Following the Equator—A Journey Around the World* which was published in 1897 and included 200 pages on India, and that constituted a major portion of the book. He called India a 'Land of Wonders'.

The most renowned travel writer of his time to visit India was Frank George Carpenter (1855–1924). Starting his career as a journalist in 1879 he began his global travels in 1888 which spanned a period of 36 years and took him to nearly every part of the world. His popular writings, accompanied by photographs, appeared as 'Carpenters' Geographic Readers and remained standard school textbooks for several decades. He travelled to India with his daughter in 1909 and was fascinated by the diversity of Indian people and the country's scenic splendours and magnificent monuments. Besides taking a few photographs with his own camera, he purchased hundreds of photographs of Indian panorama from European commercial photographers such as Bourne and Shepherd, Johnston & Hoffmann, and Barton Son & Co. Carpenter's collection is easily one of the largest of its kind relating to India. It contains pictures of street scenes in cities and towns, people of different regions in their colourful costumes, various modes of travel, shopkeepers, vendors and craftsmen at work, and their various environments. Well preserved in the US Library of Congress, this unique collection is of immense historical value as it reveals the Indian scene in the last decades of the nineteenth century and early twentieth century. Carpenter's own appearance in some snapshots marks his personal enjoyment of his own travels and adventures. Incidentally, I was the first one to write about Carpenter after discovering his visual treasure in the US Library of Congress. It was also duly acknowledged by the US Embassy in their publication *Span* which carried my feature in its May-June 1999 issue. Another notable American visitor to India in the early twentieth century was Roderick McKenzie an artist who spent fifteen years in India and has left a rich visual record with several paintings of the Indian scene.

The post-First World War period witnessed an increase in general American consciousness of India. During the interwar period, quite a few scholars and media persons travelled to India and on their return, wrote about their experiences and also on their specific subjects of study. The American magazine on the Orient entitled *ASIA*, a monthly publication, carried the writings of notable academicians, journalists, and other distinguished experts and learned persons. The amount of American interest in India became more visible when *ASIA* magazine brought out a special India Number in March 1923 with some full page illustrations of 'Monuments of Historic India'. It was the first foreign journal to do so and it gave India legitimate importance in the world. The journal later renamed *Asia and the Americas* showed support of the Indian nationalists and their struggle for freedom.

America and Freedom Movement

Americans after Independence developed a strong attachment to ideals of liberty, self-government, and republicanism, and established their own national identity apart from the monarchical, hierarchical British. This prompted them to sympathize with the plight of Indians under British rule. There were some missionaries who supported the national freedom movement but they had to adopt caution and restraint, apprehending their expulsion from India by the imperial government. Until the end of the nineteenth century, the American government was biased in favour of Britain as they were invariably informed about developments in India by British sources. In fact, there were some scraps in America who were satisfied with the British administration in India. However, we come across an outright condemnation of British rule in India by one American doctor, Josiah Harlan (1799–1871), who had worked for the East India Company and later served in the court of Maharaja Ranjit Singh at Lahore. His memoirs, published in 1842, present a critical analysis of British colonialism in India: 'Machiavellianism of the invaders, rapacity of the civil servants and the revenue collectors, a systemic looting of the country by a handful of colonizers, a general impoverishment of the population and growing indebtedness of the peasants'. According to him, the natives of India were no less slaves 'than the enslaved Africans for whom the English affect the warmest sympathy'—an analysis corroborated in the same period by French natural historian Victor Jacquemont in his journal covering his extensive travels in India.

In the first decade of the twentieth century, some Indian patriots active in the independence movement sought refuge in America to gather support and sympathy for their freedom movement. The active group among them set up the 'Ghadar Party'. The First World War (1914–18) was a turning point since the British government prevailed upon America to ban their activities. American President Theodore Roosevelt had, during his tenure from 1901 to 1908, only words of praise for the British administration in India, which he described as one of the most notable achievements of the white race during the past two centuries.

While researching in the Manuscripts Division of the US Library of Congress, I stumbled upon a typed carbon copy of a Memorandum on 'Some Aspects of Social, Religious and Political Conditions in India' prepared by Campell Bonner and dated 20 March 1918, presumably for the American authorities and policymakers. This 60 page document is quite informative and presents the contemporary American perception of British India. It contains an account of the Indian social, economic, and political scene and problems of poverty, backwardness, and overpopulation. There is a mention that with its diversity of people and scores of languages and ethnic groups, India could not be treated as a nation in the modern sense. It is worth quoting some salient points from the author's *Concluding Remarks on English Control of India*:

The government of India is absolute. It is paternal but not constitutional. It is government for the people, but not by them. On the other hand, it may be considered that the people of India have now recognized avenues for the expression to the government of their desires and needs. Furthermore, every officer of the Indian government is directly or through his superiors responsible to the British Parliament, made up of representatives of one of the most democratic and philanthropic peoples of the world.

The American critic of government in India should, before condemning a government of this sort, inform himself of the actual conditions upon which it rests. The enormous variety of the peoples of India, differing and even to same degree hostile in matters racial, religious, linguistic, and social, makes it inevitable that there should be either a considerable number of small native states or a single strong government imposed upon them all alike.

Some critics hold that India should be organized into a number of native states under native princes, assisted by councils of nobles or notables and using native laws and customs. But since in almost every part of India several religions exist side by side, it would hardly be possible to cut up the country into parts without subjecting some minority to the risk of oppression. Further, even if these native states were fairly homogeneous within themselves, they would, as they continued to exist side by side, surely fall into hostilities, unless a far greater degree of tolerance and humanity should have been attained by the Indian peoples than they can now claim. And once hostilities had begun, chaos would have come again.

There is, on the other hand, to be considered the alternative of a strong rule by a single power. Those idealistic Nationalists who would have 'India for the Indians' may fairly be asked whom they mean by 'Indians'. No sane man could maintain that government by universal manhood suffrage under a constitution would be possible in that land of swarming, ignorant, and infinitely varied millions. Any native government now imaginable would necessarily be a government by a minority and probably in the interests of a minority. The educated or partly educated champions of Nationalism, if put into power, could not control the hardier though less literate races. Neither would they truly represent the kindly, hard-working, and ignorant tillers of the soil, of whom by fate the greater part of the population of India consists.

Nationalist cries of oppression and impatient demands for self-government are prompted partly, as previously suggested, by the sensitiveness which results from a better education and by a feeling of humiliation when they are compared with other nations; partly by an exaggerated sense of their own capabilities for organization and government; partly by an obstinate, deep-seated dislike of European ways of doing things; partly by a false reading of England's dealings with India in the past; partly, in the case of the baser agitators, by a desire for greater opportunities to exploit the machinery of government to their own advantage; partly by unsympathetic treatment at the hands of English merchants and officials; but partly also, in the case of choicer spirits, by a generous and unselfish patriotism which earnestly hopes for the realization in the near future of what is probably only a distant ideal. At least two points warrant a moment's separate discussion. As regards the lack of sympathy for Indian ways of thought and Indian customs, the remedy is undoubtedly to be sought in more careful instruction of European officials in the language of the people and in their customs. It is a hopeful sign that efforts are being made to lay greater stress upon the study of oriental languages by candidates for the Indian Civil Service, and to encourage also the study of anthropology as a means of understanding the peoples of India. In a broader sense the sympathy of the government has already been shown by a constant increase during the last thirty years of the share accorded to the people of India in the councils of the government. It is probably very largely to the reforms initiated by Lord Morley in 1909 that England owes the loyalty of India during the present war. In spite of the fact that severe repressive measures have been thought necessary to restrain seditious utterances, it can hardly be believed that the relatively satisfactory condition in India would be a possibility were the natives of India in large measure living under a feeling of oppression by their rulers.

As for the patriotic aspirations of the higher class of Indian Nationalists, it is to be remarked that the wisest and soberest thinkers, both natives and Europeans, such men as Gokhale, Sinha, Risley and Chailley, all realize their value and respect them as ideals to be held up for the future, but all admit that progress toward them must necessarily be slow.

The problem of India's future seems to the writer of this memorandum to be distinctly England's own affair. The most patriotic American, in view of the more inflammable character of his people, could hardly claim that the United States would have done so well and would have been so patient had they laboured under such a problem as the administration of India. The best policy for Americans to pursue is one of benevolent non-interference. They should feel all possible sympathy for a people who are solving one of the hardest administrative problems ever presented to a nation and who are presenting an object lesson in administration for the whole world. Especially in the present crisis of European politics, there could be no excuse for interference in India. If the hands of England were to be weakened, the result would be a fatal arrest of progress and a most dangerous confusion in India. If England's controls were removed, the period of transition might easily result in India becoming prey to powers less experienced in government and less kindly in character.

Whether Russia, Germany, Japan, or even a government of natives should succeed the English government, the people of India would probably find the little finger of the new power thicker than Britain's loins.

Indian nationalists were however impressed by President Woodrow Wilson's statement in July 1918 when he called 'self-determination an imperative principle of action and affirmed that national aspirations must be respected'. Indian nationalism received support from varied American quarters. One of the most influential supporters was Revd John Hayens Holmes who in 1921 preached a famous sermon proclaiming Gandhi as 'the greatest man in the world'. He also praised Indian nationalist leaders and advocated their cause of freedom from British rule. Gandhi's civil disobedience movement in the 1930s and his dictum of non-violence attracted much attention in America. The Indian Declaration of Independence by the then Indian National Congress President Jawaharlal Nehru at Lahore on 26 January 1930 was inspired by the American Declaration and its contents.

There was considerable interaction during the 1930s and 1940s between very distinguished Americans like Louis Fischer, John Gunther, and Wendell Willkie with Gandhi and other Indian Congress leaders.

Dance and Music

American visitors to India were greatly impressed by the folklore and hectic gaiety of the Indian people and their singing and dancing at fairs and festivals which had mostly a religious flavour. Indian dance, or nautch as it was termed, caught the imagination of American observers. Professional nautch girls accomplished in their art dominated the entertainment scene and were patronized by both the Indian aristocracy as well as the British ruling elite until the middle of the nineteenth century. There is mention of them in the journals and diaries of some American mariners who witnessed their performances in Calcutta and elsewhere as it was a common form of entertainment. As the nineteenth century wore on, British patronage declined and mostly vanished as they set up their own 'little Englands' in their civil and military stations in India. The Indian ruling princes and nawabs however continued to support and patronize the talented and famous, professional nautch girls until the beginning of the twentieth century. Later, only very few patrons, mostly wealthy connoisseurs of music and dance, would organize nautch parties on special occasions to entertain their guests. We come across a fascinating account of one such party by an American lady—Lily Strickland Anderson—a prolific composer of music, a writer, and a painter. She had attended a nautch party in Bombay, hosted by an Indian Raja and was captivated by the performance of two nautch girls, who were invited from Delhi to perform. She noted that one of them was the prettiest girl she had ever seen and added that 'the

Indian nautch girl is dignified, deliberate, and serious . . . she is the mistress of the art of motion'.

Around 1900 the anti-nautch campaign, started by the missionaries and supported by the Western educated Indian social reformers, had widely succeeded in denigrating the dancing profession and its practitioners. However, while the great teachers and disciples of classical dance were languishing, there was a welcome revival of classical dance art in 1920s and 1930s which was inspired by the legendary ballerina Anna Pavlova from Russia and the dancer husband-wife team Ruth St. Denis and Ted Shawn from the USA. On their visit to India they were struck by the Indian classical dances and specially by an amazing Kathak performance of one Pt. Hira Lal at Lahore. They danced in India and even enlightened the Indians about their great traditional classical dance. The duo made their Hindu dances famous in Europe and America. Another legendary American, Esther Sherman who changed her name to Ragini Devi (1897–1982), was an accomplished exponent of Indian dance. Her career in India was unique as she was among the first to rediscover Kathakali, the Kerala dance form, and to present it in India and abroad in the 1930s. In fact she played a leading role in the revival of ancient Indian classical dance and her legacy was carried on by her daughter Indrani Rehman of international fame, and now by her grand daughter Sukanaya.

Some Americans who travelled in the hills and countryside of India were struck by the singing in the fields, village streets, and the many sorts of work done to the lilt of a song. Even the young lads who tended the cattle in the pastures were seen singing as they went about the daily chores of village life. The celebration of festivals offered scenes of crowds singing in chorus to the beat of drums. There were also songs for all seasons which did not escape the attention of some music lovers. Even the snake charmers aroused great interest when they tamed their cobras with the magical tunes of their flutes.

The later years of the twentieth century witnessed wide American interest in the study of Indian performing arts and even the learning of the classical music, both vocal and instrumental. Indian classical dance in different styles and forms is now well known in America thanks to many distinguished scholars and practitioners of these arts.

The Second World War—American Presence in India

The Second World War brought the issue of Indian freedom to the forefront of American attention in a significant way. India became an important part of the China-Burma-India theatre. Indian national leaders were encouraged by the famous Atlantic Charter agreed upon by President Roosevelt and

Prime Minister Churchill that proclaimed 'the right of all peoples to chose the form of government under which they shall live'. However, despite President Roosevelt's pressure, Churchill denied its application to India.

The war marked the advent of a new important era in Indo-US relations as well as the emerging end of British rule of India. The presence of over 100,000 American troops in India led to extensive, lively, and meaningful encounters between Indians and Americans. The Government of India were irked by their informality and friendly relations with Indians. The American war establishment in India gave employment to numerous local civilians ranging from office staff to skilled and unskilled labour. By September 1944, the number of these employees rose to about 79,000 and they were paid by the Government of India under reciprocal aid.

American opinion became a factor in Indian politics, a disturbing prospect for the British authorities. According to the British War Office records, secret measures were taken during the second half of 1942 to keep American journalists in India under surveillance. Their private mail was regularly intercepted and read for evidence of anti-British sentiment. The correspondence of individual American reporters revealed a deep hostility to Britain and its administration in India. There is an interesting case of one Mrs Bilimoria, a former Seattle schoolmistress, who ran the film section of the American Office of War Information in New Delhi. The British Military Intelligence objected to her anti-British attitude and the authorities asked for her removal but it was refused.

Not much has been written on the life and experiences of American soldiers in India during the War. The Stilwell Papers, published in 1967, are war journals written by General Stilwell which present only a factual account of the military operations. Easily, the most fascinating and delightful account of an American soldier's encounters in India is offered by John W. Wohfarth in his book, *A Modern Pilgrim in India—The Diary of an American Soldier*, published in 1995. Corporal Wohlfarth recorded his day-to-day experiences, impressions, reflections, and encounters with Indians, Americans, and the British in Calcutta, Delhi, Agra, Darjeeling, and other places. His book, covering a brief period of about one year (1945–6), provides rare insights into Indians at a crucial period in their history. Wohlfarth carries his remarkable scholarship lightly as is revealed by his discussions with Indian and English scholars on a variety of subjects like Indian music, the rise and fall of civilizations, interracial relations, and the plunder of Indian wealth by the British. He was charmed by the sights, sounds, and smells of Calcutta, which he calls the heartbeat of India as compared to Delhi where the brain resides. He is fascinated by the diversity of Indian people and their unique way of life. Among several anecdotes narrated by him, an amusing one relates to his being identified as an American by a shopkeeper simply for shaking hands with him which no Englishman ever did. He also mentions how some American soldiers were mistaken for British and assaulted during the communal riots in Calcutta. Thereafter the military personnel were directed to have the American flag sewn on the back of their uniforms. Generally, the British soldiers kept their distance from Americans.

As regards Indian impressions of American soldiers, it was appreciated that unhampered by class consciousness or racial prejudice and friendly by temperament, they mixed with Indians on equal terms. With emoluments and perks far higher than the British Other Ranks (BORs), they were valued patrons in leading stores, hotels, and fashionable restaurants. They flocked to cinema houses showing American movies, and were responsible for introducing the queue system for buying tickets. In New Delhi, American officers were provided with luxurious accommodation and had their exclusive club on Janpath almost opposite the Imperial Hotel. The soldiers occupied barracks in the vicinity of Connuaght Place and were a familiar sight riding tongas or their attractive cycles. Unaccustomed to social contact with white men of the ruling race, it was indeed an unexpected and novel experience for Indians when they met the exuberant American visitors and they were struck by their gusto and vigour. There were occasions when Indians invited them to participate in their festivities and functions. The American presence in India was also taken note of by Nehru who wrote in his *Discovery of India*: 'And then came the Americans—while the help they were bringing was very welcome, they were not liked in the highest official (British) circles and relations were strained. Indians liked them on the whole; their energy and enthusiasm for the work in hand was infectious and contrasted with the lack of these qualities in British official circles in India. Their forthrightness and freedom from official constraints were appreciated.'

The war-time goodwill between America and India continued in the post-war period during the historic developments leading to India's Independence in August 1947, so much so that Jawaharlal Nehru, even while heading the interim government, established formal diplomatic relations with the appointment of Asaf Ali as India's Ambassador to the United States. This was reciprocated by the US with the appointment of Henry Grady as the first US Ambassador to India. On assuming office as head of the interim government in 1946, Nehru in his broadcast to the nation said: 'We send our greetings to the people of United States of America to whom destiny has given a major role in international affair.'

CHAPTER 1

The British Raj in India

H.M. Hyndman

THE INVASION OF INDIA FROM THE west, in modern times, began in earnest by way of trade and commerce. There was no preconceived intention of conquering that vast territory by any of the Europeans who first landed and made settlements on its shores, except, perhaps, for a short time by the Portuguese. Nor has there ever been a successful propaganda of Christianity in Hindustan such as menaced the well-being of China and Japan. At the beginning of the rivalry of the two principal nations of Europe for influence over the Indian courts and kingdoms the French were the statesmen and administrators, the English were the merchants and traders. Such men as Dupleix and Bussy took a wider view of Indian affairs and better understood what would be to the advantage of Indians themselves than did the English of the same period. Indians, also, were first trained to war on European principles and formed into armies of sepoys by men of the Perron and De Boigne type. Yet England succeeded in establishing her rule where France failed; because her adventurers as they gained power were supported from home, which the French were not; because the English fleets eventually obtained control of the eastern as well as the western seas; and because at the critical moment the present masters of Hindustan made better use of the trained Indian

**ASIA*, May 1919. H.M. Hyndman was an English writer and politician and the founder of the Social Democratic federation and the National Socialist Party. Author of *The Awakening of Asia*.

levies and played upon the differences between the Indian courts with greater astuteness than their opponents.

Nevertheless, the conquest of India, mainly by Indian troops led by Englishmen, was achieved, as it were, by accident. There was no organized effort whatever. The *conquistadores* of South America and Mexico were born again in a new shape, and equally destitute of scruple, throughout the settlements granted as trading centres by the rajahs and nawabs of India. The East India Company was not in the least desirous of annexing and governing large and populous districts. On the contrary, the directors were never weary of impressing upon their representatives in India the permanent necessity for keeping their direct possessions within the narrowest possible limits. Above all, they should avoid war with their neighbours. Hostilities of any kind were injurious to business. The sole aim and objects of these advocates of profitable peace and lucrative persuasion was to secure the means for distributing enormous dividends on the shares of their Company. Aggression must be avoided, but adequate profits and commercial returns must be made. Agents on the spot took the most effective means at their disposal to satisfy the pecuniary demands of their chiefs in London and paid little attention to their prohibition of remunerative rapine. Thus was seen the marvelous spectacle of clerks and supercargoes developing into great generals and administrators of the first mark and winning an empire against fearful odds. This unexampled fashion of conducting the business of a mere trading company, taking possession of a civilized empire as a detail of business and waging great wars in order to pay huge dividends to shareholders thousands of miles away is quite exceptional on such a scale in all human history. Nothing like it had ever before been seen in the East; probably nothing like it will ever occur again.

From the first began that steady withdrawal of wealth from India to England which in one form or another has gone on ever since. Throughout the latter part of the eighteenth century, the wealthy English nabob, denounced by Pitt, who had returned to his own country after shaking the pagoda-tree to some purpose in his own interest, was the familiar type of the rich man of yesterday. There are the records of the East India Company to bear witness to the conduct of the fortune-hunters of that halcyon period of plunder. India was the El Dorado of the unscrupulous and cruel commercial adventurer. The legitimate proceedings of the great Company chartered by Queen Elizabeth and successfully carried on up to our own time were bad enough. There is no doubt about that. It was no rose-water management which paid such stupendous dividends and drove the stock of the lucky shareholders to such an enormous premium. But the illegitimate business of the East was infinitely worse in every respect. Even the lowest commercial morality cannot justify the robbery and rascality which pervaded every department of English administration in India from the time of Clive's rise to power until the first Governor-Generalship of Lord Cornwallis. The praises of many of the successful freebooters have been chanted for 150 years with national pride and exultation; the effect of their depredations upon the luckless Indians who suffered from their extortions, though denounced at the time by Englishmen of the highest character and reputation, has since been overlooked and is now almost forgotten.

It is unnecessary in any case to enlarge upon the crimes of the men who plundered in this way a great and ancient civilization. Whether Warren Hastings could or could not have avoided the transactions stigmatized by Burke, but disregarded by the Indians themselves in consideration of his other qualities; whether Clive and smaller men were entitled to be 'amazed at their own moderation' in the loot which they appropriated, are matters of comparatively small importance. The guilt or innocence of individuals counts for little in such a system of robbery as afflicted the provinces under immediate English control, and especially Bengal and Oudh, in the generation between 1757, the date of the Battle of Plassey, and 1786, when attempts at reform began. What the total amount of wealth may have been which was abstracted from India and transported to England without any valuable return at the end of the eighteenth century will probably never be known. It must have been quite enormous, transcending indeed the drain from America to Europe which followed upon the discoveries of Columbus and Vespucci. The wealth thus accumulated and used in the form of productive capital in English industries, especially cotton, enabled Great Britain to obtain the lead in manufacture and commerce which gave her the control of markets in the century which followed. And the Indians themselves, who provided the means for the attainment of this commercial supremacy, suffered a second time, and even more horribly than they did from direct expropriation, by the economic consequences of their original losses.

In the seventeenth and during a great part of the eighteenth century the importation of Indian calicoes into England was prohibited on the ground that their competition would have crushed the rising home industry in similar goods. At the end of the same century, however, owing to the accumulation of riches chiefly from Hindustan, England had become possessed of a virtual monopoly of new machinery run by steam power which enabled her to undersell the whole world in textile goods of every description, English handloom weavers and spinners suffered seriously from the competition of the machine-made products at their own door, but their miseries were child's play in comparison with the horrors inflicted upon the weavers of India at the same time. No protective tariff was allowed to safeguard them. Unchecked competition, free-trade in English goods in English territory, was a commercial religion. As a consequence, these poor producers of Indian fabrics saw their means of livelihood swept away from them by a process which they could neither understand nor withstand. Tens upon tens of thousands of them perished of starvation; for there was no place for them in the Indian society of that day apart from the one which they occupied. The foreign government made not the slightest attempt to regulate this fatal free-trade competition, and the effects of the English connection in this respect have been wholly harmful to the people of India. The fatal results of economic causes are carefully disregarded. Successful wars and continental annexations quite eclipse in interest the sad fate of the unfortunate Indian weavers who perished silently on the field of commercial war.

Effective steps were taken to check this objectionable form of the exploitation of India by England and to regularize the methods by which the dominant power in Hindustan remunerated itself from Indian resources for the services rendered to the subjugated territories. The improved system of administration was set on foot in 1786 and, after having incidentally conquered the Mahrattas, the native states which rose to great prominence on the decay of the Mogul authority, the Governor-General, Lord Cornwallis, finally established English administration in India in much the same shape in which it exists today. Honesty was favoured, if not insured, by payment to the Europeans employed of such high salaries that the temptation to accept bribes, or to indulge in illegal appropriation, became less and less inducive in proportion to the risk of removal and punishment. Whether the form of government thus created was suited to the character of the people, whether foreigners were capable of sufficiently sympathizing with the social system into which they had burglariously forced themselves, or whether the European ideas, laws and economic conceptions imposed upon the population were not likely to prove injurious; these were points which the new government never stopped to consider.

For 130 years, from 1786 to 1916, the official class of foreign administrators have done their utmost—alike in India and in England—to convince the world that British rule has conferred immense benefit on its subjects and that the inhabitants of Hindustan are quite incapable of governing themselves. This has never been the view of the mass of Indians themselves, ignorant, peaceful and submissive as the great majority of the cultivators may be, who constitute more than four-fifths of the entire population. And there are the great 'protected' Indian states, with nearly 70,000,000 of people, to prove still that administration of India is by no means the hopeless business that Englishmen as a rule believe it to be. The Montague-Chelmsford Report, unsatisfactory as Indian radicals have pronounced it, constitutes important evidence in the case, for it bears official witness to the necessity for wide-sweeping reform, as well as to the honest conviction that the Indians themselves must more largely share in and uphold a responsible government.

During the whole of the period (1786-1916) referred to conquest by force of arms and annexation by that means or by chicane have gone steadily forward. Some of the military operations, always carried on in the main by native troops, exhibited great skill and courage on the part of the European leaders; though such a disaster as that of Ferozeshah showed that Indian troops under Indian generals had not degenerated from the earlier days. But the most remarkable fact, brought out by those of the English administrators who were in closest touch with their subjects, was that the worst rule by their own people was preferred to the best management by foreigners. Thus, Sir William Sleeman of the old East India Company was a man so thoroughly versed in Indian languages and customs and so completely at home in Indian dress and manners that he succeeded in doing that which even the great Akbar at the height of his power was unable to achieve. He was able to put down that extraordinary semi-religious sect of stranglers, the Thugs, whose members had been the horror of all Indian travellers for hundreds of years. The capacity of disguise, the astounding coolness and courage displayed by Sleeman in the course of this triumph of detective enterprise and repression of crime have never been excelled, if ever equalled. But, in addition to this marvelous performance, Sleeman was one of the ablest and best of the Company's civil servants. Naturally, too, he was loyal to British rule.

Yet what does he tell us of a specific instance with which he was familiarly acquainted? Native rule in the great province of Oudh was in every way abominable. It is doubtful whether in time of peace any worse tryanny was ever seen in any part of Hindustan. Robbery, torture, the most fiendish barbarities of every kind, were inflicted daily upon the wretched inhabitants. If ever interposition by a neighbouring state under peaceful and law-abiding foreign control could appear not only justifiable but inevitable, this was such a case. Interposition and annexation, therefore, actually took place. What followed? Though all this anarchy and misgovernment were suppressed and life and property were secure under English law and justice, the people were bitterly opposed to the change, which seemed to foreign eyes to be so much for the better. Amid all these horrors, so shocking to Europeans of the nineteenth century, Indian habits, Indian customs and Indian laws were in the main upheld. The land-tax was roughly and not unreasonably assessed and levied, the rapacity of native moneylenders was checked, the existing legal methods were simple and generally understood.

To give Sir William Sleeman's own words: 'There were neither accumulating arrears of land revenue nor ruinous back debts to weigh down the proprietors; there were no unsatisfied decrees of Court to drive debtors to hopeless despair . . . arrears were remitted when the impossibility of payment within the year was clearly demonstrated. . . . There could be no black despair in those days of changeful misrule.' Never was there a more crushing exposure of the idea that honesty of administration and peace within the borders of a subject country really justified foreign domination. 'The people,' so this master of Indian affairs openly declared, 'the people generally, or at least the greater part of them, would prefer to reside in Oudh . . . . than in our own districts, under the evils they were exposed to from the uncertainty of our laws, the multiplicity and formality of our courts, the pride and negligence of those who preside over them. . . . I am persuaded that if it were put to the vote among the people of Oudh, ninety-nine in a hundred would rather remain as they are, without any feeling of security in life or property than have our system introduced in its presented complicated state.'

This was in 1856. Two generations have passed since then and the system is more complicated than ever. No fewer than twenty-five thousand new laws were put on the statute-book in the first ten years of this century alone!

Annexation, therefore, to the British Empire in India has never been welcomed by the people annexed. Yet the direct government of Englishmen who did not interfere with Indian habits, but did their best to ensure honest and prompt judgement in case of difference and used their authority to

LORD CLIVE (1725-74), WHO LAID THE FOUNDATIONS OF THE BRITISH EMPIRE IN INDIA

WARREN HASTINGS (1732-1818),
THE FIRST GOVERNOR-GENERAL OF BRITISH INDIA

restrict economic hardship and to secure fair play, has often been immensely popular. Such men are never forgotten by the inhabitants of the provinces over which they have once exercised their benign sway. Whole districts would turn out to welcome them, men, women and children would cover them with flowers and chant their praises when they returned after the lapse of many years. This one-man rule called, of course, for thorough knowledge of the country and the language, as well as long and continuous residence among the people themselves. But such instances of individual success were not rare under the Kumpani Bahadurs. The servants of the Government who were given appointments found themselves at the early age of seventeen or eighteen thrown among a strange population and often entrusted with powers which rendered it imperative that they should become thoroughly acquainted with those over whom they were placed. It is creditable to our race that after the early days of rapine and rascality so many were successful under such trying circumstances.

Moreover, the East India Company itself, though it kept up a European and a powerful Indian Army, was not lavish in its expenditures; nor, in spite of all drawbacks and the general objection to the new methods gradually gaining ground, was it regarded with hatred by its subjects. The drain of produce without return from India to England was trifling in Company days, compared with what it afterward became. Some of the most capable of those who rose to high appointments remembered what India had been and might be again. A few saw that European domination could be only temporary and endeavoured to prepare their countrymen for the withdrawal which they knew sooner or later was inevitable. But the general opinion both in India and in England was that the Indians, split up into many races and peoples, with at least four antagonistic religions professed by millions of people and with the caste system which shut out whole sections of inhabitants from any close contact with one another, were quite incapable of common action against the foreigners, however much they might dislike their rule. The great past of Hindustan was already being forgotten in any estimate of the future of the Empire. Already it was taken for granted that Europeanization was the one thing needful to make of India a greater empire than ever before, and thus to increase the power and wealth of England.

Yet many hundreds of years before the nations of India had been a collection of wealthy and highly civilized people, possessed of a great language, with an elaborate code of laws and social regulations, with exquisite artistic taste in architecture and decoration, producing beautiful manufactures of all kinds and endowed with religious ideas and philosophic and scientific conceptions which have greatly influenced the development of the most progressive races of the West. One of the noblest individual moralists who ever lived, Sakya Muni, was a Hindu; the Code of Manu of the ninth century before the Christian era is still as essential a study for the jurist as the Laws of the Twelve Tables or the Institutes of Justinian; Akbar the Mohammedan was the greatest monarch who ever ruled the East; while even in later times nations over whom the English held supremacy have proved that there are among them no unworthy descendants of the authors of the Vedas, of the Mahabharata and Ramayana, of the architects of the Taj Mahal and Bejapore, of Toder Mull and Nana Furnava, of Baber, Hyder Ali and Runjeet Singh. Nevertheless nine-tenths of what has been written about India in English is so expressed that we are led to believe stable civilized government in Hindustan began only with the European Raj and that nothing short of wholesale Europeanization can save Hindustan from permanent anarchy.

It is now recognized that the revolt, which goes by the name of the Indian Mutiny, was in reality a national rising against the growing extension of European domination. The native troops of the East India Company were roused against their officers by misrepresentations calculated to outrage the dearest feelings and prejudices of soldiers of all creeds and castes. But the scope of the upheaval went far beyond the army itself. A considerable part of India was directly hostile to English rule, so far as the more intelligent and well-to-do classes were concerned. The plans of the leaders were all laid; the discontent upon which they could reckon was widespread; the recent referral of the ancient right of adoption by the Government and seizure of the territories of Indian chieftains on that ground had alarmed all the princes; the date of the attack had been well chosen, being a hundred years after the manifest superiority of the white man in arms had been first admitted; the secret of the conspiracy was, on the whole, well kept. Yet the insurrection failed. This circumstance resulted from several causes. The original muntiny at Meerut began before it was intended, and before the general outbreak which was to follow, or to occur simultaneously, was ready. The agricultural population over the greater part of India did not sympathize sufficiently with the revolt to oppose actively, or even passively, the operations of the Government troops; the vast number of camp followers required to enable an army to move under European leadership never fell short for want of recruits. The insurgents developed no really capable leader, with the exception of Tantia Topee and that famous princess, the Ranee of

THE LONDON SALESROOM OF THE EAST INDIA COMPANY
INDIA'S WAS THE EL DORADO THE ADVENTUROUS ENGLISH TRADER
AT THE END OF THE EIGHTEENTH CENTURY

Jhansi, who were not sufficiently supported. On the other hand, the English soldiers and officers exhibited wonderful vigour, courage and endurance, while individual civilian officials of the government who had long been in the country and were known and trusted by the Indians under their control kept quiet whole districts that would otherwise have joined the insurgents. But above all, the English government owed its successful suppression of the outbreak to the fact that the Sikhs, the great people who had most recently been defeated by the foreign rulers, took sides with their conquerors and rendered invaluable assistance which ensured victory to the Europeans. The rising was, therefore, put down, and all Hindustan came under the direct or indirect control of the British Crown.

India with its 300,000,000 inhabitants has for 60 years been under the management of the most extraordinary and fortuitous system of foreign domination known to the memory of man. The rulers of these people come in succession from without, educated, until their appointment at the age of more than twenty-one, in accordance with methods as remote from, and as irreconcilable with, Asiatic ideas as it is possible for them to be. Alike in their work and in their pleasure, they keep as far aloof as possible from the people they govern. Very rarely do they marry Indians: still more rarely do they settle permanently in the country. The head of the government, who himself is brought out fresh from Europe and entirely ignorant of India, does not remain in office for more than five years. His subordinates return 'home' frequently for their holidays and go back to England permanently, to live on a considerable pension, after their term of service is completed.

I quote an English writer who knew India well: 'Not only is there no white race in India, not only is there no white Colony, but there is no white man who purposes to remain. . . . No white man takes root in India and the number even of sojourners is, among these masses, imperceptible.'

The longer this reign of well-meaning but unsympathetic carpet-baggers continues, the less intimate do their general relations with the Indian people become. The colour and race prejudices, which existed not at all, or to a very small extent, at the beginning of English dominance, now become stronger and stronger every year. In India itself men of ancient lineage, beside which the descent of the oldest European aristocracy is a mushroom growth, are considered in the presidency towns, as well as on the railways, unfit to associate on equal terms with the young white bureaucrats just arrived in the country. And these 'competition-wallahs', owing their position too often to desk-work, though clever enough in their own way, lack nowadays that indescribable quality of the *sahib,* or 'gentleman', which is nowhere so instinctively recognized as in Asia.

And what is this alien supremacy based on? Upon 1,500 foreign administrators isolated among the hundreds of millions of Indians—*rari nantes in gurgito vasto*—not one of whom, with the best intentions in the world and even enjoying a far closer intimacy with his subjects than a modern civil servant claims, can exercise any lasting influence on the people committed to his charge. These are the district officers, the real rulers of India, upon whom the true responsibilities of government fall. Each is in his way a governor, and these are some of his duties. He is: collector of the land revenue, registrar of the landed property in the district, judge between landlord and tenant, ministerial officer of the courts of justice, treasurer and accountant of the district, administrator of the district excise, ex-officio president of the local rates committee, referee for all questions of compensation for lands taken up for public purposes, agent for the government in all local suits to which it is a party, referee in local public works, head of the police, ex-officio president of municipalities, and magistrate, police magistrate and criminal judge.

It is utterly impossible that all these multifarious duties, with the endless reports that have to be written and the questions with superiors which have to be discussed, can be performed satisfactorily. Many of the ablest of the civil servants themselves admit that this is so. Constant transfers from district to district and frequent furloughs to Europe make things worse. Here again is a criticism by an English official in India when the situation was by no means so critical as it is today. This official himself was brought into contact with Indians much more familiarly than most of his countrymen. His family had been connected with India for more than a century and furnished two or three directors to the East India Company:

> It is in general sadly true that Englishmen in India live totally estranged from the people among whom they are sojourning. This estrangement is partly unavoidable, being the result of national customs, language, and caste. . . . The English contempt proceeds . . . from English ignorance, and English ignorance is accomplished, as so often happens, by English bluster. Those who have known the natives well have generally liked them, even loved them, and their love has been returned with a remarkable wealth of unselfish affection. The natives are worth the effort of knowing . . . but because . . . it does take some effort to know them, most Englishmen keep aloof. This tendency to aloofness is increasing. . . . Certain it is, the natives consider the sahib is not what he used to be—certain, too, that English rule is not popular. This is the great social calamity attending our Raj in India. . . .

Over and above the Europeans immediately concerned in administration there are many more occupied directly or indirectly in other branches of government affairs. But in all India there are no more than 200,000 Europeans and Eurasians altogether. These are, for the most part, entirely outside the official class. The British Empire in India consists, therefore, of the bureaucrats spoken of above and in pre-war days, 75,000 English troops, of whom 50,000 at the outside can be reckoned as fit for active service at any given moment. A peaceful upset of the entire English system is quite possible, seeing that, as has been truly said, the Indians themselves have only to refuse to work for Europeans and the whole white empire would be brought to an end within a month. Certain it is that if the agricultural population, hitherto so quiescent, with the exception of a few local outbreaks were to become even passively hostile, British rule would soon be a thing of the past.

CHAPTER 2

Eastern Craftsmen and Western Markets

M.D.C. Crawford

NOT SINCE THE VOYAGE OF VASCO DA Gama in 1497 has Asia been so important to the Western world. In our commerce we need Asiatic merchandise as much as in our arts we need the Asiatic traditions. On the other hand, Asia requires many of the objects we produce in America, though in many ways our need of Asia is greater than Asia's need of us. But if we are to develop markets that will endure, they must be established on an intelligent basis of exchange, and this means emphatically the modification of certain preconceived notions now entertained by both worlds.

Intelligent trade must be built upon a mutual understanding of the needs and preferences of peoples and the prevailing industrial and economic conditions. But more particularly does trade depend upon a knowledge of the ability of peoples to make certain articles in demand. This is the day of the specialist in commerce as in other matters, and the time has come for a broader commercial vision and more scientific application. Let us, therefore, turn away as rapidly as possible from the fallacy of the 'dumping-ground idea'.

We must study Asiatic commerce in the light of present-day problems and avoid the myths of the past. Out of these confusing reconstruction times, two solid facts are recognized as the basis for sound reason. All over the world there is greater need for production, and production that follows

**ASIA*, October 1919. M.D.C. Crawford (1882-1949), was the curator of the costume department at the American Museum of Natural History, New York.

the line of least resistance. In other words, the all too evident shortage of labour makes it necessary that we regulate production as far as possible so that the tasks may fall upon those best qualified to perform them with the least waste of labour time.

If one race or nation is trained to handwork and another has a similar penchant in favour of mechanical production, these very pertinent factors deserve as much consideration as the more obvious problems of propinquity to raw material. Therefore, at this time to divert established productive forces into exotic, unaccustomed fields of endeavour, in an attempt to build up industries through sheer material force, regardless of local conditions, is as senseless as trying to grow oranges in Dakota or wheat in Florida. The world has now no leeway for such diminishing of resources and waste of material substance.

If I have chosen an obvious example in the use of material, the facts are no less obvious in the matter of human penchants and adaptabilities. The commercial history of the world has been a series of dreadful disasters due to the fact that stronger nations and peoples have often attempted to dictate or restrict the forms of commercial endeavour among weaker peoples. While at times this control may be paternalistic, generally it has been dictated with regard to the interest of the stronger people. It is high time that we learn the lesson that good business consists as much in buying as in selling—and in buying those things which are produced to the best advantage in the foreign market—and in selling such as are produced most advantageously in the home market. In each instance the selection of commodities should be regulated by the ascertained needs and tastes of the people who are to receive them.

America has an unusual genius for serial production by mechanical agency, while the Orient has a correspondingly-developed inclination for individual and group craftsmanship. True, there is in this country a very important group of craftsmen developing definite forms of art of the highest importance. On the other hand, in the Orient (especially in Japan), there are powerful groups of modern manufacturers operating factories in the most efficient manner. But these, in both instances, are the exceptions, and while they deserve consideration, and may grow in importance in the near future, for general purposes the distinctions I have made hold true.

There is a market in the Orient for many of our machine-made commodities. We have advanced standards of production to such a degree that our merchandise is of the highest quality with the lowest consistent price. At the same time, the taste of the Western world in all matters of industrial art also has advanced greatly during the last generation. New mechanical discoveries and greater familiarity with the machine has made it possible for us to supply a certain part of this demand mechanically, but it is equally true that the potential demand for handmade merchandise of higher artistic quality has increased at a greater ratio. This is not difficult to understand, since our desires for ornament are limited only by our intellectual appreciation which has been vastly stimulated by educational forces of comparatively recent development. At present our needs greatly exceed our productive possibilities.

Many of the buyers from America who have gone to the Orient, particularly to India, have approached the problem with a rather superficial knowledge of prevailing conditions and the traditions of craftsmanship or the history of her great arts. The fact that labour per day or hour is cheaper in India than in Europe or America has led them to seek the cheapest kind of material in the market. What we need in the Orient is the same type of buyer that goes from this country to Europe. In other words, the successful buyer in the Orient must be an individual of taste who understands thoroughly the types of design, colour and composition which will be desirable in America, and has had at least the rudiments of training in the ancient and modern history of the Orient. There are unquestionably large groups of craftsmen all through the Orient, more particularly in China, India, and the Malay Archipelago who, with some little instruction, can be directed into modifying their present crafts so as to make materials highly desirable in this country.

Costuming in the Orient has settled into more or less definite lines which are prescribed by custom, religion and limitation of material. Design on fabrics has become regulated by these costume needs. In America, however, styles vary constantly, although within much narrower limitations than the public believes, and in addition we require seasonable changes. The point of difference, however, is that we cut our materials, whereas in the East it is a more general practice to use an entire piece of goods, without cutting it. Therefore, the main point is to show the craftsmen in India that we desire continuous patterns by the yard, rather than separate pieces. Many of the materials that already come to us from India in colour and design are highly desirable, but the particular composition places them in the class of exotic objects. What both India and America need is that we should treat these objects as articles of contemporary commerce.

It is surely unfortunate that the East should imagine that our taste is entirely for the garish and untasteful in ornament. We have been misinterpreted in many instances. This is very unjust, as much of the good taste now developing in America is the result of the reaction from the earlier, greater periods of Oriental art. We have learned, and learned deeply, from the great collections of Oriental art which now exist in this country. Asia is the mother of loveliness. There is hardly an expression of ornament, scarcely a philosophy that adorn and enriches Western intellectual life, that cannot be traced to some Oriental source. Yet it all belongs to the past. Asia today is not the Asia of the golden centuries, any more than Europe today is the Europe of the Middle Ages or the Renaissance. If at first sight it seems presumptuous to think of the West teaching the East, it must be admitted that even Europe, with its traditions of art second only to Asia, has been able to learn something in the practical application of taste to production for commercial exchange from the criticisms and advice of the intelligent American buyer.

In such relationship there is nothing that endangers the traditions or imperils the skill of Oriental artists. Indeed, they will gain in vitality and vigour from modern contact. Oriental artists of the sixteenth century learned much from the Portuguese, Spanish and Italian arts of that period. The arts of one people as a rule must be interpreted before they can fit the needs of another, and where this interpretation is brought about in an intelligent, rational manner, it can do no harm to the arts of either people. Every race and every age have produced various modifications in expression. Art is a mobile rather than a static force. Surely at a time when the arts of all the world are at the lowest ebb, we should be very stupid to attempt to compel an awakened Orient to continue in the use of forms which have largely lost their meaning, or to prohibit them from extending their research and creative power into new fields.

Let us briefly outline the situation as it applies to fabrics: it is a conservative estimate that an export business of $250,000,000 in fine cottons alone was destroyed in northern France by the war. In England, though a far more hopeful condition exists, disorganization and unrest have diminished production to a great extent. In our fine yarn mills in America there has been a retrogression of almost a quarter of a century, due to the fact that our mill owners have paid more attention to immediate profits than to future possibilities. In other words, decorative cottons of distinction have become extremely rare. This is a great pity, since for many purposes cotton is the ideal fibre, and its absence from the market has a detrimental influence on other industries. In my belief, the East can supply a large part of this valuable material.

Almost all forms of decorative cottons a century ago came from India; the collection of fabrics which possesses even a few of these early specimens is rich indeed. But it is a great mistake to think that the art of the cotton print in India is dead. Even to-day we are importing block printed curtains that, in point of design and colour, lack little of the ancient traditional value. The Oriental block printing method differs from the European counterpart in that the pattern is composed from a number of small blocks rather than from a single composite. Many of the details could therefore be used just as they are in making fabrics for dress wear. Colour, design and texture are perfectly satisfactory, but the composition is not adapted to our needs. This is little to be wondered at, since in India, and the East generally, there is not that sudden change in type of garment which, however to be deplored in certain respects, lies at the basis of our prosperous fabric business.

The static condition of costuming in India has led to the adoption of certain conventions in design. Therefore the Indian printed cottons, while beautiful in themselves, have the charm of exotic textures rather than of fabrics of general use. What the director of Indian craftsmen should do is to induce the craftsmen to compose these units and certain others that will naturally suggest themselves, for printing by the yard. Our conditions of wear, and requirements as to fastness in washing, also require consideration. It is not a difficult problem, but one that will solve itself very quickly. It should not be approached, of course, from the idea of inducing the Indian craftsmen to substitute our more or less banal decorative art for their own, which has stood the test of centuries of good taste.

The gold and silver brocades of India are another example in point. Indian gold and silver threads do not tarnish, and are made so that they do not fray to the same degree that the European threads do. I have before me as I write a collection of weavers' samples from Ahmedabad which are 40 years old, and every piece is as bright as the day it left the loom. But a great many of India's most delightful and most useful designs are woven as borders to the scarfs. Here again a slight modification in composition would make fabrics that would be marketable in large quantities.

What has been said in respect to weaving can be applied with equal, if not greater, force to embroidery. All-over patterns by the yard, a little stronger perhaps in line, a trifle less exquisite in texture, would fill a great need. We are to-day buying brocades from the handlooms of Lyons that run in wholesale price from $50 to $85 a yard, and the prospect is that even these high prices will advance. An embroidered blouse purchased for a few rupees in India a decade ago would cost $100 to duplicate in America to-day.

More attention has been paid to the adaptation of fabrics for interior decoration, but there is still much progress that can be carried out even in this connection. There was a time when the American home had the appearance of a curiosity shop, and anything of an exotic character had a place. But during the last few years there has come a change in the type of house, method of lighting, and general interior arrangement, and this change has been for the better. Quite naturally, therefore, we require different materials, modifications of colour schemes, and simpler composition in fabrics. If the East is to hold her position in this market, she must pay some attention to these changes.

There has been, and still is, in this country, a large market for block printed French, English and Belgian cretonnes. The limited supply of such fabrics prevents a development of a much more interesting market. Many

MODERN DESIGNS FOR JACQUARD BROCADES, SUGGESTED BY OLD MATERIALS, IN WHICH VERY LITTLE MODIFICATION HAS BEEN MADE

of the coarser cottons especially such as were made on handlooms, would lend themselves admirably to this purpose. Again, however, our method of cutting material makes it necessary that the design run by the yard, not in individual pieces.

Perhaps the finest opportunity lies in rugs. It is a matter of comment that the restlessness of the more intricate oriental designs makes them more or less undesirable for the modern type of house and system of lighting. Of course, in this generality I do not include the true antiques which are, properly speaking, objects of art, and assert their position by their esthetic value. But since Persian rugs are being made in India and Chinese rugs in Bokhara, and all types in Japan, the original significance and romance of the knotted carpet has in a measure been destroyed. Indeed, even the laity have come to understand that most of the modern rugs, while woven in the East, are designed in London, Paris or New York, and the thought naturally arises, why can we not have rugs which, in design, are more sympathetic with contemporaneous environment? It has ceased to become an antiquarian problem and has become frankly a commercial matter, and it is the part of good sense, as well as good taste, to accept it in this spirit. No floor covering

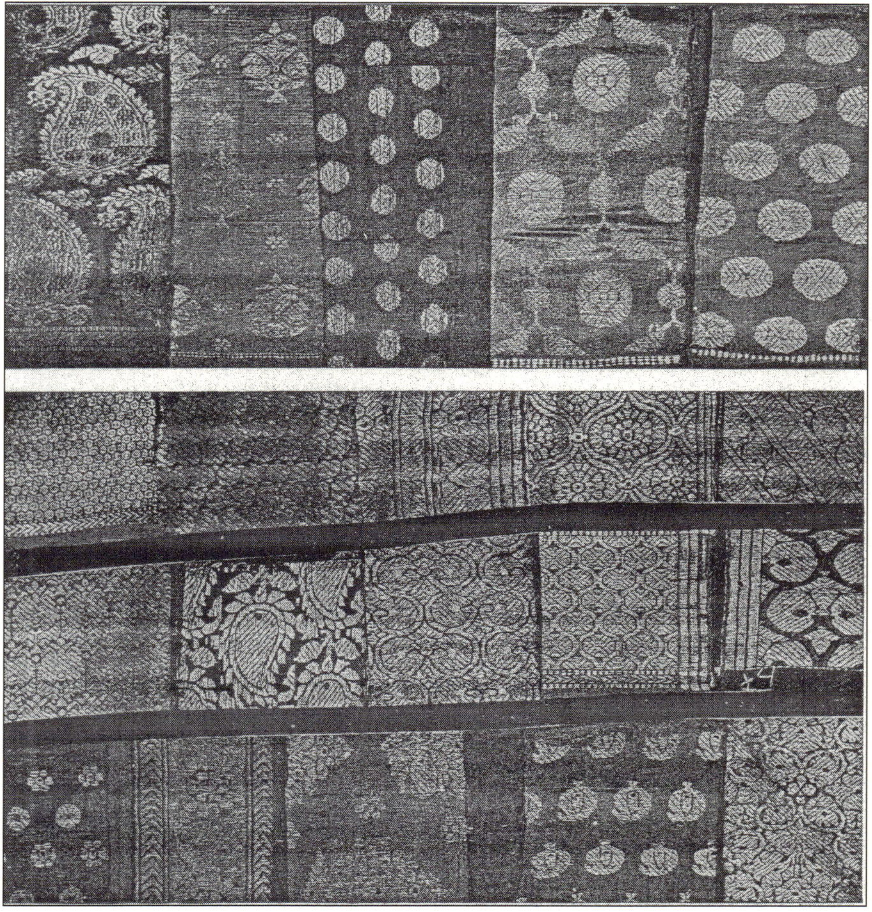

SAMPLES FROM AN INDIAN WEAVER'S PATTERN BOOK OF 40 YEARS AGO

Eastern costumes, as a rule, are draped rather than cut. This means that their designs are constituted with reference to the piece, instead of goods by the yard, and thus come under the head of exotic art. American buyers hope to influence eastern craftsmen to study the needs of Western markets and supply the present deficiency in textiles.

that exists can compare with the pile knot carpet; and yet, certain qualities that are creeping into the design and the colour schemes are gradually creating a popular feeling against the rug. It is a very serious matter and one which, if permitted to take its own course, may in time come to be a disaster.

It is far from my thought to create the impression that such a change in commercial relations as I have suggested can be accomplished either quickly or by simple methods. Obviously the subject is too great for hasty generalizations, and we must be patient in awaiting results. But surely it should not require argument that commerce which is mutually beneficial ought to be built upon a knowledge of the needs of the peoples concerned. Surely the anomaly can escape no intelligent person that the average modern Oriental shop is filled with objects that have little relationship either to our lives or our taste, and that the objects of art from the same people of other ages are among our most priceless possessions. Therefore, it seems to me that really the most vital service we can render to the East today is to lead her craftsmen back to the appreciation of the fact that there is a market in this country for their finest workmanship, and that all that is necessary to bring about a revival of those arts in India is a little change in the method of expression.

If we bought and sold goods in India with the same intelligence that we buy and sell between Chicago and New York, or Boston and San Francisco, the problem would almost solve itself.

CHAPTER 3

Democracy and India

Charles Johnston

Britain's Policy of Self-Government in India

The following statement by the Right Honourable Edwin Samuel Montagu, Secretary of State for India, was given out by him in London on September 15 to the Associated Press correspondent, before leaving for the East to consult with officials and native leaders in regard to the furtherance of self-government in India:

My journey is the direct outcome of the government's announcement in parliament that its policy in India is to develop self-governing institutions with a view to the progressive realization of a representative government. This ideal of ours must be approached by easy stages. The man who thinks home rule for India is a practical policy is either wholly ignorant of the situation or designedly mischievous. Steps toward responsible government will be taken at different rates by different parts of India. Great provinces will fit themselves for it at different times. But the great thing is that we are going ahead firmly on the path toward the end which we all, British and Indian alike, desire. . . . We have set ourselves avowedly to the enormous task of improving the condition and life of the people, to guarding them against famine and against wars, external and internal, so that they might live and learn and develop their great resources unhindered and in peace. One of the most striking

**ASIA*, December 1919. Charles Johnston (1867-1931), joined Indian Civil Service in 1888 but left two years later and became an eminent Sanskrit scholar. Translated *Upanishads* (1896) and wrote extensively on oriental historical and literary subjects.

evidences of our work in India is found in our enormous irrigation enterprises, which are even vaster than the greatest of your own enormous irrigation exploits, and which have reclaimed literally thousands of square miles of desert. But it is still a country of poverty. The majority of the people live on a few rupees a month, and it takes three rupees to make an American dollar. Their country has vast resources awaiting development, but the people are still very poor. Only about 10 per cent of the population can read and write. India's greatest terror, the spectre of famine, has practically disappeared, owing to irrigation and the development of transport by railway, canal and river. A season of famine, which a generation ago meant hundreds of thousands of deaths, now means only discomfort and strain. As we have conquered famine, so we shall surmount the educational difficulties. . . . Today the British people have begun to realize that India has proved herself worthy of a larger part in the imperial plan. India is now assured of a place in all future imperial war conferences. Further steps toward responsible government will be taken as a result of my trip to India, steps which I trust will be convincing and satisfying to the great body of educated public opinion in that country.

The beginnings of democracy in India were the self-governed village communities, which manage their own affairs and appoint their own police. And these self-contained, self-governing village communities are the most venerable institution in India, one of the most ancient and universal in the world. They were here, practically in their present form, not only before the Portuguese, Dutch, English and French navigators arrived beginning with Vasco da Gama in 1498, but before the coming of the Moguls, the Arabs, the Persians—the whole list of medieval invaders and conquerors. More than that, they were in all likelihood firmly settled on the soil of India before the coming of the Brahmans and the Rajputs, the white and red races of early colonists. Sir Henry Maine has likened the organization of these village communities to the crystallization of sugar; a drop of syrup, wherever you put it, will presently crystallize, and always in exactly the same way.

The village community was the beginning of democracy in India, and practically the end also, so far as indigenous institutions are concerned, since every larger political unit was originally based on conquest and ruled in practice as an Oriental despotism.

The English traders of the East India Company reached India practically at the same time as their fellow-traders reached the Atlantic shores of North America, and as a part of the same great commercial movement which grew out of the naval activities of Sir Francis Drake, Sir John Hawkins and the worthies of great Elizabeth. It would be an interesting parallel to trace the result upon the natives of the two regions, the Indians of India, and the 'Indians' of North America. And the question would be distinctly relevant, if it came to a discussion of rights and equities in the two regions.

The two groups of Englishmen, therefore, sailed east and west about the same time. Then, for about 150 years, they did little more in either region than establish trading centres on the coasts. Curiously enough, it was not so much any local conditions or events that set in motion the large movement of expansion which followed after this century and a half of comparative inertia in both regions; it was the fact that England and France became involved in a great European war, precipitated when Frederick II of Prussia laid violent hands on the inheritance of Maria Theresa, the young princess who had come to rule over Austria. There is 'a scrap of paper' in that story also. England's contest with France extended to India and to North America; and Washington and Clive were fellow-officers in the same campaign, though at opposite sides of the world.

There were in India, at that time, three groups of powers. The first was the disintegrating Mogul Empire, founded by the invader, Baber, and raised to a height of splendour by Akbar the Magnificent, Queen Elizabeth's contemporary, but now falling into decay and breaking up into semi-independent states under vigorous, predatory viceroys: Nawab Nazim was their title in the legal Persian of the Mogul court. Their gorgeous courts turned the title Nawab into a noun, which became Nabob in English, a synonym for wealth and lavish display.

Bengal was one of these semi-independent viceroyalties. Its Nawab, whose name is generally written Surajah Dowla, had his headquarters at Murshidabad, in the very region where the magnificent mosque of Murshid Kuli Khan is now crumbling into ruins.

Surajah Dowla fell out with his relatives, who fled to Calcutta, the English trading post on the Hugli, a branch of the Ganges in the delta. Surajah Dowla pursued them with an army, seized Calcutta, and threw some scores of the English colonists into a dungeon, where most of them died in torture, suffocated. So, in 1756, the 'Black Hole of Calcutta' brought on the conflict between the Nawab and the English traders. In 1757 Clive settled it decisively by his victory at Plassey.

Mir Jafar had helped the English; he was set up in Surajah Dowla's place, and, inevitably, was more or less under English influence. This was the first important political tie established by the English traders in India. But they heartily desired to keep out of politics; they were, first and foremost, merchants, and many of them made large fortunes by trading in silk and spices, spices then meaning predominantly pepper. It was a fight over pepper, between the Dutch and the English traders, which swerved the English from the great Malay islands to the Indian mainland.

So an empire grew from little peppercorns. The English traders at Calcutta soon found themselves involved in Bengal politics, and presently they were induced to undertake the collection of revenue in certain districts, at first on behalf of the Nawab of Murshidabad and, nominally, as his vassals, though probably not intending to remain such. This was a godsend to the natives, for this reason: Moslem rulers have often possessed splendid qualities, but they have always had a rotten fiscal system, whether in India, Egypt or European Turkey; they have farmed out the taxes, and the tax farmers, paying large sums in advance, have then recouped themselves by plundering the natives. No single factor is more certain to bring misery and ruin in its wake. The traders at Calcutta began by establishing a fixed rate of taxation over the region of Bengal they had become responsible for, with the benign result that every native knew exactly how much he would have to pay; everything beyond that was absolutely his own. The tax rate fixed was notably low; it is extraordinarily low in India still, something like a dollar and a quarter of revenue per head per year, for which India gets one of the best governments in the world, a government in some ways far more democratic than democracy, since the interests and wishes of even minute minorities are sedulously guarded.

Not only is the taxation exceedingly low; over large areas the English bound themselves never to increase the one great tax, the land tax; and this engagement has been kept for a hundred years, even though the cost of government constantly rises. But, in spite of this phenomenally low taxation, great spaces of India are, and remain, exceedingly poor. The reason is, that so large a part of the population, 225,000,000 out of something over three hundred millions, live by agriculture alone, and over many regions in northern India, in the Indus and Ganges valleys, the strictly rural population is more than a thousand to the square mile. Belgium and England, both with large urban populations, are the most densely peopled countries in Europe; but, if we take the population of England to the square mile, and add to it the Belgian population for the same area, we shall still fall short of the numbers who, over many thousand square miles in northern India, are trying to gain a living from the soil. And, cultivators for many millenniums, they practically refuse to change. Further, this dense population grows steadily denser, with almost the highest birth-rate on earth, due, in large degree, to the religious custom of abnormally early marriage; due also to the fact that, under the Pax Britannica, they are no longer killed off by native wars. That is why India is, and remains, pitiably poor.

The second group of powers which the expanding English merchants found in India was the old Hindu States, and notably the great States of Rajputana, some of whose princely pedigrees go back to the Mahabharata war; the States which most genuinely represent the great Ancient India. These Hindu States had been hard hit by the Arab, Persian and Mogul (Mongol) invasions. They were hard pressed also by new powers which were just then growing up in India: the predatory tribes of the Mahrattas, chiefly in the Vindhya mountains; and the intolerant religious organization of the Sikhs, in the Punjab (Panch-ab, 'five rivers'), the valley of the Indus and its tributaries. The English came into collision with both Mahrattas and Sikhs; in both cases, the native power was the aggressor. The Mahratta States, their predatory impulses checked, have been preserved; the Sikh territory was reluctantly taken over about a decade before the great Mutiny, and has since been administered by Englishmen.

The removal of the pressure of the Moguls, the Mahrattas and the Sikhs made it possible to restore and conserve the older Hindu States which they were absorbing, notably the Rajput States. One-third of the area of India is, today, made up of Native States, in which the old princely lines or their representatives still hold Oriental court. The Sikhs were so completely reconciled to English Administration that, in the great Mutiny of 1857, they fought heroically on the English side against the mutinous native troops and their adherents. In the year following the Mutiny, the affairs of the old East India Company were wound up, and the Imperial Government of India was established.

So we come back to modern India, to the chowkidars and punchayets. The Mogul administrators who, in spite of their rotten fiscal system, had certain good ideas, had divided their viceroyalties into a great many smaller units; these they called Zillahs, and there were, perhaps, 50 of them in Bengal. These units were preserved by Warren Hastings and his successors, when they began to collect the revenues of Bengal, and they are still the units of government. They are now called Districts, such as Murshidabad District; and a District has, on the average, a population of a million. The Head of the District, whose primary duty was to gather revenue, is called the Collector and District Magistrate; a part of his duty is to wander, camping, through its confines. He is aided by a District Judge, who sits in court at the 'Sudder Station', the small metropolis, trying both civil and criminal cases. There is a District Superintendent of Police, with an English assistant or two; there may be a Joint Magistrate and one or two assistant magistrates. And that is all. Outside this white handful, every part of the administration is carried on by natives, and, for the most part, carried on well. The Collector, the Judge, the Joint and assistant magistrates, belong to what is called the 'Covenanted' Civil Service, because they enter into a Covenant with the Government of India. Of these people, there are some 900, managing the practical administration of a varicoloured population of over 300 millions. The practical force behind them is an army of British troops which, before the war, amounted to 75,000, or, say, four divisions; there was an army of native troops, about twice as large.

The British hold their position in India, therefore, not by force, but by virtue of the work they do. Peace and justice are the first parts of their work.

After a millennium of fighting, there has been no war in India for 60 years. This is the Pax Britannica, affecting a greater population than the old Pax Romana. Certain and equal justice to everyone in India, native or foreign, white or brown or black; civil and criminal justice alike, rapid, impartial, costing little, and unpurchaseable, is the second part of their work.

Law, in India, falls under two heads: first, the criminal law, with modern commercial law, like the law of contracts, is based on English principles and is universal in application. Then there is that part of civil law which touches home affairs, inheritance and so on, law which, in the East, is always interwoven with religion. Every religious community in India, and they are countless, preserves and administers, under English rule, its own traditional law. Thus questions of inheritance among Mohammedans are decided according to the Koran and the derived law-books; questions of inheritance among Hindus are decided under the Laws of Manu and the law-books which ancient Hindu jurists deduced from them. And so with every people, nation and language throughout the length and breadth of India. And to ensure the smooth working of this system, every one of the 900 Covenanted Civil Servants is asked to study not only the general laws of India, based on English principles, but also Hindu and Mohammedan law, and to pass a stiff examination in them. And every law case is tried in the local language or languages, which the Civil Servants are also set to study and to study hard. One part of their examination consists in reading the badly written petitions of nearly illiterate peasants, so that everyone throughout India may have a certainty that his wants will be learned and understood. Another part consists of conversation with these same peasants, a native official being the examiner; and some of those peasants talk a bit quaintly too. A magistrate may be called on to take testimony in three or four native tongues in a single case, meanwhile recording this testimony in English for possible revision by a court of appeal. The result of all this is that, under British rule, every element in India, however small, is free to develop, and is encouraged to develop, along the lines of its own genius, in its own tradition, speaking its own tongue. This is, as I have said, far more democratic than democracy, under which minorities, even if they make up 49 per cent, are compelled to conform to the wishes of majorities, even of bare majorities. As a rule, the government in a democratic country represents only the majority, though the war had led to minority representation in several governments, notably those of England and France. Under democracy, the safeguarding of the rights of minorities is the most formidable difficulty. Under the British government in India, the rights of minorities are ideally preserved, as against the ruthless tyranny which they suffered under native rule.

The village community with its elected Committee of Management is about as far as India ever got in representative government. I believe it is still the only element of representative government in the Native States, making up one-third of India; with the exception, perhaps, of self-governing municipalities in some of them. In the Native States, picturesque Oriental despotism, tempered by the presence of a British Resident, is still much what it was in the golden days of good Harunal Rashid.

But in the two-thirds of India directly administered by the British Covenanted Civil Service, efforts are continually being made to teach the natives the English principle of representative government, and to induce them to adopt it. We spoke about the unit of administration, the Zilla or District, with about a million inhabitants. In most of them the English have organized an elected District Board, which has charge of roads, bridges, hospitals, schools and so on, levying a light tax to pay for them. In order to keep the thing running smoothly, the Collector is Chairman of the District Board, but he works hard to get as much effective help as possible from the elected native members.

A district is generally divided into four or five subdivisions, as they call them, with, say, a quarter million brown inhabitants. In his second year, an assistant magistrate is generally given charge of a subdivision, where he settles down to a thorough study of the native tongues (at some risk of forgetting his own) and the rudiments of statesmanship. The subdivision also has its little parliament of elected natives, its local board; and the assistant

THE SACRED GOLDEN BULL IN THE GOLDEN TEMPLE AT BENARES

In Benares, as in many other Hindu cities, the sacred bull is revered in the flesh and idolized in metal and stone.

magistrate presides at its meetings, and takes a vivid interest in its discussions and decisions. So, in hundreds of these small local parliaments, the natives of India are learning something that, throughout the long millenniums of their history, they never devised for themselves: the principles and practice of representative self-government. They are learning under the guidance of the nation which created representative self-government, the world's greatest discovery since the beginning of our era.

The governors of India have done the same thing in the towns. They have created self-governing municipalities, to the number of over 700 (and towns in India are few and far between). A majority of the members, in the governing bodies of these municipalities, is always elected; there is practically always a majority of natives. These municipalities have charge of streets, of sanitation, of schools. And it should be clearly understood that the welfare not only of the natives, but also of the English inhabitants of these Indian municipalities, has been put into the hands of these preponderantly native governing bodies. The English have given the natives authority even over English well-being. So completely do the English apply a principle that they believe in. On the whole, the business works well. Towns in India are, generally speaking, very orderly, clean, healthy, so far as the climate allows. The self-governing municipality is, therefore, the next step in the great system of self-government which her present rulers are slowly and steadily introducing into India.

The zillas or districts, the units of administration in India, are based on the old Mogul fiscal divisions, and it is interesting that a great many words belonging to the administration of a district are still preserved from Mogul times; they are, for the most part, Persian words, brought to India by Mohammedan invaders. But the districts are merely convenient slices of older and larger territories, some of which go back to very ancient kingdoms, and have, to a considerable degree, the same boundaries as the native languages.

The languages of India fall into two great groups: those of the north, Punjabi, Mahratti, Gujerati, Hindi, Bengali, Uriya, all largely derived from Sanskrit, or dialects akin to Sanskrit, like the Pali of Buddhism, or the Prakrit of the dramas. The languages of southern India are wholly different; they are the tongues of the black aborigines whom it is the custom to call Dravidians; the most important tongues being Tamil, Telugu, Canarese, Malayalam. Then there are all the languages of Burma; of the Afghan and Baluchi frontier, of the Himalayas, of the old aboriginal tribes; a series without end. Hindi stands first, spoken by 82,000,000; Bengali stands second, spoken by about 50,000,000. Telugu comes third, with 23,000,000 speakers. If we skip to the thirty-third language in the list, we come to Manipuri, spoken by 310,000. English comes next, spoken, in various fashions, by about 300,000.

The ancient kingdoms or nations which express themselves in these multicoloured languages (which differ far more among themselves than do the tongues of Europe) are grouped into provinces, which now number 15. Beginning with the oldest, they are Madras (speaking Tamil and Telugu), Bombay (speaking Gujerati), Bengal (speaking Bengali and Uriya), the United Provinces of Agra and Oudh (speaking Hindi), Punjab (speaking Punjabi), Burma (speaking Burmese), and so on.

If there be a question of 'nationalism' in India, these are its natural basis. Broadly speaking, the only thing which keeps the people together politically is the English rule including them all equally. Apart from that, they are separate in speech, race, history, tradition; to an overwhelming degree, they are mutually unintelligible. Whoever talks of an Indian 'nationality' which is supposed to include all these divisions, is talking of something which has no existence.

But, taking these old bases of nationality as the larger units of its administration, the British Indian government has for a long time been working to introduce the representative principle at this point also. The head of each of these provinces, the Governor or Lieutenant-Governor, as his style may be, is assisted in his work by a Legislative Council, and this Legislative Council always includes elected natives side by side with official members. They have, therefore, at least the beginnings of parliamentary life in each of these resuscitated ancient nations, and the practice of it is steadily spreading and expanding.

In the Legislative Council of the Governor General of India, there are also elected native members, many of them men of high ability and great influence; and their views invariably carry great weight. So far, then, representative self-government has already gone in India; while real, effective democracy, safeguarding the rights and wishes of even small minorities, penetrates into every corner of the whole British Indian Empire, taking care of races and tribes so various, that they form a vast museum of ethnology.

To apply to a country like India the system which works fairly well in England, would be unjust, if it were possible. The British system has been developed within the limits of England, gradually and slowly through centuries. It is based on the character and the needs and wishes of the average Englishman. And the average Englishman is really a thinkable, practicable unit. But the average native of India simply does not exist. What race does he belong to, Rajput, Brahman, Mahratta, Punjabi, Bengali, Madrassi, Burman? What language does he talk? What is his religion, his tradition, his historic heritage? There is really no analogy at all; the solution which is good in one case, is quite illusory in the other.

Thirty-fourth among the languages spoken in India, and next after Manipuri, comes English. Excluding people of European birth, English is talked primarily by the officials, those who, at the Sudder Stations, help out the Collector and his staff. It is talked by students of the universities which the English have founded in India, the students whose natural destiny it is to get government jobs at the Sudder Stations and elsewhere. It is talked also by a handful of native princes, and by a few native professional men and merchants.

But by far the largest element among the English-speaking natives consists of Brahmans and the castes who depend on them; the great and powerful priestcraft, whose tyranny English rule has done so much to check. It is precisely this class which has developed an artificial 'nationalism', not corresponding to any reality in Indian life; and it is this class—the old priestly oligarchy—which would be put back into power, were their demand granted. The immediate result would be a civil war between Hindus and Mohammedans; India would be thrown back into the chaos from which she has been, slowly and painfully drawn by a century and a half of English rule.

CHAPTER 4

The Economic Basis in India

H.M. Hyndman

THE AGRICULTURAL POPULATION OF India is the most poverty-stricken mass of human beings in the whole world. It constitutes four-fifths of all the inhabitants of Hindustan. The true test of the prosperity and good government of any country is not the average income of the whole population in which the great revenues of the millionaires, big landowners and heads of industrial or transport combines balance the wages received by the artisans, small cultivators, or agricultural labourers, but the real well-being of the whole of the producing class. Now this in India is steadily deteriorating decade by decade and year by year. William Digby's book with the misleading, ironical title, *Prosperous British India,* which I implored him not to use, was published in 1901. It contains the most terrific indictment of British rule in Hindustan that has ever been penned. The facts and statistics contained in its 650 pages are drawn almost entirely from official reports, documents and calculations. The whole constitutes a social, economic and political investigation of surpassing interest and value. One categorical statement alone is enough to condemn our entire system:

In the year 1850, seven years before the Mutiny, the estimated income of British India was 2d. per head per day.

In the year 1882—a generation later—the officially-estimated income was 1½d. per head per day.

**ASIA*, June 1919.

In the year 1900 an analysis of all sources of income gives less than ¾d. per head per day.

What the real impoverishment of the Indian ryots or agriculturists of British India actually must be, when the incomes of all the well-to-do population in the cities and districts of Anglo-India are deducted can scarcely be imagined by the inhabitants of the poorest European state. Digby's previously quoted 12/6d. per head per year is probably now an overestimate. Can we wonder that a sense of deadly dulness, depression and ruin weighs on that portion of Hindustan where Europeanization is supreme? It is not poverty alone that occasions this sad state of things. Everything tends in the same direction. Native Indian arts are disappearing, education is neglected, there is no life or pleasure available, no outlet for energy, no hope of change, no variety of occupation. An American traveller in a recent book full of glorification of Europeans and European rule has described the vivacity, colour and magnificence of the court of Udaipur in all its ancient splendour, side by side with ancient indifference, ancient abhorrence of the new, ancient customs and ancient devotion to a sacrosanct ruler possessed of a pedigree directly traceable for thousands of years. And then he cannot restrain himself from comparing this un-Europeanized relic of the past, still holy to scores of millions of Hindus, with the squalid monotony and unending sadness which pervades British India.

It may be, as the majority of Englishmen and European visitors believe, that India can never emancipate herself without external aid from her present position of subjugation. Whether it is consonant with the claims of England to be the champion of justice and freedom in other directions that she should keep what might be a great and glorious empire under her permanent and ruinous domination, is a matter which must soon be considered. It will be seen also that of late years a school of extremists, as well as a school of moderates, has grown up, both of which demand self-government and in the long run complete emancipation of India.

When these criticisms on European rule are made and evidences of continuous and increasing poverty of the ryots are adduced, the defenders of the British government bring forward a number of facts and figures which are conclusive of prosperity to the ordinary Western mind. Against the contention that so far 150 years of European management and teaching have produced no enduring effect on the Indian mind and have introduced no permanent improvement in Indian affairs, one great argument also is used. 'See', say the optimists,

how we have introduced everywhere the blessings of peace! From the Himalayas to Cape Comorin and from Burmah to Bombay, wars have ceased, internecine struggles are unknown, religious riots are at once quelled, life and property are secure as they never were before in the history of Hindustan. The Pax Britannica is more profound and affects a larger population than the Pax Romana ever did. Here all these numerous nations and peoples and religions and castes dwell together, if not in unity, at any rate with trifling differences. Hindu and Mohammedan, Sikh, Pathan and Mahratta go on from year's end to year's end with no more than local squabbles which are easily suppressed. Raids and organized robberies are almost equally unknown. Justice is administered without the suspicion of bribery or the possibility of dangerous disputes out of court because of the decision reached. The military caste no longer exercises any influence. Peace, the greatest boon that can be vouchsafed to the hundreds of millions under the suzerainty of the Emperor-King, is secured so long as the British remain masters of the country. But only so long. Let that superior power be once withdrawn, or even greatly shaken, and all the anarchy of the past will be revived, all the infinite passions now kept down will be reawakened.

Such is the tone not only of Englishmen but of most Europeans who visit the country and rush by rail through the Europeanized towns and cities and garrisons and health resorts which constitute the white man's India. That the horrors of peace may in many ways be worse than the horrors of war is a consideration which never enters their minds, still less affects their judgement. All the tests of prosperity which they are accustomed to apply are fulfilled. Population is increasing rapidly, poverty is favourable to generation. Exports are rapidly increasing: what is the amount of return? Railways have been built over a large portion of the country: transport does not necessarily increase wealth. Vast irrigation works have been built: old irrigation tanks have been allowed to decay throughout huge areas and the charges for the new water are heavy, rendered still heavier by the enforced use of government water to the exclusion and shutting down of Indian wells. These counterbalancing drawbacks are never noted. Foreign-manufactured peace is a doubtful benefit at best.

All that is great and admirable in India was created during the period when she was an independent empire with groups of fine provinces, first under local rulers and then under the central domination of the Moguls. With all their drawbacks and hideous cruelties, they lived in the country. Though they themselves were Mohammedans, they employed Hindus of all races in the very highest posts as financiers, as administrators and as generals. Asiatics ruling Asiatics, they knew how far it was safe to go without bringing ruin upon the people and being overthrown themselves. Even in their period of decay, when debauched incompetents sat on the throne of Akbar and Aurangzeb, the rule which they maladministered was native rule and the dull despair of the upright foreign despot never settled like a miasma on the country. The Mahratta chout levied by the bold reavers of the Deccan and the West was hard to bear. But impoverishing as it was in its degree and in its time, it reckoned as child's play beside the persistent transfer of wealth to a faraway country year after year, which was the inevitable consequence of costly foreign rule. Moreover, all home-bred rulers encouraged native art and native manufacture, and the best of them, such as the great Bahmung dynasty of Bejapoor, developed local irrigation works to such an extent that the menace of famine in the irrigated districts became more and more remote. There were terrible famines indeed in some districts and provinces in these days prior to European invasion. But they came at long intervals and in the periods between them there was no steady, continuous reduction of the amount of food available for the people whose persistent labour provided the whole of the agricultural produce.

Peace, in fact, may be purchased too dear, and law and order, however admirable theoretically, may become a grinding economic and racial tyranny if enforced by foreigners who fail to comprehend alike the nature of the many diverse races beneath them and the best means of raising them to a higher level of prosperity—foreigners who never remain permanently in the land they control. Suppose a succession of capable Chinese mandarins, supported by a Chinese army and an Italian army under Chinese officers had ruled in Italy, imposing peace, perfect peace, upon the City Republics a few hundred years ago. They would have imposed also Chinese ideas of morality and justice, industry and culture—and very high ideas they were and are—upon the countrymen of Dante and Petrarch, Borgia, Machiavelli and Leonardo da Vinci. But is it not clear that the world would have been infinitely poorer for the repression of Italian initiative and for the sombre, dead level of monotony and dependence thus brought about? Would not Italians have been justified in resorting to any means in order to relieve themselves from such a rule, however high-minded and well-intentioned its Chinese representatives in Italy might have been? Would not this have applied in like manner in England during the Wars of the Roses, to France at the time of the anarchic and bloody struggle between Catholics and Huguenots and even to Germany when devastated by the Thirty Years' War? There can be but one honest answer to these questions. Yet India was never in a more perturbed condition, never suffered more from internal misrule or attacks from without than the different countries named at the above periods. And the rigidity and miscomprehension of Chinese domination in Europe could scarcely under any circumstances have been greater than the rigidity and miscomprehension of European despotism in Hindustan.

It was the economic pressure which perhaps first roused the more intelligent Indians to a full comprehension of the permanent injury which persistent Europeanization was inflicting upon India as a whole. And this was first appreciated and forcibly expounded not by Indians themselves but by English merchants and administrators in the days of the East India Company, long before the Mutiny or the National Revolt of 1857 had openly manifested the discontent that existed on other grounds. Thus even at the time when the real significance of the yearly drain of produce to England from India was far less, alike in amount and effect, than it is today, an Englishman, Montgomery Martin, pointed out what the wholesale transfer of Indian wealth to England really meant. During the early times of unregulated appropriation, the amount paid away to the West, in one shape or another since legal methods had been introduced and enforced up to 1857, amounted to many hundreds of millions of pounds sterling, without any commercial return. That is to say, India had been depleted of her wealth to that extent for the benefit of England, as a consequence of European conquest and rule. Even the abolition of suttee by Lord William Bentinck, the check to female infanticide and the suppression of the Thugs made no economic amends for this ruinous impoverishment of a poor country, all the territory of which was already occupied, some of it tilled to the point of exhaustion and some very densely populated. But this drain of produce enormously increased after the assumption of direct government by the Crown and the great extension of Europeanization in every direction.

The higher minds in the government service strongly insisted upon the great and increasing danger of this economic policy. Civil servants and military men alike enlarged upon the ruin that was being wrought. James Geddes and A.O. Hume, Major Bell and Colonel Osborne, William Digby and Knight, all in their various ways did their best to represent to the government in England and in India the irretrievable mischief that was being done. So did others. The famous Parsee, Dadabhai Naoroji, only too fast a friend of British rule in India, devoted himself also for many years to this question. All to no purpose. At one point, during 1878-80, the English government at home did appreciate what was going on, and Lord Salisbury and Lord Iddesleigh, with the concurrence of Lord Cranbrook, Lord Beaconsfield, Edward Stanhope and Sir Louis Mallet, made the first steps toward the gradual restoration of Indian rule. A beginning had been made most successfully in this direction in Mysore in 1868 to the permanent advantage of the population. There the removal of the rigid system of taxation and the revival of the old Indian system of consideration of Indian needs at once uplifted the well-being of all the inhabitants of that territory.

But the influence of the hide-bound Indian bureaucracy and the personal interests of the middle class at home were too strong to be resisted. On the return of Gladstone's Liberal administration to power, all the preliminary reforms introduced were swept away, and from that time to this, Europeanization has become more and more the panacea for all evils, the foreign government has become even more expensive and extravagances such as the creation of new and wholly unnecessary capital cities at Delhi and Dacca encouraged waste to the extent of many millions sterling.

Naturally, to keep pace with this fatal system, the land tax is more cruelly exacted than ever and the agriculturists get poorer all the time. Compare this with the statement of Chester Macnaghten in regard to the comparative results of Indian rule:

The fact is, that under existing circumstances, a Native State under British superiors is almost an ideal of prosperity. This remark is a general one, applying to Travancore, Mysore, etc., as well as to Baroda. While the people are governed in their own simple way, the revenue is not wasted. The peace and prosperity which characterize the rural population of India are maintained, while the corruption and dishonesty which characterize native courts are checked. The system is an inexpensive one to the states which enjoy it and contains all that is best in British and native methods. I believe it is only true to assert that there is not a single Native State in India which, if so administered, will not show a surplus.

And these Indian states have little if any drain of payments to Europe. Even so, there is in some of these states too much meddling by the European residents with a tendency to the current bureaucratic belief in Europeanization.

But the phenomenon of the economic drain calls for closer investigation. This is especially injurious, of course, to a poor country. It may arise to all appearance advantageously and without the additional drawback of foreign rule, and yet be a very serious hindrance to the country which suffers from it. On the other hand, it may constitute comparatively so small a proportion of the total wealth of the country increased by the investment of loaned capital on which the economic drain represents the interest that the advances can be redeemed with ease at maturity. Both the United States and Russia have been large borrowers—the former to a comparatively small amount in relation to its wealth of late; the latter has constantly required loans. But the United States was an undeveloped country, rich in virgin agricultural soil and vast mineral resources, developed by the constant exertions of a vigorous and in the main not needy population from Europe. Railway communication afforded profitable outlet for all products and if the lines were overloaded with indebtedness the companies simply did not pay. As the wealth of the vast territory grew, the loans and bonds were bought back or the capital borrowed again at a lower rate of interest for new enterprises. It is the same with municipal borrowings and state loans issued in Europe.

With Russia the case has been different. The country outside of Siberia was already settled; the people were poor and ignorant, the development, except in the oil regions, did not keep pace with the borrowing; the body of agriculturists, mostly emancipated serfs, got no richer. Therefore the unwieldy Muscovite Empire with all its wealth of undeveloped resources could not sustain the drain of produce to the West for the interest on the money that was advanced. Thus it befell that even more and more loans were needed to keep up payment of interest. Prior to the war of 1914 Russia was fully £150,000,000 behind in the payments to meet her liabilities to Western creditors, mostly French. Her yearly debt on this account was not far short of £55,000,000 sterling. So, as shown in her account of exports and imports, she was nearly three years overdue in meeting her indebtedness—a deficit which had been covered by all sorts of shifts. Russian agriculture, the mainstay of that great country, had lost instead of gained strength, as was clearly shown by Professor Miliukoff. The difference between the United States and Russia is obvious. In one case the imported capital had enhanced and quickened production far beyond the amount needed to pay the yearly interest: in the other case the interest represented for the most part a deduction from production which had been little increased, if not diminished in agriculture and not sufficiently expanded in manufacture and mining. Hence, the drain of Russian produce has been ruinous and the inevitable outcome is bankruptcy and repudiation.

But the real economic condition of India is far worse than this. Putting aside the profits on tea-planting, gold-mining and other enterprises established and financed by English capitalists, which cannot be fairly regarded as withdrawals from actual Indian wealth, seeing that these ventures are purely European, the total amount of the payments made in produce from India to England without any commercial return is not less than £30,000,000 every year. This is an understatement of the truth. Moreover, the drain does not apply to the so-called Native States—that is to say, to states under British protection but not under direct British rule. These great provinces not only are relatively wealthy, in comparison with the rest of poverty-stricken Hindustan, so far as their agricultural population is concerned, but also they have practically no remittances to make to England on civil and military account and little for interest on railways. Their trade, therefore, is relatively greater per head of population. But, as the English trade returns are made out, it is practically impossible for any outside investigator or critic to discriminate correctly between the commercial dealings of British territory, proper and those of these great Native States which contain considerably more than one-fifth of the entire inhabitants of Hindustan. The drain of produce, therefore, is derived not from the 315,000,000 of people in India but from 245,000,000: the 70,000,000 in the protected territories should be deducted (Census of 1911). And the trade of these 70,000,000 constitutes in reality much more than one-fifth of the total trade. This is a very important fact in considering the economic effect of European rule in Asia and it is not generally recognized. For, in the calculations which follow, it must always be borne in mind that certainly not less than one-fourth of the trade imports and a very much greater proportion of the treasure imports go into the countries which are not under direct British rule—the great Native States with 70,000,000 inhabitants.

Under pre-war conditions the total amount of exports by sea of private merchandise of Indian products from British India and the Native States together for the five years 1909-10 to 1913-14 was £731,657,602, or an average of £146,331,520 a year. The total amount of imports by sea of private merchandise during the same period of five years was £486,157,310. Here is a difference of not less than £245,000,000 between the exports and the imports of private merchandise, or a yearly disparity of £49,000,000 without return in the form of merchandise, although the imports for 1912-13 and 1913-14 reached the exceptional figures of £107,000,000 and £122,000,000 respectively. Against this extraordinary discrepancy the almost equally remarkable import of treasure, ranging from £25,000,000 to as high as £41,000,000 in the years under consideration, is naturally put forward by official apologists for India's desperate poverty. But the Government of India has always refused to make any distinction between the exports and imports of the Native States and those of British India. I am Quite confident that at least half of the imported treasure, as well as a great deal more than their proportional part of the imports of merchandise, goes into these Native States. The yearly drain from British India of commercial produce for which there is no commercial return I put at upward of £30,000,000 a year.

If India with its vast population were even a moderately rich country this drain of produce to a foreign power going on year after year and increasing rather than diminishing would be a matter of concern, especially as it has proceeded now for just 150 years. But when the amount thus calculated is extorted from the poorest population on the planet, then it is clear that the name which I gave to this process nearly 40 years ago, 'Bleeding to Death', represents what is being done.

Lord Curzon estimated the average income of the Indians at not more than £2 a year. William Digby put the average value of the production of the cultivators at not more than 12s. 6d. a year per head. It is inconceivable to us that human beings can exist upon such a miserable pittance. Yet out of this despicable return for constant work upon the soil the Government Land Tax, which produces the Land Revenue, deducts no less a sum than £21,000,000 a year. Moreover, the British government insists upon this tax being paid by the cultivators before the crops are grown, and paid in silver calculated at a factitious rate. This means that while the actual value of a rupee on the markets of the world may be not more than 11d. or 1s., the defrauded Hindu ryot is compelled to pay his Government Land Tax in rupees at the rate of ¼d., or above 30 per cent more than the rupee is worth—this, I repeat, before the crops are grown and reaped! What is the result of this? Inevitably that the cultivators are forced into the hands of the native moneylenders at rates varying from 15 to 60 per cent. And then official apologists for the government hold up their hands in horror at the exactions of the usurious moneylenders. The result is that the position of Indian cultivators and their families is becoming more and more hopeless.

It is preposterous to argue that irrigation is remedying this state of things. Nothing of the sort. Irrigation applies to a very small area as carried out under European engineers. Sometimes the quality of the water supplied has proved actually injurious, owing to miscalculation as to the nature of the silt it would carry with it. In other cases the charges have been in excess of the value of the water to the cultivators, who were compelled to take it and to close down their own wells in order to do so. If the soil is constantly being exhausted by overcropping, irrigation by itself does no good. It was not an Indian but an Englishman, Thorburn, holding a high official post in Bengal, who said: 'We are driving a juggernaut car of Western progress over the fortunes of the people of India.' The word 'progress' is evidently used there in an ironical sense. Mr. Donald Smeaton, too, declared that England was working up in India to a revolt beside which 'the Mutiny would be child's play'. That is my own conviction.

CHAPTER 5

Dropping the White Man's Burden

H.M. Hyndman

DURING THE GREATER PART OF THE nineteenth century the peoples of European race claimed to have a manifest superiority over Asiatics. But history demonstrates conclusively that such superiority does not exist. Nor was this the attitude of European travellers and adventurers in the East in the first instance. Most of these men, persons of ability, knowledge and repute in their own countries, were amazed at the civilization, wealth and magnificence of the Courts they visited and the general well-being of the populations under native rule, which also they admired. For many a long day deference rather than arrogance was the tone of the white men towards the Emperors and Kings, Maharajahs and Nawabs, Viceroys and Mandarins whom they encountered. The high qualities and great attainments of these potentates and their ministers then obtained due consideration. The arts and sciences, philosophy and jurisprudence of these remote societies were appreciated and respected. The infinite obligations of the West to the East were still recognized: the capacity of Asia, in war as in peace, was not forgotten.

Then the Eastern world lay dormant for a time. Europe advanced rapidly in material development and scientific knowledge and acquirement, while Asia ceased to discover, or invent, or even to adopt and absorb. Improved weapons and the new great machine industry gave Europeans the

**ASIA*, October 1919. This article is the concluding chapter in H.M. Hyndman's *The Awakening of Asia*, published by Boni and Liveright.

temporary advantage in war and in trade. But how long will this last? What security have we of the permanence of this superficial predominance?

It is well to recall that, within comparatively recent times wave after wave of conquering Asiatic armies broke in upon Europe; and barbarian as most of these warlike hordes were, great generals, great organizers, great administrators rose up from among them, both in West and East, whose equals could not be found in the Europe of their day. The Arabs of Spain, the various Moslem rulers of Bagdad, Egypt and Adrianople left, directly or indirectly, their mark on the civilization of the West. The Moguls of Delhi, the Bahmani dynasty of the Deccan, Kublai Khan in China, and the rulers of the Khanates of Central Asia showed splendid capacity, in arts as in arms. These men and others built up empires which the white races saw and heard of dimly from afar. But whether as distant rulers or as terribly near invaders, these Asians were formidable foes, and in the changing course of time we may yet have cause to fear them again.

We now know to our cost what a war to the death between nations and races, provided with equal means of destruction, really is. In the long run, should no exceptional military genius manifest himself, nor any incalculable spirit animate one of the combatants, the number of the trained soldiers on either side determines who shall be the victor. In numbers the East has an enormous advantage over the West. And there is no reason why a really great admiral, or general, should not appear in the countries which border upon the Pacific Ocean, as well as in those whose outlet is the Atlantic.

While all the Powers of Europe were engaged in a desperate war of resistance to Teutonic aggression, and we were looking on, practically helpless, at the internecine butchery of the white race, there has been a steady revival among the vast populations which inhabit the territories extending from the Persian Gulf to the Sulu Sea, and from the Amur River to the Straits of Singapore. Nevertheless, we still talk with confidence of capturing more of Asiatic trade and influencing for all time Asiatic development.

Not long ago, European nations were calmly discussing and deciding among themselves how much more of sleepy Asia they should appropriate, for the benefit, no doubt, of the peoples brought under this foreign rule. But now our sense of conscious superiority is being shaken, and when we find the inscrutable Asiatic learning to meet us successfully with our own weapons, we draw back a little. We even begin to see that he may have good grounds for regarding his white rivals as the uncultured and discourteous barbarians that, in many respects, we really are.

Compared with the madness of Europe, also, the comparative quietude of Asia has been sanity itself. Yet this may not endure. With all the facts before us, and with prejudice thrown aside, we are still unable to lay bare the causes of the gigantic Asian movements of the past. They were certainly not all economic in their origin, unless we stretch the boundaries of theory so far as to include the massacre of whole populations and the destruction of their wealth within the limits of the invader's desire for material gain. And, whether these movements arose from material or emotional causes, they have been before, and they may occur again. Forecast here is impossible. A new Mohammed is quite as likely to make his appearance as a new Buddha, a reborn Confucius, or a modern Christ.

Asia owes to Europe little or nothing. At most, white men are teaching her improved methods of slaughter, and providing her with more perfect appliances for creating and distributing increased wealth for the few. As against these very doubtful services, the record of the white man's atrocities is ugly indeed. Trade has been opened up with unwilling peoples, in almost every instance, by bloodshed or threat of bloodshed. Thenceforward, it was spread by all the horrors of war and the permanent evils of unjust annexation. The traffic itself was often by no means advantageous to the country upon which it was thrust. Where the poisoning of millions of industrious and simple Chinese folk was profitable to the foreign traders and merchants, there poison was forced upon these peaceful people at the cannon's mouth. In cases where emigration for the coolies meant certain death within a short period for the unfortunates who were kidnapped and shipped off, all the remonstrances of the Government of China, whose subjects were thus outraged, failed to obtain redress.

Japan herself, whose leadership of Asia, afield and afloat, may yet, unless we are very careful, teach white men a lesson all over the world, was driven into close contact with Europe and America against her will, first, by Commodore Perry's dexterous diplomacy, supported by the power of the United States, and then by the much less justifiable measures of other white nations. Japan was, in fact, compelled to enter upon foreign commerce with Europeans by the familiar process of bombardment and butchery, which their immensely superior weapons of offence rendered merely a passing amusement for the civilized aggressors. That was but yesterday. It would be a desperately dangerous experiment to repeat today. Well for us if it is forgotten tomorrow. Asia raided and scourged Europe for more than a thousand years. Now for five hundred years the counter-attack of Europe upon Asia has been going steadily on, and it may be that the land of long memories will cherish some desire to avenge this period of wrong and rapine in turn. The seed of hatred has already been but too well sown.

The continent which has long regarded itself as the home of the progressive peoples and the hope of the entire planet is beginning to forfeit its assumed supremacy. The warlike and industrial potentialities of the near future are passing slowly but surely to the Far East. However the recent stupendous war may finally end, the whole of educated Asia can read its meaning written across the map of the world. If all those portions of the globe which are inhabited or dominated by the white races are seriously taking account at the present moment of their strength, their population, and their possibilities for the increase of their wealth on a larger scale than ever before, we may be sure the ablest men in Asia are not blind to what can be achieved in their own countries in peace and in war. It is true that the differences between the Asiatic peoples are as acute as any which exist in Europe. But against the white man they are practically all at one.

Yet the white man still holds control over nearly half of Asia and its vast population. Asia comprises, including its islands, little less than 1,000 million of the human race. England, France, Russia, Holland and the United States are all deeply concerned in the future of this mass of people, in view of the scope of territory and population they control. All will be greatly affected by the general political, economic and social movement of Japan, China and India. In a word, the position of Great Britain foremost, and of the other powers in their degree, is now being steadily undermined. The determined effort to secure Asia for the Asiatics, once begun as earnestly in action as it is now being seriously considered in thought, might spread with a rapidity which would paralyse all attempts at reconquest, if, indeed, such attempts could ever be effectively made. The West deprived of British India, the Asiatic Provinces of Russia, French Tonkin and Cochin China, Dutch Java, Sumatra and the Celebes, the Philippines under the United States, would be a very different Europe from that to which we have been accustomed.

That is a possibility of which the West, with forces now weakened and depleted to a wholly unprecedented extent, must soon take account. Unconsciously, but nonetheless certainly, it is making way. Where fifty or even twenty years ago the continuous expansion of Western domination over the East was taken for granted, now an uneasy but not yet openly admitted feeling is growing that the tide has turned and that ere long the area of European influence in the East will be considerably reduced. The partition of China among the 'Great Powers' is not today within the sphere of practical politics, and Japan pursues her policy in respect to that magnificent country with little regard to the susceptibilities of the white man and his burden. The appeal of China herself to the White Powers, that they should aid her to resist the unwarranted demands of Japan, has met, at least temporarily, with a cold rejection. But while 'The League of Nations' is being generally discussed it is certain that, in the opinion of the Chinese, the national independence of China is seriously menaced if the much-cherished Open Door is being carefully, though silently, closed.

All this is more remarkable since the Ottoman Turks, for centuries the advance guard of Asia in Europe, are at last being driven from their hereditary camping-ground. Even their mastery over Asia Minor, irrespective of the baffled German programme of appropriation, is obviously threatened by Great Britain and France. What, under other circumstances, would undoubtedly be considered additional evidence of the growing predominance of Europe, seems today scarcely a makeshift against the probable insecurity of the white race in the Far East. The practical occupation of Persia now proceeding attracts little attention when the permanence of British rule in India is questioned, not so much from without as from within. Russia is incapable of any warlike policy and will probably be so for a long time to come. The French, too, will not long be able to retain undisputed possession of the territories they have seized from China. The difficulties to be faced at home, with a decreasing population, increasing financial burdens and the probable inability of Russia to pay interest on her enormous debt, so largely in French hands, will be such that withdrawal from her Far Eastern possessions can scarcely fail to be a matter of imperative necessity. The retention of the Dutch Archipelago, were Holland's ownership ever directly challenged, would be impossible. Certainly, without a powerful European ally, or active support from unready China, America would have to strain all her great wealth, extraordinary energy and enormous industrial resources in order to continue to hold what is really no use to her in the Philippines.

Asia, in short, is already far from being the Asia which was fair game for adventurous European experiments. New conditions must be dealt with by a new policy.

And who shall say that the frank abandonment of the fallacious polity of Imperialism will not greatly benefit the countries which boldly enter upon this honourable course? The possession of India has been a curse to England, alike in her domestic and foreign affairs. Democracy at home has greatly suffered from the maintenance of despotism abroad. The two can never be harmonized, nor kept simultaneously in being, without danger to the popular cause. The fear of what might happen to the English in India has frequently perverted the action of British policy. In economics also the tribute from Hindustan, which must be paid, no matter at what price, in saleable commodities, has done mischief to the producers of Great Britain as to the ryots of India.

So with France and her Asiatic possessions. What have the French peasants and *bourgeoisie* to gain, from any point of view, by retaining provinces that must be defended at the cost of their blood and treasure, and must introduce a dangerous military sentiment into the management of their affairs?

Happily the same views as to the madness of modern warfare which are now being forced upon the rest of the world are also making way with Asiatic statesmen. They, too, see that friendly cooperation for common advantage might be far more advantageous to all than rivalry for power or competition for gain. Freedom of nationalities, equality of rights, respect for treaties and conventions, international arrangements for securing permanent peace are as important for Asia as for any other continent. But the responsibility for adopting them, should the Japanese democratic party prevail, and India and China press their demands without violence, rests entirely with Europe. The Asiatic nations are so far threatening no legitimate European interest: they ask only that the principles for which the Allies justly claim they fought Germany should be applied in the most populous regions of the world.

But it is useless to disguise from ourselves that this concession would involve of itself a complete revolution in the East. For such policy honestly applied would mean:

1. The emancipation of India from foreign rule by peaceful agreements with its numerous peoples.
2. The cessation of attempts to force foreign capitalism and foreign trade upon Asiatic countries.
3. The recognition that Japanese and Chinese are entitled, in countries and colonies inhabited or controlled by Europeans, to rights equal with those of Europeans in China and Japan.
4. The granting of similar rights to Indians on the same basis.
5. The acceptance by Europeans of the principle of 'Asia for the Asiatics' as a rightful claim.

But no student and no statesman would contend that such a wide policy of justice can be suddenly realized. Yet if in the near future public opinion in Europe and America were to endorse such a programme, and the nations interested would take the first steps towards its realization, much of the antagonism which is already manifesting itself in Asia might be removed. Past injuries cannot now be remedied. The most to hope for is that, in the Asiatic mind, they may be held to balance those Eastern attacks upon the West which belong to a past more remote.

We are turning over a new page in the history of the human race. What will be written upon it depends on the men and women of the rising generation. If, in international relations, the old race and colour prejudices are maintained, if trade and commerce, interest and profit, continue to be the principal objects of our statesmanship, then troubles may easily ensue beside which even the world war may take second place. On the other hand, should wider views and nobler aspirations animate both branches of civilized mankind, then indeed a magnificent vista of common achievement will open out before our immediate descendants.

CHAPTER 6

Gandhi, Religious Politician

Gertrude Emerson

I was waked by a deafening shout.
'Mahatma Gandhi ki-jai! Mahatma Gandhi ki-jai!'

It was five o'clock in the morning. White-clad, white-capped figures ran here pushing, elbowing one another, peering in at the lighted train windows, clambering up the steps of the various carriages. They were all eagerly searching for that latest heralded apostle so altogether upsetting to British peace of mind in India, the reincarnated Holy One worshipped by countless numbers of simple souls with superstitious reverence: a thin, unprepossessing little man, who would have walked through life unnoticed from beginning to end, had he not been endowed with an incandescent spiritual energy, with a burning sense of what he looks upon as India's economic and political wrongs, probably the man most despised and best loved in India—Mahatma Gandhi.

When I climbed down at the Punjab city of Ferozepur an hour before dawn on the morning of November 9, I had not yet seen Mr. Gandhi. I had heard of him in China and in Siam. In Singapore I had read accounts of meetings in Bombay and Calcutta where he presided over the burning of huge piles of foreign-made cloth. In Java I had listened to an experienced

⋆*ASIA*, May 1922. Gertrude Emerson (1893-1982) was an early twentieth century expert on Asia and editor of *ASIA* Magazine. Author of *Voiceless India* (1944) and *Pageant of Indian History* (1948).

'MAHATMA' GANDHI

India's national leader has recently been arrested and is now serving a six years' term of imprisonment

colonial administrator, just returned from India, denouncing him as 'a dangerous mischief-maker and breeder of rebellion', who ought to be locked up without a moment's delay. According to the generally accepted view of governing peoples in the Far East, this mysterious personality was an incalculable influence for evil. Yet in India, as far as I could judge, he was worshipped as a saint. Why? That was what I purposed to find out.

After several weeks of vain effort to settle upon a time and place of meeting convenient to us both it had finally been arranged that I should see and talk with Gandhi in Delhi. When I arrived in that city, however, I found that he had changed his plans and was leaving that same night for Lahore, stopping off in the early morning to address a mass meeting in Ferozepur. I bought my ticket to Lahore by the same train. Since Mr. Gandhi had just announced during the session of the All-India Congress

Committee at Delhi that he expected to inaugurate 'civil disobedience', that is, a programme of non-payment of taxes as a means to compel surrender on the part of the 'Satanic Government'. It seemed to me that very possibly the police might also be seeking an interview with him. It was partly for that reason and partly for the sake of seeing him first as he appeared at one of his great Indian mass meetings that I also decided to stop off at Ferozepur.

While I stood on the platform, trying to decide what plan of action to adopt, Abdul Aziz, my Bengali Mahommedan 'bearer'—the term for the travelling servant in India was surely invented by a humourist—was directing in his best style the apportionment of my luggage among two or three humble station coolies and its balancing on their turbaned heads. By this time the crowd had swarmed to a second-class carriage in the rear of the train. Since I could detect no movement of any one within to get out, I was beginning to fear that there had been another change of plans and that once again Gandhi had eluded me. Fortunately at this juncture a young English military police officer appeared and asked if I were in need of assistance. When he learned my object, he told me that the Gandhi meeting was to be held in the 'City', a station some five minutes farther on. He added that since no Europeans were ever allowed in the City, it would be unwise to go there, particularly at this time, and he strongly advised me not to think of it. I am always thankful when people merely advise me not to do the things I want to. I thanked the young man politely, checked my luggage in the waiting-room, found a *tonga* outside and told the driver to take me to the City.

As we left the station, three gigantic silhouettes of mysteriously burdened camels loomed up on the road ahead. With faint clinking of camel bells, they ambled past on their great padding feet, loosing little clouds of dust behind them. Though it was still quite dark, the whole city was astir. Hundreds of people were walking along all in one direction. The crowd at the station had consisted of men and boys dressed in the ugly white Gandhi skullcaps and *khaddar,* a coarse cotton variety of *swadeshi* cloth, the hand-spun, hand-woven product that is Gandhi's debatable panacea for all India's economic ills. But here were men, women, children and babies, garbed in all the heterogeneous, infinitely picturesque costumes of the countless tribes and races and creeds whose home is northern India: Marwari women in gipsylike skirts of every colour of the rainbow; men with huge, baggy trousers and turbans piled mountainously on their long curly black hair; men with nothing but a crumpled *dhoti* caught up between thin legs and tucked in at the belt behind; *purdah* women, those sheeted ghosts of India, who go out only when they are swathed from head to foot in an opaque white garment with two tiny drawn-work lattices serving as windows for the *kohl*-blackened eyes; graceful women in fluttering *saris,* embroidered or printed, silk or cotton, purple, yellow, rose and green; lastly, children in silver anklets and bracelets, with little amulets tied on strings around their bulging middles—if adorned by any costume other than this, most frequently wearing gay little Mahommedan caps of dark coloured velvets encrusted with gold embroidery. Most of this multitude walked barefoot, after the Indian fashion, but for those who had the means, there were two-wheeled tongas like mine, there were carts drawn by water-buffaloes or mild-eyed oxen with painted horns, there were moth-eaten donkeys as single mounts and occasionally there was a motor-car laden with Ferozepur aristocrats and shooting past with utter recklessness.

We crossed a bridge over the railroad tracks and continued down a straight road, at times hemmed in by the blank, mud-walled Indian houses, at times open to the ploughed fields whence must have come all those cartloads of cauliflowers and carrots processioning by. Presently we came to a place where several thousand people were squatting on the ground in a natural amphitheater surrounded by trees, with a flower-decorated platform at the lower end. Our tonga-driver deposited us somewhat unceremoniously at one side of the road and, leaving his horse to eat leaves up and down the hedge in unexpected holiday, pushed his way eagerly into the crowd. This was the moment when, according to my pessimistic adviser at the station, I might have expected some violent anti-foreign demonstration to take place. Nothing of the sort happened. On the contrary an usher with a green, yellow and red *Khilafat* band across his chest came up and informed me that undoubtedly I would find a place in the purdah section reserved for ladies, and there another usher went out of his way to see that room was made for me as close to the platform as possible. The women with whom I was surrounded were all extremely friendly. They bombarded me with questions in Punjabi which I could neither understand nor answer, and went on chattering just the same. Now and then they could not resist the temptation to reach over and surreptitiously feel my dress or finger some bit of jewellery. They held up their poor little half-smothered babies for me to admire, and when the press of people searching for room threatened inundation, they linked their arms back of me by way of protection. I shall not forget the courtesy of those uneducated countrywomen.

The sun was up sufficiently high to make us thoroughly uncomfortable before Gandhi finally arrived, in a carriage drawn by two horses covered with necklaces and chains of flowers. As the grass in a field is sometimes bent all one way by the wind, so the people swayed forward. A few more or less self-appointed directors jumped up waving their arms frantically, shouting to the masses to keep their seats. The air was shattered by the familiar cry of 'Mahatma Gandhi ki-jai!'—'Victory to Gandhi Great of Soul!' Then those of us in the purdah section saw how on the opposite side a passage was being cleaved through the crowd and someone was slowly making his way toward the platform amid showers of far-flung petals and strung marigolds.

There emerged a small, almost emaciated figure, with bare head and feet, wrapped in a nondescript shawl such as Lincoln used to wear. He sat down cross-legged, indifferent to the shouting, acknowledging by neither word nor gesture the acclamation with which he was being received. It struck me that this was not a man to be tempted cheaply. He probably weighed mob enthusiasm for what it was worth—compounded of mere love of shouting, of violent waving of arms, of curiosity, of tribute-paying instincts expressing themselves primarily in homage to the man rather than his ideas. For himself, he was oddly scornful of all this, or perhaps only rather tired. Nevertheless Mr. Gandhi is not, as he is so often described, an impractical idealist. He knows only too well the strength of mass support to his cause. He knows that, particularly here in India, the ignorant masses can be made to reflect in multiple images the well-thought-out ideas of the leaders. For the sake of the goal he has set himself, realizing his singular power to weld the masses to at least a semblance of unity of feeling, he suffers himself to be adored. I am not one of those who believe that he really likes it. As he sat there in the attitude of an ascetic deep in contemplation, he remained curiously aloof from the crowd; nor did he ever descend to it. The craning of necks ceased a little as the people fulfilled their ambition to see their hero in his humble glory. Somebody passed up to him a small spinning-wheel. A child near me began to wail, refusing to be comforted by the sticky sweets his mother coaxed him to accept. He continued his dismal howling. While this little domestic incident distracted my attention for a moment, Gandhi had risen and was preparing to address the crowd.

Unfortunately the time had come for me to leave, if I was to get my luggage from the Cantonment Station waiting-room and catch the nine o'clock train for Lahore. I had had my first long range view of Mr. Gandhi, but later in the day I was to see him at closer quarters under extraordinary conditions. We continued the journey to Lahore by the same train, Gandhi making his connections at the City Station, where he had got off. In answer to a note delivered to him by Abdul, one of his three sons presently came back to my compartment to say that if I would come to the house of Mr. Lajpat Rai at six o'clock that evening, he would be glad to see me. Meanwhile we made a triumphal progress that surely the Prince of Wales might envy. Vast crowds had assembled at every station. A cordon of volunteers had to protect the door of Mr. Gandhi's compartment from being broken down. If, as might have been expected, the shouting proceeded from the students and the element that Gandhi himself brands as hooligan, many country people were there in a spirit of profound reverence. They clasped the palms of their hands together with fingers pointing upward in the Indian gesture that is both worship and greeting, and if they could not be sure that they were greeting Mahatma Gandhi himself, they were content just to pay their respects to the train that was carrying him.

In my concern to arrive in good time for my appointment, I found myself drawing up in front of the house of Mr. Rai half an hour too early. It seemed best to wait where I was, and I had just instructed the chauffeur accordingly when a car came swinging out of the gate with Gandhi and half a dozen people crowded into the seats and on the running board. When he saw me, he stopped his car and explained that he was then on his way to a big mass meeting in the Badshahi Mosque. 'If you would care to come', he said, 'we could return to this house afterwards. Then I will answer any questions you wish to ask me.'

He made room for me to sit beside him, and off we drove to the mosque through streets lined with the cheering populace of Lahore, including many schoolchildren in Gandhi caps, singing a national song. Fifteen thousand people must have been packed into the mosque. There was not anywhere a square foot of unoccupied floor space, and those who could not get inside had scrambled all over the outside of the building, so that every cornice and projection and even the roofs were swarming with motley Gandhi throngs. We entered by a side door, and almost before I realized what was happening, I found myself obeying Mr. Gandhi's request to precede him along the narrow temporary bridge erected from the back of the mosque to a small square platform in the centre. As we hurried along this structure, I was pelted with a generous share of the flowers intended for Gandhi, and my feet narrowly escaped the eager hands reaching up on every side to touch in superstitious reverence the bare feet behind me.

An *imam* opened the meeting, followed by one of Gandhi's coworkers, who made a full report on the results of the 'national schools' founded in opposition to state schools a year ago. At the close of his address several graduates of the 'National University' of Lahore received .their diplomas from Mr. Gandhi's own hand.

As he rose for the first time, dropping off his blanket shawl and appearing clad only in a very short dhoti, in accordance with a recent resolve he had made to share the utmost poverty of his people, I saw, to my surprise, an expression of sophisticated amusement run across the faces of those nearest the platform. But if for one moment a few people laughed, the laughter ceased abruptly. Mr. Gandhi began to speak in a voice that at first sounded a note of great physical exhaustion but after a few moments shook off this weariness and rang out with arresting urgency. He is not an orator. His thin right hand with fingers bent flexibly backward at the tips made the same automatic gesture again and again. He did not plead his audience. He made no attempt to flatter it. Rather did he seem to be speaking in anger and bitterness of heart. He was asking the people how they expected to have *swaraj* when they would not work for it; when they would not adopt the vow of swadeshi and thus make India self-sustaining as she was of old; when, through incapacity to deny themselves comforts or to suffer, they showed themselves unprepared for true self-rule. Some of the familiar catchwords I caught. A stout Moslem gentleman who sat near me on the floor of the platform occasionally acted as interpreter.

But the text of Gandhi's face was what chiefly interested me. I am almost tempted to call him ugly. To begin with, his head is small, even for his short stature, though possibly the proportionately broad Indian shoulders make it seem more so. Close-cropped iron-gray hair with the long wisp generally worn by Hindus—I never saw Gandhi himself wearing the cap his followers have adopted—a forehead with very deep horizontal lines, a long nose shadowing a distinctly oriental mouth with a clipped moustache, thin cheeks, dark eyes rather far apart with indefinite eyebrows and heavy eyelids—such is his general appearance as well as I can describe it. Perhaps it is the effect of sharp features too much crowded into the lower half of the face that is its most distinctive characteristic. Perhaps it is the troubled forehead and the deep-set lines running from nose to chin. The lines are those of suffering and old age, now not very far away, although in years Mr. Gandhi is only just fifty-two. When he smiles, one notes with a shock how the lines in his face deepen and how the absence of two or three teeth in the lower jaw accentuates the impression of advancing age. There was something inappropriate about that smile. Gandhi once remarked to me that it was his sense of humour which kept him going sometimes. But I have heard many people lay claim to a sense of humour when I could never discover a trace of one. So it was with Gandhi. His smile was not of the troubled soul. It broke around the mouth and passed quickly, like a veil thrown for a fraction of a second across the settled melancholy of the face. Many Indian faces wear that same melancholy. Sometimes it is sunk in apathy, often it expresses itself in conscious discontent, but whatever its varying shades, it has seemed to me fundamental to Indian thought. It is a flag of the mind. You never see it reflected on a Malayan face, for instance. As for the eyes of this man, they suggest a stern and critical appraisal of everything coming within range of their vision, and a curious detachment. It is so that one looks out on a glittering tropical sea or toward the desert horizon.

The windows in the mosque darkened, and the lights hanging from the ceiling gleamed with hostile brilliancy. Many men in the audience were now weeping. The slight, half-naked figure of Gandhi, saying again for the thousandth or the ten-thousandth time all that he had to say about the *charka* and swadeshi and swaraj, seemed to shrink even smaller. Was it that something of himself was actually spent, something material and physical, as his indomitable will battled against the mass mind, striving to lift it to the plane of his own strange vision?

I am aware of having drawn a picture that commits me to a certain sympathy with Gandhi's personality. This sympathy has nothing to do with my critical estimate of his balance or his political judgements, which I shall attempt to give in a succeeding article. For the present I shall not discuss any of the involved questions that have made Gandhi a dangerous person in the eyes of the English world. It is worth stating, however, that, although I talked about him with a great many English people in all parts of India, I never heard any except two general expressions of opinion concerning him. To the larger number, he is nothing more nor less than an arch hypocrite, a man who talks non-violence and indirectly incites to violence, who professes to love mankind and all the time stirs up the bitterest feelings of race hatred. To the rest he is an incomprehensible religious fanatic whose psychology and point of view are so apart from the usual understanding that it is impossible to meet him on any sort of common ground; in short, a fool. Both sections of opinion agree that he has let loose forces beyond his control, and that it would have been better if he had been shot a long time ago. Very few of those with whom I talked had either seen or heard him. They said they did not want to do either. For three years he has been publishing a weekly paper in English called *Young India,* containing signed articles by himself on nearly every development of the political, social and economic situation in India. Almost no one in the English community is sufficiently interested to follow that expression of his opinion. I except the censors, naturally.

Over against this almost universal Anglo-Indian attitude there are a great many different Indian attitudes, the why and the wherefore of which I shall discuss in another place. But I can remember only three Indians who accused him of out-and-out insincerity. Sir Surendranath Banerjee, who has rendered distinguished services to the liberal party in India and is now occupying an important post in the government of Bengal, made no effort to disguise his feeling that of late Gandhi had turned into a mere politician. A Gurkha cook who looked after a little tea-house in the Himalayas where I sometimes dropped off my horse to have a cup of tea and get warm after a ride from Darjeeling, insisted that, Gandhi's real object in life was merely to become *maharaja* of all India. And the superintendent of the model prison at Jaipur expressed his convictions with equal certainty. 'He is a malicious disturber of the peace', said that gentleman. 'If he ever dares to come into our state, I will see that very good care is taken of him, very good care indeed!' Rabindranath Tagore and the great scientist, Sir J.C. Bose, neither of whom agrees with Gandhi's narrow nationalistic bias or his economic conceptions, definitely stated to me that his integrity could not be questioned. Whatever the truth of this issue may be, the fact remains that the ignorant masses have come to look upon him as a god. He has cast his shadow over India as a banian-tree—widespread, deep-rooted.

One day the director of the Royal Library in Calcutta told me a story indicative of the extent and the character of Gandhi's influence. In the interest of the Library, the director had sent a Tibetan from India to visit various monasteries in an attempt to persuade some of the lamans to sell their holy books. This man kept a diary, and in it he recorded that he was very often asked whether it was true that the Second Buddha had been reincarnated in India and was known as Mahatma Gandhi. The Tibetans said they had heard that he was now waging war with the English King, but that, when his enemies tried to shoot him, their arrows passed harmlessly through his body. When they tried to crush him by running iron trains over him, he merely stood up twice as strong as before. The other answered that, though he had not heard of anything like this and did not believe it was true, certainly there were many marvels in this distant country of India. For instance, he himself had seen automobiles that flew in the air. 'Now,' said the Tibetans, 'we know that you are lying to us. Now we do not believe anything you say.' Thus had the Gandhi legend spread in roadless, trackless Tibet.

In a country where 96 per cent of the people are illiterate, it is something quite different from any fundamental understanding of Gandhi's political aspirations on behalf of India that gives him his support. Last winter we all read in the papers one morning how a certain tree in Calcutta was supposed to have sprouted swaraj leaves. 'Swaraj' is a word of Sanskrit origin meaning self-rule or self-discipline. It has been incorporated in the ordinary political vocabulary to signify home rule. The leaves in question had some curious white markings that somebody had deciphered as 'swaraj', and at the same time fibrous strands of a cotton-like substance appeared on the branches. In other words, when the people took to spinning their own cotton and weaving their own cloth, they would have swaraj! I intended to go and inspect that tree, but the evening papers announced that there had been a stampede of several hundred people who wished to possess the sacred leaves and that they had stripped the tree absolutely bare. Another story that impressed me indicates the tragic possibilities inherent in this blind acceptance of a faith. Gandhi has laid great insistence on the fact that India must be self-sustaining if she is to be self-governing. Toward that end he has preached the necessity of developing spinning and weaving as home industries and has urged that every one discard foreign-made cloth and put on the swadeshi, or home-made, product. One ignorant country woman who had heard him make this plea returned to her mud-walled house and obediently flung out of the door her single garment of English cotton. Then she remembered that she had nothing to substitute for it. Two days later her son-in-law wondering why she had not been to visit her daughter, came to see her, and before he could be warned, entered the house and beheld her in her pitiable condition. He at once rescued the discarded sari and, threw it to her and went in search of the daughter. When they came back, they found that she had hanged herself with her sari, as the only means of expiating her disgrace.

After I had been in India a few weeks and had tested out the cloth bazar districts and the slums of some of the larger cities, I was on the point of believing that every one of the 319 million inhabitants of India knew all about Gandhi. That the mass of people cannot read does not stand in the way of their learning of the events of the times. In every village there is, of course, some person who is familiar with a written dialect, and he it is who sits of an evening by the well or in front of the shrine to the Monkey God, or whatever god may be worshipped in that village, and reads out the news from old papers that find their way, no one knows how, into the district. Moreover, the National Congress, a body of several hundred Indians who meet annually to pass resolutions as an expression of public opinion, furnishes both paid workers and volunteers who have spread Gandhi propaganda assiduously for the past few years. Nevertheless I did find two people in India who had never heard of Gandhi, and there must be many hundreds of thousands to whom his name means less than it does to the casual reader of a metropolitan newspaper at home.

Biographical details can no more tell the essential points in a man's life than a tombstone screed can sum him up after death. Nevertheless, without them we are at a loss how to interpret the manuscript of what he is. Mohandas Karamchand Gandhi was born in October 1869, in the province of Gujarat on the north-west coast of India. His family seem to have been local officials of sorts for a few generations back. There is nothing particularly to record of either his father or his mother except that they belonged to the third of the great Hindu castes, the Vaisya or trading caste, and were exceedingly strict in the observance of caste principles. Among these the doctrine of *ahimsa,* non-killing, is one of the most important. A biographer of Mr. Gandhi relates how Gandhi as a boy used to steal off with some of his school friends to the bank of a stream, for occasional meat-eating feasts, very much against the vegetarian tenet of his religion. It is the solitary sin I have found recorded against his name unless his brief effort, in his London days, at conversion to the standards of an Englishman must also be set down. Gandhi had early conceived the wish to go to England to study law. His mother opposed the scheme, and it was only after she had made him take three solemn vows in the presence of a Jain priest, to abstain from meat and from wine and to observe chastity, that she gave her consent to his leaving India. In London a friend took him in hand and tried to turn him into an imitation English gentleman. Under his tutelage Gandhi studied French, music and dancing, but there was something incompatible in all this with his deep-seated religious nature. Once at a dinner party as he was eating meat soup a sudden abhorrence came over him. He rose abruptly and left the room, much to the disgust of the friend who had brought him there. After this little incident he abandoned the attempted compromise with his principles and devoted himself solely to his studies.

When he returned to India, at the end of seven years, after he had been called to the Bar, his mother had just died. According to Indian custom, he had long before been married, at the age of twelve, to a child wife. He now prepared to settle down and began his practice of law in the Bombay High Court. Within a few months, however, a chance offer came to conduct a case in South Africa in which some Indians were concerned, and Gandhi embarked on that long chapter of his life which was to last for 20 years and to foreshadow in surprising detail his recent activities in India.

Just as the case on which he had gone out to South Africa was brought to a satisfactory conclusion and he was on the point of returning home, it became apparent that serious anti-Asiatic legislation was likely to be enacted in the colonial legislature. Gandhi decided to give up his personal career, so far as becoming merely a successful barrister was concerned, and to devote all his strength and ability to serving his ignorant countrymen, of whom several thousand were at that time settled as indentured labourers, working in the mines and on the plantations, in Natal and the Transvaal.

Two aspects of Gandhi's life in South Africa are of interest in connection with his subsequent leadership in India. He began as a champion of the rights of labour, and it is among the labouring classes that he has chosen to spend practically the whole of his life. But in that isolated Indian community where the conflict between the white rulers and the Indian workers was necessarily a bitter one and where the Indians were at an appalling disadvantage, the sense of nationality and of patriotism emerged under the white heat of the fire. Mr. Gandhi became an ardent patriot.

In the second place, in organizing his campaign of Indian resistance to oppression and of open warfare on behalf of principles of justice, he made use of all the familiar Western machinery of opposition, employing such coercive measures as strikes, refusal to recognize discriminatory legislation and voluntary imprisonments. But always he laid emphasis on the more spiritual side of the struggle. It was not primarily a material end they were fighting for, and the means to be employed must reflect that truth. One sees rapidly emerging all those ideas that have since given colour to the movement in India. Physical force is to be met with soul force, that is, passive resistance. If non-cooperation on one side, instead of persuading those in power to give in, results in their using violence and physical force, those against whom this force is used will fearlessly bow the neck and offer their bodies to the will of their conquerors. Their souls yet remain their own. In the end soul will win. Through concentrating on this conception and on that of self-discipline as a means of attaining the self-control essential to the successful working out of his programme the labour leader and patriot began to allow the religious side of his nature to expand. Mr. Gandhi became an austere, a great, religious teacher.

Both these attainments are the result of fine emotional capacities.

In 1914 Gandhi returned to take up the broken thread of his life in India. He came back a hero in the eyes of the Indian people. In South Africa he had earned four terms of imprisonment and the stigma of being considered an agitator, but he had succeeded in what he was trying to accomplish, namely, the protection of the right of Indian immigrants to settle down and own property and to be treated, as far as the law is concerned, on a basis of general equality with other inhabitants. He now turned his attention to the condition of affairs at home.

There, on the outskirts of the great industrial city of Ahmedabad in his own province of Gujarat, he founded at Sabarmati the *Satyagrah Ashram,* or asylum of truth seeking. It is here that he has lived with his wife and several grandchildren, when not off on one of his exhaustive tours. His oldest son, who is not in complete sympathy with him, is a merchant in Calcutta. The second son has been active in carrying on various sorts of work in connection with the movement, particularly the teaching of Hindi as a national language, in Madras and elsewhere. At the time of my visit to Ahmedabad, in December, made the acquaintance of the youngest son, who had just returned from South Africa where he has continued to publish *Indian Opinion,* the paper founded by his father years ago. He was trying to decide whether he would now remain in India with his father. Gandhi himself has spent the better part of five years in holding big meetings in every section of India, in travelling up and down in the interests of the campaign against the government and in performing the other acts of leadership that have devolved upon him.

As I jolted along, in a springless *ghari,* on my way to a talk with Gandhi in his own home I felt how old a city Ahmedabad is and how surely, if I had time to hunt, I should find in it traces of Indian splendour. Long since it has outgrown its walls and pushed its way through its own gates in a clutter of small mud houses and dusty streets. Dirt and flies are everywhere and that profusion of cheap lives characteristic of the East. I rode through the city, then across the river, where strips and squares of many bright coloured pieces of cloth were being laid to dry on the banks and out into the country. The road passed between brown sun-burned fields. Wherever a tree grew, it cast a welcome shade. Little hammocks generally swung from the branches and here the babies of women in trousers, working in the fields beyond, slept or wailed according as their stomachs were full or empty. Wild peacocks occasionally trailed across the road, and once I saw a large monkey with a very long tail turning himself upside down by the gate-post, of a landowner's property. I drove for about an hour and a half and then I came to a cluster of isolated houses, some of them yet unfinished, scattered in haphazard fashion on both sides of the road. This, my driver told me, was the Satyagrah Ashram. It was a bare spot, with no beauty except that, of the dusty fields and wide horizon and sandy river. I saw no one about; so I followed a path that led through a garden of papaya-trees and magenta flower-beds to the covered veranda of one of the houses. The place looked rather neglected, clean enough, but evidently not occupying the attention of those who lived there. In a swinging settee sat Gandhi's son. He arose and, after disappearing for a moment into a room on the left, returned to say that his father was waiting to see me.

The Mahatma was sitting on a mattress on the floor, in front of a low table covered with books and papers. He took off his steel-rimmed spectacles and without getting up smiled pleasantly and invited me to sit on a square stool. I preferred the floor, however, and sat down on the piece of faded red cloth that did service as a carpet. A small spinning-wheel and some carded cotton were near the table. Otherwise the room was bare of furniture.

This home of Mr. Gandhi's outside Ahmedabad must, I think, be very similar to the one he founded nearly eighteen years ago in Natal. At that time he had been reading Ruskin's *Unto This Last* and conceived the idea of some sort of settlement in the country, where a small community of men and women might live together in spiritual unity. They were to divest themselves of all the artificial trappings of so-called civilization, and in this haven of sanctity and peace, through contact with nature and by rigid discipline of the body, come nearer to an understanding of divine principles. It was during this period that Gandhi laid upon himself and his family an iron yoke of habit. He gave away his fortune. He wore the simplest, raiment and took only enough food to sustain life. He slept outdoors on a coarse blanket. If one knows India, one can appreciate why the superstitious report has spread that, he possesses miraculous powers and that the arrows of his enemies have no power to do him injury.

At the Satyagrah Ashram Gandhi has gathered around him a curious group of disciples. They have taken eight vows: the vow of truth-seeking, of non-killing, of fearlessness, of 'a celibate life, whether married or unmarried', of poverty and of control of the palate, the vow to use every influence to do away with caste regulations against the Untouchables, which Gandhi believes to be the greatest blot on Hinduism, and finally the swadeshi vow—patronizing and encouraging home industry. About a hundred persons have become members of the community, but since many of them go out to carry on the work of organization in different parts of India, there are never so many at hand.

Just now, or at least when I visited the settlement, the tension of the political situation and Mr. Gandhi's determination to identify his religion with the government of India were reflected in the daily routine. Everybody was spinning. It is one of the fundamental points in his propaganda that India must become self-sustaining if she is to be self-governing. Agriculture is therefore to be supplemented by the creation of a spinning and weaving industry on a vast scale. Instead of exporting cotton to be bought back in the form of manufactured goods from Manchester, India will supply herself with what she needs, or as much of it as she can. But why advocate a return to the handicraft stage? Why must everybody possess a charka, or spinning-wheel, and produce his own hand-spun, hand-woven clothing? Mr. Gandhi gives two answers.

'I am not opposing the establishment of mills in India, but I am doing nothing to encourage it,' he said to me. 'Flooding India with mills will not solve the problem of the poverty of millions. Thirty million people at least live on only one meal a day, consisting of a *chapati* containing no fat and a pinch of salt. Our vast agricultural population is idle four months in the year. These are the people who suffer. Formerly we had a great spinning and weaving industry, but it was deliberately killed. It must be built up again.'

Mr. Gandhi advocates the revival of cottage industries because he believes also that the material civilization of the West stifles the soul. He says of civilization: 'People living in it make bodily welfare the object of life. . . . Formerly men were made slaves under physical compulsion; now they are enslaved by temptation of money and of the luxuries that money can buy.' And elsewhere, 'According to the teaching of Mohammed this would be considered Satanic civilization. Hinduism calls it the Black Age.' In contrast to the materialistic creed of Western nations he says that 'Hinduism, Islamism, Zoroastrianism, Christianity and all other religions teach that we should remain passive about worldly pursuits and active about godly pursuits.' In Gandhi's own tongue, Gujarati, the equivalent for civilization is best translated as 'good conduct'.

I should like to quote at length one passage from his book on *Indian Home Rule,* because it seems to me to sum up his idealistic view of life and at the same time to reveal his inherent mental weakness:

We notice that mind is a restless bird; the more it gets the more it wants, and still remains unsatisfied. The more we indulge our passions, the more unbridled they become. Our ancestors, therefore, set a limit to our indulgences. They saw that happiness was largely a mental condition. A man is not necessarily happy because he is rich, or unhappy because he is poor. Millions will always remain poor. Observing all this, our ancestors dissuaded us from luxuries and pleasures. We have managed with the same kind of plough as it existed thousands of years ago. We have retained the same kind of cottages that we had in former times, and our indigenous education remains the same as before. We have had no system of life-corroding competition. Each followed his own occupation or trade, and charged a regulation wage. It was not that we did not know how to invent machinery, but our forefathers knew that, if we set our hearts after such things, we would become slaves and lose our moral fibre. They, therefore, after due deliberation, decided that we should only do what we could with our hands and feet. They saw that our real happiness and health consisted in a proper use of our hands and feet. They further reasoned that large cities were a snare and a useless encumbrance, and that people would not be happy in them, that there would be gangs of thieves and robbers, prostitution and vice flourishing in them, and that poor men would be robbed by rich men. They were, therefore, satisfied with small villages. They saw that kings and their swords were inferior to the sword of ethics, and they, therefore, held the sovereigns of the earth to be inferior to the Rishis and the Fakirs.

It is in statements like this that we see the Indian mind at work. In the West there is no fundamental scorn of life in itself. But the ancient East has grown weary of the struggle. All Eastern philosophies teach that life is a process of pain from which we must seek to escape. Over against an unhappy reality mankind will always create in imagination that state of perfection for which the soul yearns. Some of us invent a Bright Heaven yet to come, and some look back to a Golden Age that never was. Mr. Gandhi is of this latter sort. Only once in all his writings or speech did I ever find the slightest suggestion that perhaps this Vedic India he so persistently paints as an actual historical reality was not that, after all. He was elaborating his conception of the joy and beauty to be found in cottage industry and the happiness of village life worked out on this principle. 'I always hear divine voices telling me in my ears that such life was a matter of fact once in India, but even if such an India be the idle dream of a poet, it does not matter. Is it not necessary to create such an India now? . . . I cannot bear the heart-rending cry of the poor.' And when he left South Africa to return home after his 20 years of voluntary exile, he wrote as his final word, 'I believe that it is in India that the nearest approach to perfection is possible.'

All that morning that I spent with Gandhi at his Ashram, he himself sat spinning. He looked like the fifteenth century poet Kabir, thin, bare from the waist up, one hand holding the twirling cotton and the other turning the wheel.

The day at Sabarmati begins at half past four in the morning, when all the members of the community gather outdoors for prayers. There are no monastic rules requiring that everybody do the same thing at the same time. The Satyagrah philosophy encourages independence. It is merely the bond of a common effort that brings together the various persons associated with the Ashram. But since the spirit is one, the day falls into a natural order. Between the early prayers and breakfast people busy themselves as they please, performing the simple tasks of cooking, cleaning or attending to other personal matters. According to Indian custom, each family or individual prepares food separately and eats alone. After breakfast the work of the day begins in earnest, and continues until evening prayers at six. Until lately there was a school attached to the settlement, but Gandhi has become somewhat indifferent to the idea of the school. Even the young, he says, must make their sacrifice at this critical time and devote themselves to national work of some kind. So when I went through the grounds and inspected some of the other buildings, I saw little evidence of anything going on except work in connection with the swadeshi part of Gandhi's programme. A curious twang echoed from a number of cell-like rooms opening off a covered passage on an open court. When I put my head inside one or two doors, I saw young men carding raw cotton with a tightened string. In the weaving school a child six years old was busily spinning. From this home made thread cotton cloth of several varieties was being produced on handlooms, operated by weavers of the neighbourhood and poor women paid to do the work. Two of the women were rocking their babies in hammocks beside their looms, swinging them by a rope fastened to the big toe. All the cloth is sold, and the money goes into the swaraj fund.

It seemed strange that a movement of tremendous political destruction should emanate from such a place. But it was after all only the background of a different sort of activity. Gandhi himself, although he has taken to spinning a great deal of the time, also writes his weekly copy of *Young India* at the little desk in front of his lowly pallet.

All the time I was at Sabarmati people were coming and going, making reports on the progress of the non-cooperation movement in all parts of India. The organization has long been an elaborate one, reaching out to every village. I saw a little by what process this organization is carried on, although I had only my eyes to interpret for me. Gandhi's room gradually filled up with persons waiting to interview him. I remember being struck by the variety of these people, both as to apparent position in life and occupation. There were several barefoot Hindu gentlemen in swadeshi skirts and shirts and Gandhi caps. So far no one has copied Gandhi's style of entirely dispensing with an upper garment. These men were obviously political organizers. A Jain priest, wearing his yellow robe over a coarse shirt, came in and sat down by the wall, depositing near him his red lacquer begging-bowl and his drinking-cup made from a coconut shell. I felt sure that a Jewish-looking man, perhaps Persian, was, like myself, a stranger. He kept looking around with a nervous, pleasant smile. He wore a high white cap and a long coat, with an agate watch-chain, and carried a black walking-stick with a silver top. Then there was a strange-looking man with curly black hair reaching to his shoulders and black glasses, which gave him a fantastic appearance, as if he were masquerading. And then there were two very neat gentlemen dressed in sheer white linen with red and gold borders to their dhotis and flat red turbans tightly folded. They looked like wealthy merchants, but one, from the fine red lines painted between his eyes was evidently a Brahman. He wore a large diamond ring. Yet he had intimate business with this man whose vow of poverty was a visual reality before us. Besides these visitors, who had all come on business, there was a constant stream of silent women, presenting themselves just within the doorway, kneeling down and touching their foreheads to the floor in humble reverence, gazing a few seconds with awe upon Gandhi—spinning at his wheel and never even looking at them—and then making way for the others who had collected at the door. Occasionally Gandhi greeted some one who entered the room, but for the most part he did not lift his eyes from his work. He seemed to have great power of concentration. Once he remarked that he had set aside the hour from three to four to see strangers, and he seemed annoyed that the streams of silent women had somehow found their way into his presence at a time not set aside for them.

While we were discussing his idea of the right type of education for India, suddenly he looked up and asked me abruptly whether I would excuse him while he went to take his bath. 'Otherwise the whole of my day will be upset,' he explained. He was gone about twenty minutes and then came back, followed by his wife, a thin little woman with a personality curiously reflecting that of her husband. She, too, has known her prison sentences in South Africa. With other Indian women there, she led in a fervid refusal to recognize the new law that legislators attempted to pass when the anti-Asiatic feeling was running high, declaring void the Indian marriage laws and customs. From the first to the last she has stood stanchly by the side of her husband, obeying without question and with such understanding as may be derived only from the school of life and the promptings of her heart, his exacting requirements. For no one may live near Gandhi and enjoy a life of ease. Now she brought to him his noonday meal, milk in an old silver bowl (this was the solitary object in the house even whispering that Mr. Gandhi had once known and enjoyed wealth), and the equivalent of a biscuit, which he ate as he continued talking to me. When he finished the milk, he took some sliced orange and his meal was over.

At the time when I went to see Gandhi, it seemed evident that the non-cooperation programme was about to adopt new measures of some sort. The government had recently abandoned its tolerant policy under which Gandhi had been free to say everything he pleased wherever he pleased; with one brief exception, since his return to India in 1915. The Viceroy had recently declared that government was determined to put down this confused opposition, which had for its aim not any concrete reforms, but a policy of forcing the government to yield large measure of control. To whom? In what manner? To what end? Those are questions that the Indian politician never seriously confronts. Force the government to give in. That is the sole cry.

When I asked Gandhi what steps he now proposed to follow in his policy of non-violent non-cooperation he made an astonishing answer:

> I expect to have peace established in India at the end of three months, but this will depend on our ability to exhibit real strength, that is, to suffer. We will flood the gaols of the country. Now that the government has taken up repression in earnest, all we need to do is to follow the government gaols as soon as possible. Then the administration will come to a standstill, not because of the arrest of a few thousands, but because it cannot face such an expression of deep discontent. You see, I still give the government credit for feelings of sincere humanity.
>
> There are three reasons for this programme of voluntary arrests. It will bring the government to a standstill. This is the lowest reason. A higher reason is that we need discipline in suffering. If we weaken at facing imprisonments the little pin-pricks in store for us, then we cannot expect peace in three months. The struggle will be infinitely prolonged. We must remain dignified and calm. With quiet dignity we must go into the gaols. Lastly, we feel uneasy, remaining in so-called freedom in a state we hold to be corrupt.

I asked Mr. Gandhi why it was that he himself had not been arrested, when so many subordinate leaders of the movement were now in gaol. Only that morning had come news of the arrest of C.R. Das, president of the National Congress.

'My turn will come,' he answered.

'After the Prince leaves?' I queried.

'No, before then. I hope to be able to precipitate my arrest. It will come in January, I think.'

'But do you not think that, if you are arrested, there will be serious outbreaks of violence all over India?' I asked. It was an important point. On it hung my final judgement as to Gandhi's sincerity in his non-violent pronouncements.

'The people of India are receptive to the doctrine of non-violence,' he answered quickly. 'For hundreds of years they have been trained in it. I find no difficulty in making people here listen to that doctrine, but I should be laughed at all over Europe if there I gave expression to such an idea. Big audiences here have listened to me with attention and with understanding. It is because the people themselves know and love this ideal of non-violence that they attribute to me extraordinary powers. They have always believed in it. It will be India's salvation.'

'But we would have sent in thousands to the gaols before this, if up to this time we had not been afraid of the outbreak of violence. Now the time has come for the final test. The leaders are going to gaol, and the people too will offer themselves gladly for imprisonment.'

'But if you are making a mistake? If your arrest does precipitate revolution?'

For a moment Gandhi was silent and thoughtful. 'Then,' he said, 'everything that I have done will have been in vain. I shall have lived my life in vain. There will be no more use for me or for my work. I shall die in prison. I shall declare a perpetual fast.'

The three months have nearly passed, but peace as predicted by Gandhi is not established in India. Gandhi was arrested three weeks ago. We have heard of no violent demonstrations. One report has said that everywhere the people are waiting expectantly for the locks to fall off the doors of his prison. But to those of us who have just left India, the calm seems rather like a lull before a storm. Between the high points of Gandhi's religious and patriotic ideals lies something futile that is part of the man. But he himself has said: 'See me please in the nakedness of my working and in my limitation; you will then know me . . . my path is destined to be through jungles and temples. The glamour produced by the saintly politician has vanished. Let us be judged eye to eye.'

CHAPTER 7

Intransigent India

Gertrude Emerson

INDIA'S QUARREL WITH ENGLAND IS OF long-standing. I asked Gandhi, when I went to see him at his home near Ahmedabad shortly before his arrest, in what way he considered English rule to have been definitely harmful to India. He found no difficulty in drawing up his case for the prosecution.

'In my opinion,' he announced, 'the activity of the Government of India has been wholly mischievous in all that vitally affects India. Personally I do not consider that any good has come from it. Handspinning and handweaving, India's principal industry next to agriculture, has been absolutely ruined. It did not die a natural death. It was deliberately killed in the interest of England. When the destruction of cottage industries took place in England, there were corresponding advantages to be gained by the people, but in India the destruction of handspinning and handweaving resulted in poverty for millions. What difference does it make if machine-made cloth imported from England costs a few cents less per yard than Indian cloth, when actually there is a great drain of something like £60,000,000 paid to England by India every year as the price of this cloth?

'I consider the emasculation of millions by making them totally dependent on foreign aid for self-defence a sign of decay rather than health. There is much talk of *Pax Britannica*, but who would contemplate with equanimity the dead peace that meets you in a graveyard?

**ASIA*, July 1922.

DUKE OF CONNAUGHT AT THE INAUGURATION OF THE NATIONAL LEGISLATIVE ASSEMBLY

Parliament considered the Government of India Act, of 1919, providing for Greater Provincial Autonomy, a real step toward self-government; but Indians insist that the government veto destroys the powers granted

'I condemn the system of administration of justice, for it has made justice practically impossible. The manner in which cases are fought protracts trials indefinitely. A pettifogging case may take two years for settlement. I do not call that justice which is obtainable only if you spend thousands of dollars.

'The English system of education has created a complete break between home life and school life. Education has not reacted on the homes. In most instances it is the source of tragedy, for it creates a mental separation between husband and wife. My wife was brought up in the orthodox style. She is not what you call an educated woman. We have lived a happy domestic life only because I have not allowed myself to be influenced by my Western education. Education in India is imparted through a foreign medium. Its substance also is largely foreign. I am not taught to regard anything belonging to my own country with veneration and affection, but on the contrary I am induced to regard everything Indian with either indifference or contempt.'

'But after all it is the English,' I ventured to interrupt, 'who have restored India's beautiful monuments of the past.'

'I was waiting for that remark,' Gandhi answered quickly, looking up from his *charka*, upon which he had been spinning for nearly an hour. 'The monuments have not been preserved on behalf of the people, but for the benefit of tourists. The motive has not been to fire the imagination of Indians or to see that they did not forget their ancient things. If that were so, Indians would be educated in a true appreciation of Indian art. Little benefit is to be derived from the preservation of ancient monuments, when no care is taken of the living tabernacle.

'And finally,' he concluded after a pause, 'the system of government itself is so expensive that it has reduced India to pauperism, under which thirty million people at least live on only one meal a day.'

These are accusations which need careful examination, although it is safe to say that, when Gandhi makes them, his followers believe them without further warrant. In India, where the vast millions are totally illiterate, the attitude of the educated leaders of the country is doubly significant. What they think about government will, in the end, determine the nature of government, for they have power to exert control over the masses for a long time to come, through exploiting their prejudices and ignorance and sense of race hatred, as well as their legitimate pride in India's past achievements and in her dawning nationality. Indian leaders of today are divided into Moderates and Extremists, those who advocate constitutional progress in reform along the lines laid down by the Government of India Act, 1919, and those who express disbelief in the sincerity of the government, brand the reforms as empty rhetoric, and demand either immediate home rule in India, on the dominion status, or complete independence.

At the present moment the Extremists, under the leadership of Gandhi, who was arrested early in March and sentenced to a six-year term of imprisonment, unquestionably dominate the Indian masses. But on account of their policy of non-cooperation with government and the boycotting of the new elections to the National and Provincial Legislative Assembly and Councils held in November a year ago, the most active agitators themselves are unrepresented in the actual organization of government. Present members of the legislatures will hold office until 1924, and until that date, when new elections take place, it will be impossible to determine the real scope or strength of the Nationalist Party, as the extremists have come to be known. Officials of the government express a belief that recent radical measures of the Nationalists have already produced a reaction in favour of the Moderate Constitutional Party. The Nationalists, it would seem, are planning to precipitate a crisis in the government in which the choice for their compatriots will lie not between Moderates and Nationalists, but between England and India. In such an event there is little room for doubt as to the issue; for at heart all Indians are nationalists in the broader sense of the term.

Unfortunately there is sufficient ground for the assertion that English policy in India, up to the past few years, has been determined primarily in the interest of England, and has considered the interests of India, generally speaking, only in so far as they coincided with those of the Empire. The mistake is in assuming that England, when her Indian policy was taking shape in the eighteenth century, should have possessed and acted upon the enlightened political wisdom which is being forced upon the world in the twentieth. Missionaries preaching the gospel of Political Democracy are newfangled and have to contend, in their proselytizing, with the Imperial Idea, which seems to have originated in the Valley of the Nile about the year 3000 BC, and which thus has a handicap of 5,000 years. Today the Mahommedans have united with the Hindus in an outcry against the abuses of alien domination, but it is well to remember that but yesterday the Mahommedans, during the period of the Mogul invasions, were the haughty aggressors. It is recorded that under Akbar, for instance, certain rebellious Rajput villagers objected to paying tribute, until they had been overcome by force of arms, and that later, pillars were erected on the imperial highway with accommodation for a hundred heads each, by way of emphasizing Akbar's point of view. The Venetian chronicler of Mogul Court days, Signor Niccolao Manucci, offers food for interesting speculation on, say, 'economic policies under Shah Jahan', in this casual sentence: 'We remained for seventy-five days in that port [Surat] the revenues of which had been given by Shah Jahan to his daughter, Begam Sahib, to meet her expenditure on betel.'

The chief trouble with England's attempted compromise with the new order of things is that probably it has come too late. The new Act of 1919 was based on pre-war conditions, and already circumstances have changed. There have been, too, as a result of the war, unfortunate incidents in India, which have had the effect of heightening Indian self-consciousness and widening the breach between the government and the people. What might have satisfied the Nationalists of the last century will not placate the intransigents of today. There has been a general Indian attack on the economic and educational phases of British Indian policy, and on the costly, unwieldy and discriminatory character of the administrative organization.

It is to be expected that a government which originated in commercial enterprise should reflect that fact to a large extent in its economic policy. The chartered traders of the East India Company, whose object was handsome profit-making, found French and Portuguese and Dutch competitors already on the ground, and a struggle began for superior advantage which would insure a permanent trade with India. Political influence from home was brought to bear, and factories of the Company were founded at Bombay, Madras and Calcutta. These establishments meant the acquisition of certain territorial 'rights' with semi-political privileges attached. In this case the flag followed trade. The Mogul Empire was already decadent and military conquest went on apace. Because England possessed a stronger navy than the rival foreign Powers and because London backed the Company more energetically than Paris backed the French traders, who were also trying to found an Indian Empire, the Company emerged supreme. But coincident with growth of power had come growth of responsibilities. A trading and military organization had had to transform itself into a civil government no longer answerable for its administration either to itself or to the sovereignty of a board of directors in London, but to the British Parliament. This was accomplished with the definite transfer of India from the jurisdiction of the Company to the Crown, in 1858.

India possessed raw materials that England needed. It offered a market for English manufactures. The policy of free trade was adopted. Most of the bitterness on the Indian side has centred in the question of cotton and cotton manufactures, which constitute the largest item in Indian export and import figures. Throughout the trading-world, Indian textiles were formerly noted for their excellence. Manucci in his chronicle refers several times to the superior quality of white and printed cloths manufactured in certain centres, where Armenian traders were generally to be found, 'who buy the cloth and send it to various parts. Sometimes European traders come there to do business in this cloth'. The popularity of Indian handloom cloths early aroused the jealousy of the English cotton producers. One cannot argue with simple fact. *The Indian Year Book* states that the trade 'grew so large that it excited alarm in England, and it was killed by a series of enactments, commencing in 1701, prohibiting the use or sale of Indian calicoes [the name is derived from Calicut on the west-coast of India, where this kind of cloth first became known] in England'. With the invention of the spinning-jenny, handloom cotton was doomed, and in earnest England set about making India dependent on Lancashire for her main supply of cheap cloth. When the Lancashire cotton manufactures foresaw in 1870 that the infant mill industry growing up around Bombay might eventually become a threatening rival, they began an agitation for the adoption by Parliament of a free trade policy in India. It was pointed out not only that home interests would be served but that undoubtedly the Indian consumers would derive benefit; for a customs duty which might be considered as a protective tariff would inevitably push the price of cotton up in India.

After a period of free trade, a 3½ per cent duty was finally placed against cotton entries toward the close of the century, when the question of finding more funds for the Government of India had become acute. But at the same time, in order that this might not be considered in the light of a protective tariff for Indian cotton manufacture, an excise duty of equal amount was placed on all the productions of the Indian mills. Finally, in 1917, the House of Commons agreed, again as a measure of finding finances for the struggling government, that English cotton imports should bear the burden of an additional duty of 4 per cent, for which there should be no countervailing excise charges. Last year, the Indian legislature passed a measure increasing the general ad valorem customs duty to 11 per cent, including cotton manufactures, and the record of that move brings the history of cotton legislation up to date.

The position of the Nationalists is that since India is the second largest cotton producing country in the world, there is no reason to cancel the value of its cotton exports by the cost of importing cotton back again in the form of manufactured goods from England. Why not let India's producers absorb India's cotton-crop and make India self-sustaining so far as its main textile requirements are concerned? Gandhi has given a new turn to the vexed question by suddenly advocating a return to the hand-loom, on the ground that flooding India with mills would do nothing to distribute among those who are the neediest the millions thus saved, but would merely tend to create a capitalist system in India modelled after that of the West, with the wealth concentrated in the hands of a few. It is not probable that Gandhi's economics can stand out against the pressure of normal industrial expansion. India cannot isolate herself from world influence, good or bad. But certainly Nationalist economic policy, when it obtains the opportunity to function, will reverse the English policy of free trade and adopt a protective tariff.

Without a flexible revenue derived from customs imports to fall back on, the Government of India has had to fill its exchequer from other sources, chief among them the Land Tax. This is complex, owing to the two systems of land settlement recognized in India, known as Permanent and Temporary settlements. In certain sections of India, notably Bengal, landlord ownership was acknowledged and the Land Tax fixed in perpetuity at the end of the eighteenth century. This system, now recognized as a thoroughly bad one, has produced a class of rich landlords, who exploit their cultivators and who do not pay a fair tax to the government, because the tax was determined in perpetuity, regardless of rising values of land and increased productivity, more than a century ago. Under the temporary settlement, which holds good for four-fifths of British India, the land was considered as belonging to the State, and landlord and peasant tenures were recognized on the basis of a tax, which was really in the nature of a rent, fixed for a limited time, generally 30 years. At periodic intervals the tax becomes subject to revision according to a revaluation of the land, so that the State shares in a general rise of prosperity. Under the temporary settlement scheme, the proportion of the net product of landlord holdings claimed by the government averages 50 per cent. In the case of peasant holdings, one-fifth of the gross produce may be taken as the extreme limit.

English influence in land legislation in recent years has been directed toward the protection of the cultivator against the exploitation of the landlord and the extortion of the moneylender, but progressive measures have too frequently had to meet the checks of powerful interests vested in the Indian landlords. The land problem of India, be it noted, has never been complicated by any attempt at English occupancy or seizure. Englishmen generally have considered India as a temporary resting-place, a caravanserai on the road to trade and commerce. On the other hand, the taxes imposed on the basis of evaluation of crops have not infrequently been challenged as exceeding an economic rent, so that the standard of living, instead of rising with prosperity, tends to remain fixed at its present very low level. Agrarian disturbances, which are becoming increasingly troublesome, suggest that the Indian cultivator will refuse in time to bear his present burden of economic oppression. On the whole, however, the Land Tax is light as imposed by the various provincial governments, though it may be unfairly distributed. The revenue of £24,000,000 derived last year from the land is £10,000,000 less than that collected by Aurangzeb on a much smaller empire, at the close of the Mogul period.

It is frequently stated that Indians are the most lightly taxed people in the world, and the figure of something like ten *rupees* as an average tax is quoted in evidence. 'The official apologists,' says Mr. Ramsay Macdonald, 'keep reminding us of the low taxation of India, but that has nothing to do with the matter. The question is what is the taxable capacity of the Indian people, and as regards the great mass the answer must be: "Practically nil." Englishmen may be taxed, on the average, £10 a head and Indians only one shilling, and the Indian impost be heavier than the English one.'

When it comes to the question of education, mistakes on the part of the government must be laid at the door of ignorance and short-sightedness. In the first years of English contact, it was thought that all India needed for wholesale conversion to Christianity was education, whence would spring enlightenment. Missionary influence was strongly in favour of introducing an English form of education as a bridge to Heaven. According to Gandhi, it has led in quite the opposite direction. Controversies waged hotly until the question was settled in 1835 by the famous Minute of Macaulay, which, in sum, pronounced Indian culture useless baggage, the sooner thrown overboard the better. Confessing to his ignorance of both Sanskrit and Arabic, Macaulay affirms that after reading translations and conversing with men proficient in eastern tongues, he has never found one among them 'who could deny that a single shelf of a good European library was worth the whole native literature of India and Arabia'. The introduction of an educational system which did not include modern science would be tantamount, in his opinion, to countenancing, at the public expense, 'medical doctrines that would disgrace an English farrier, astronomy that would move laughter in girls at an English boarding school, history abounding with kings thirty feet high and reigns thirty thousand years long, and geography made of seas of treacle and seas of butter'. Macaulay won the day.

There was a practical issue of an expanding government organization in need of clerks trained in English methods, and the schools and colleges established soon acquired the character of a government nursery or clerical factory. A graduate expected his appointment to a government post as a matter of course. Unfortunately there are no longer enough government positions to go around. There are approximately fifty thousand students in Indian colleges, of whom twelve thousand pass out into the world each year to face the problem of earning a living. Nothing like that number of civil service or provincial posts become vacant; the professions of the lawyer and the writer (which make the greatest appeal to Indian abilities) are already overcrowded; and the result is that an increasing number of educated young men, able to apply the 'higher criticism' to every aspect of the political and economic life of their own country, are set at large to infect the community with their dissatisfaction and resentment. Their position in the main is justified. The government has stressed higher education, has invited them to enter the contest for the laurels it affords, but is unable to furnish them the opportunity to earn a living after they have obtained their degree. Probably the average university or college graduate falls back on the position of a commercial clerk earning thirty or forty rupees a month.

Instead of giving its support to this type of education, under the false illusion that education is going to filter down to the masses from the top, and meanwhile leaving these masses severely alone, to become a prey through their ignorance to whatever political propagandist may choose to tell them the tallest story, it would have been better if the government had at least made an effort to introduce elementary education with a practical bearing on the lives and needs of the very poor millions of India. Lack of funds, rather than deliberate policy, is probably the true explanation of the situation, but the fact remains that more has been done for general education in the Native States of Baroda, Cochin, Travancore and Mysore, than in British India, and that the government has laid itself open to a reflection against which it is difficult to find adequate defence.

The cost of legal redress is another grievance of the poor. The Roman-English system of law is held by many Indians to be inappropriate to Indian life. And out of two million annual civil suits, about three hundred thousand relate to sums of ten rupees or less, and over a million to sums of fifty rupees or less! All these cases have to pass through the courts, many of them appealing to the higher courts, and lawyers who are unscrupulous too often prey upon their ignorant clients. Tagore told me bitterly that a poor Indian was generally poorer for winning his case.

The complaint from Indians is loud and grievous over the matter of the Indian Civil Service. They maintain that the pledge given by Queen Victoria, 'And it is our further will that, so far as may be, our subjects, of whatever race or creed, be freely and impartially admitted to offices in our service, the duties of which they may be qualified by their education, ability, and integrity duly to discharge,' has not been lived up to. Until a revised method of recruitment was inaugurated, in 1920, official positions were open to competitive examination, but because these examinations were held in London, the larger number of otherwise eligible Indians were precluded from taking part. In 1913 only 46 of the 1319 civilians filling the reserved posts of the Service were natives of India. The Indians have had to contemplate the fact that almost all the higher salaried positions have been kept out of their reach. Taking all the posts under the Indian administration in 1913, including provincial and central governments, only 8 per cent of those carrying salaries of 1,000 rupees per month and upward, only 19 per cent of those carrying salaries of 500 rupees and upward, and less than half of those of 200 rupees, were held by Indians. Under the present arrangement, inaugurated as part of the government reform scheme in 1920, the Service has been divided into what is known as the Indian Civil Service and the Provincial services. Simultaneous competitive examinations for the ICS are held in London and India, and provision has been made for a percentage of listed appointments and of promotions from the ranks of the Provincial services. The most important modification, perhaps, is the new percentage established to cover the total Indian recruitment. This is now fixed at 33 per cent, rising by 1½ per cent annually for ten years to a maximum of 48 per cent.

The heaviest expenditure of the Indian government, next to that for military purposes, is for 'Salaries and Expenses of Civil Departments'. The viceroy draws a salary equal to that of the president of the United States, and the men with whom he is surrounded are all highly paid officials. Up to the present, Indians have been largely debarred from sharing in the more lucrative posts of the ICS, and they have felt injustice in the fact that it is the Indian taxpayer who supports an expensive alien administration. Added to the salaries are the pensions, which stand for an annual drain of Indian money to England, of no mean figure. Before the passage of the new Act, the secretary of State for India in England was also paid out of Indian funds. Indians maintain that in view of the general poverty in India, the expense of government might be considerably curtailed through having more Indians in the administration and establishing a basis of salaries more commensurate with the general scale of Indian living. On the other hand, the policy of excluding Indians from the Civil Service, as it has hitherto been put into practice, is defensible in the interest of the efficiency of the Service. It is one of the melancholy signs of the times that under the changed conditions the Service has become less attractive to Englishmen of the finer type, and there is a perceptible shrinkage in the number of new men presenting themselves for the ICS examinations. It is going to be no easy task to replace, in ability and in integrity, these men trained in the traditions of a vanishing order of gentlemen. Their Indian substitutes will bring other gifts to the Service, perhaps, but they cannot outdo their predecessors in the qualities that have so far given the ICS its enviable reputation.

On the military side, there is widespread opposition to the 'British occupation' of India, also at the cost of the Indian taxpayer. The strength of the Indian Army before the war came to about 200,000 fighting men. The British Regular Army in India is normally 77,500. The maintenance of this great army, which is used mainly as protection along the North-Western Frontier and for the suppression of disorder within the realm, cost the Government of India £46,000,000 out of a total revenue of £127,000,000 in 1918-19, and £60,000,000 out of a total revenue of £145,000,000 in 1919-20. The contrasting figures in allotments during the same years for education and sanitation (which, however, may be considered matters of provincial rather than central control and appropriation) were, for education, £4,000,000 and £4,500,000 respectively, and for sanitation £500,000 and £750,000. I have been unable to collect provincial accounts that would offer a fair basis of comparison. Last year, under the separation of government and provincial revenues, nearly two-thirds of the national revenues went for military purposes, while this year a sum equal to 52 per cent of the total has been requested by the commander-in-chief.

There is no question that India, poor as she is in the matter of national revenue, finds a bill of this size for her defence—often interpreted by Indians as repression—a rather staggering load to carry. Indian Moslems, who contributed so largely to British successes in the Eastern field during the war and who are particularly dissatisfied with the Turkish settlement, assert that the military organization India supports is really but an instrument of British imperialism, which may at any time be used against India itself. In order to cut down the appropriation, over which it has no direct control, the National Legislative Assembly has, within the past few weeks, refused to pass certain proposed taxation measures, designed to yield the funds for this expenditure. The governor-general, under the Government of India Act, retains the power, in cases of emergency, 'to authorize such expenditure as may, in his opinion, be necessary for the safety or tranquillity of British India', and the action of the Legislative Assembly does not constitute, therefore, a direct check on the government. It can merely be taken as a very decided expression of national opinion on the military policy of the Government of India.

These are the vital points of Nationalist opposition to British policy in India. Like the Nationalist whose position I am attempting to make clear in this article—but for different reasons from his—I slight the constructive accomplishments of the British *raj,* such as its tremendous irrigation projects, its cooperative village banks, its famine relief organization, its projection of an electoral machinery, its insistence on ideals of impartial justice and its refusal to favour one religious group at the expense of another. Bad in many respects as the English government has been, it is better than any other we know that has preceded it.

The new Act, creating Provincial Legislative Councils and providing for a greater degree of provincial autonomy, was considered by Parliament as a substantial step forward toward the goal of eventual self-government for India. It was not so considered by Indians, who insist that the system of government veto and of checks and counterchecks effectively destroys any new power that may seem to have been granted. On top of the Act, India was stirred to the depths by the Punjab crisis. The Khilafat situation augmented the troubles. India grew sullen, and the Nationalist Movement suddenly acquired momentum.

It is at this point that I return to Gandhi, whose psychology, coloured by centuries of purely Indian influences and evolutions, has brought the Nationalist Movement to a head and given to it a character quite distinct from that of any other revolutionary movement on an equal scale. Without Gandhi, the movement would in all probability have followed the methods at work behind the overthrow of the old regime in Russia. With Gandhi, it assumed, at least at the start, the aspect of a unique experiment to secure, under the banner of non-violence, the liberation of a subject people.

In the beginning of the struggle, its religious significance was constantly put before the people. Gandhi announced that he was but following in the footsteps of the Indian patriot, Gokhale, when he urged the necessity of an attempt to express Indian religious concepts in the field of political activity. He maintained that religion could not be divorced from politics, and that, because, under the foreign administration of India, its institutions were losing their religious character, it was essential to spiritualize politics. 'I believe in God,' Gandhi wrote to a friend, 'as I believe that I am writing this letter.'

While declaring himself a determined opponent of modern civilization, and everywhere urging upon his audiences the rejection of western culture, he nevertheless frequently made public avowal of his loyalty to the British Empire. He did more than avow his loyalty. In the days of the Boer War, though he had just been engaged in fighting the anti-Asiatic legislation of the colonial legislature of Natal, he abandoned his programme of opposition and organized an ambulance corps of Indians under the British flag. When recruits were being sought for the European war in India, Gandhi made speeches urging his Indian fellow-countrymen to enlist in the cause of the Empire. This was in 1915, and for four years afterwards his attitude did not change in a fundamental sense. Even now he has refused to permit the National Congress to embody in any of its resolutions the proposal of certain members of the Congress that the Constitution be amended to include as its object the attainment of *swaraj* outside the British Empire. Since 1919, however, Gandhi is one of those who have lost faith in the sincerity of parliament in offering India a reformed government. 'The history of British rule in India is a history of broken promises,' Gandhi said to me with a conviction which removed from the assertion all aspects of histrionism. I doubt whether ever again he will reaffirm his loyalty to the Empire. Although he has not advocated out-and-out separation in his campaign for swaraj, he has left the matter open for later decision. What he does stress is that India must be absolutely free to choose whether she will or will not remain a part of the British Empire.

Lately, the organization and the methods adopted by the Nationalist Party have absorbed most of the public attention both in India and abroad, and the fundamental religious inspiration that lies back of Gandhi's work as a political leader is almost forgotten. When I hear Americans who have never been in India and who have no conception of the real significance of Gandhi's religious impulses, ardently support Gandhi against the British government on purely theoretical principles, I sometimes wonder what attitude they would adopt if they realized that, as far as American civilization and practical ideals are concerned, Gandhi would be even more contemptuous of us than he is of the English. We are both of the West, and it is the West that Gandhi despises at heart. 'India's salvation consists in unlearning what she has learnt during the past fifty years,' he has written. 'If British rule were replaced tomorrow by Indian rule based on modern methods, India would be no better, except that she would be able then to retain some of the money that is drained away to England; but then India would become only a second or fifth edition of Europe or America.' No compliment is intended in the tentative comparison.

The Nationalist Party has presented India with a very definite programme of activity, by which it promises that India will soon attain the freedom to fashion her further political evolution according to her own lights. The ten-year period of probation fixed in the terms of the Act of 1919, before the question of more substantial Indian home rule shall again be brought up for examination and decision, at the discretion of parliament, is deemed entirely inadequate to the situation. 'We want absolute power to govern ourselves. We want complete fiscal autonomy and control of our revenues and foreign trade. We want the control of all the departments of government, including justice and police. We want full control of the military situation. We want control of foreign relations so far as India is concerned. We do not ask for complete severance from Britain, if we can come to a satisfactory settlement of the Khilafat question.' Such is the challenging position of the Nationalists as interpreted in Gandhi's words to me five months ago. If Gandhi had concentrated on religious reformation and had let politics alone, he would not now be in jail, nor would India have reached that stage of political cohesion which threatens to disprove the official assertion that India can never be considered a nation.

The Gandhi movement has two aspects, a constructive one of social reform within India, and a destructive one designed to paralyse the efficient administration of the present government. Unfortunately, it is the second rather than the first, that has received the organized attention of the Nationalist Party, and the destructive work of the Nationalists has far outstripped the constructive programme. Internal reforms have advanced only because Gandhi has advocated them.

On this constructive side, Gandhi has preached character-building as the greatest essential to the attainment of true swaraj. The 'truth-seeking' ideals embodied in the *Satyagrah* Movement, which preceded the political activity of the Nationalists, have remained as a fundamental influence behind all Gandhi's personal acts and words. By example and precept, he has done much to break down the social barriers erected against the Outcastes in the Hindu social and religious system. Those who identify themselves with him as leaders of the Nationalist Movement have had to follow his practice of democratic relationships. Hand in hand with this, Hindu-Moslem 'fraternization' has gone on apace. The position of women in India is undoubtedly undergoing a change through Gandhi's invitation to them to share in the work of national organization. 'India is like a man walking on one leg,' he said to me. 'The women of India must be educated to take their part in the responsibilities of the new swaraj.' He has organized a number of 'national schools', where, among other subjects in the curriculum, Hindi is being taught with the idea that it is better fitted to Indian self-expression than an utterly foreign language like English. Social purity is one of the strongest reforms urged by Gandhi, who condemns among other things child marriages, the position of widows in India, and the Hindu religious institution of giving yearly to the temples, for 'the service of the gods', many hundreds, or thousands, of little girls. Gandhi supports a prohibition movement for India. He also advocates a return to the village *punchayets,* or arbitration councils, as a substitute for the expensive and complicated machinery of judicial procedure under the Roman-English system of law.

At a special meeting in Calcutta in September 1920, the National Congress, an entirely unofficial organization of elected representative Indians who have met in yearly session since 1885, for the purpose of passing resolutions as an expression of public opinion on Indian affairs, adopted the negative programme of non-violent non-cooperation first launched by Gandhi as a means of bringing about the paralysis of the present working of the government. The Congress went on record as of the opinion that the only effectual means of vindicating national honour and of preventing a repetition of the Punjab and Khilafat wrongs was the establishment of *swarajya,* and advised certain steps in support of non-violent non-cooperation to bring about immediate home rule:

1. Surrender of titles and honorary offices and resignation from nominated seats in local bodies;
2. Refusal to attend government levees, *durbars* and other official and semi-official functions held by government officials or in their honour;
3. Gradual withdrawal of children from schools and colleges owned, aided or controlled by government, and in place of such schools and colleges the establishment of national schools and colleges in the various provinces;
4. The gradual boycott of the British courts by lawyers and litigants and the establishment of private arbitration courts by them for the settlement of private disputes;
5. 'Withdrawal by candidates of their candidature for election to the reformed Councils and refusal to participate in the elections;
6. The boycott of foreign goods.

At the same time it was urged that *swadeshi* in piece-goods should be adopted on a vast scale.

When the regular session of the Congress was called three months later, the whole programme was adopted. It was further provided that committees should be organized in each village or group of villages, with provincial central organizations in the principal cities of each province to accelerate the progress of non-cooperation. Also, a proposal was made for an All-India Swarajya Fund. Within the past six months an appeal has been made to Indians to withdraw from the army, and non-payment of taxes has been advocated in those districts where prescribed conditions of a general adoption of swadeshi clothing have been fulfilled.

In my next article, I shall answer the questions that at once arise: How far has Gandhi been successful in enlisting the support of the masses in his astonishing programme of non-violent non-cooperation? What is the attitude of the Government of India? How will the drama unfold?

CHAPTER 8

'Non-Violent Non-Cooperation' in India

Gertrude Emerson

THE LITTLE TABLES IN THE LOUNGE OF the Great Eastern Hotel in Calcutta were pleasantly crowded last September with foreign residents and visitors drinking their *chota* pegs and their lime squashes. Outside in the glaring sunlight the sacred cows sauntered down the pavement in serene assertion of their right of way. Dusty-throated scavenger crows perched on the upper railings, watching their chance to swoop down on the basket of a fruit or fish vender below, and a million bare brown feet shuffled busily through the city thoroughfares on all the small, nameless errands of poor folk. Life seemed to run in channels worn smooth by centuries. There was little, so far as casual appearances were concerned, to indicate that India was in the throes of a serious political revolution. Yet one can give no other name to the activities of the Nationalists, under the enigmatical leadership of Gandhi.

At this time the non-violent non-cooperation programme, which had been adopted by the National Congress at its special session held in Calcutta, in September 1920, as a means of checkmating the government, had been in operation just a year. This programme had for its avowed objects the righting of the Punjab grievances, that is punishment of the officers and officials responsible and money payments to the families of the four hundred victims of Amritsar, a satisfactory settlement of the Khilafat wrong, as the Turkish question is commonly referred to in India, and the attainment of *swaraj*. These ends were to be secured within a year through

**ASIA*, August 1922.

pressure of public opinion upon government. In the time-limit set by Gandhi, however, nothing had resulted in connection with the Punjab affair; Lloyd George was still juggling with his pro-Greek policy in the Near East; and India did not have swaraj.

Obviously, since the possibility that there could be anything wrong with the programme itself did not occur to the leaders, responsibility for failure to attain its objects rested with the people. With great naiveté, for no popular leader should put himself in the position of repeatedly promising something that in all probability he has not the power to grant, Gandhi promised India swaraj on the first of August, then on the first of November and then on 1 January 1922.

It was a strange and perhaps a pathetic faith, this that Gandhi pinned to the government. According to the provision of the new Government of India Act, 1919, the question of a further advance in the 'progressive realization of responsible government in British India as an integral part of the empire' is not again to arise until the expiration of a ten-year probation period, that is, in 1929. As provided in the Act, the Secretary of State and Parliament are then to appoint a commission 'for the purpose of inquiring into the working of the system of government, the growth of education, and the development of representative institutions, in British India'. It is specifically stated that the action of Parliament in such matters must be guided by the cooperation received from those on whom new opportunities of service have been conferred and by the extent to which it is found that confidence can be reposed in their sense of responsibility. The idea back of Gandhi's programme has been that by making it unmistakably clear to the English authorities that their presence in India is unwelcome, and by bringing enough pressure to bear, Indians will force the English to yield large measures of control at once, regardless of the Act passed by parliament some two and a half years ago. This hope has thus far met with signal lack of realization. The English show no intention of evacuating India tomorrow, or next week or next month.

At the time of my arrival in India, reports as to the success Gandhi had achieved in winning national support for his ideas were curiously conflicting. The strength of the movement was debated hotly on both sides. I set out to discover as far as I could the actual results of non-violent non-cooperation in the year in which it had been in existence.

To begin with, the Tilak Swarajya Memorial Fund of a *crore* of rupees, an amount not far from $3,000,000, had been easily subscribed in less than the allotted time. Thus the leaders found themselves in possession of plenty of money. Besides the sums spent in creating and maintaining a party organization which spread like a vast network over all the villages of India, large amounts were appropriated for publicity at home and abroad. Further immense sums were used to buy and distribute *charkas,* or spinning-wheels, in support of the economic aspect of the programme, and the Congress organization had also undertaken to employ weavers and to dispose of *swadeshi* cloth that they or private individuals were able to produce.

Indians had not, apparently, shown much inclination to begin non-cooperation by surrendering their titles. Out of an approximate total of 5,000 holders of honorary titles, some 21 only, including Rabindranath Tagore, had resigned their titles in the wave of indignation that carried over from the Punjab troubles. The movement for the secession of lawyers from the courts had met with more marked success, but the administration of the law was by no means paralysed. It is still functioning, and recently the courts have done a thriving business in the prosecution and sentencing of political prisoners, including a large number of the 'resigned' lawyers. With regard to the boycotting of elections to the newly created Legislative Councils, an interesting situation developed. The non-cooperators made strenuous efforts to render the elections of November 1920, abortive by breaking up meetings, picketing the booths and intimidating candidates who had refused to recognize the Nationalist appeal to withdraw their candidature. As a result, only about 20 per cent of the total number of those exercising the privilege of the franchise made use of it. In only 6 cases out of 637 where elections took place, however, was an election rendered impossible, owing to the absence of a candidate. Instead of wrecking the electoral machinery, the non-cooperators merely succeeded in excluding themselves from a position where they might have made their influence directly felt in the administration of government. As it is, Liberals, rather than Extremists, have held the legislative posts and have been able to contribute valuable work to the first years of the new system.

The part of the Gandhi programme which involved the withdrawal of students from government institutions succeeded in introducing considerable disturbance into the educational system of India. Bengal has long been the cultural centre of India and, as one might expect, showed the greatest sensitiveness in its immediate response to this appeal. In a report on the situation issued by the Vice-Chancellor of Calcutta University in September 1921, it was stated that 42 per cent of the students below college grade had left the recognized schools of Bengal between September and March, a number equal to between forty and fifty thousand, and that by August 1921, only 14 per cent had returned. The names of three or four thousand college students had also disappeared from the registration lists, and the number of those presenting themselves for matriculation examinations had been cut off by 20 per cent. The magnitude of the disturbance in Bengal was obviously alarming. Elsewhere in India, however, it was not felt with anywhere near the same degree of acuteness.

The original plan was that national schools, founded on an entirely different educational system, would be organized to take the place of government schools, but although three or four 'national universities' were successfully started in different parts of India, these could not possibly accommodate the main body of students suddenly called upon to leave the schools and colleges. When it was found that a situation had been created which it was impossible to cope with, students were urged to join the Congress volunteer movement of picketing cloth shops, themselves taking to weaving and otherwise demonstrating the force of Nationalist sentiment. Gandhi announced that in a struggle like the one then in progress throughout India, every one, including even the young, must bear his share in the great sacrifice out of which the nation was to be built up. But sober-minded opinion in India did not back this attempt to involve students in a political movement. As the enthusiasm created under the excitement of the moment has somewhat abated, a tendency to return to the schools has manifested itself. But Gandhi's direct appeal to Young India to participate in the Nationalist Movement has produced its crop of unrest. On several occasions the student bodies have declared *hartals* or strike demonstrations which the authorities have shown themselves quite unable to control. One of the most remarkable, perhaps, was that of the students of Mysore University on the day of the Prince's arrival in Bombay. Later the Prince's address to the students of Benares University was chiefly marked by the absence of most of the students from the meeting.

The Nationalists had been able to bring over a large section of Moslem opinion to the cause by definitely espousing the Ḳhilafat issue, together with prohibition. Gandhi's championship of the Untouchables and his effort to include these Outcastes in the Hindu social order made an appeal to another wide section of the community. In the interest of national self-expression, he aroused the sympathy of the impressionable educated section of the country. But his economic policy, which had for its inspiration the amelioration of the pitiful condition of the masses, rather than the industrial development of India as a whole, to which Gandhi was bitterly antagonistic, persuaded vast, inarticulate India that the champion who was about to right all the accumulated wrongs of untold centuries, had at last revealed himself. The spinning-wheel was simple enough to be understood by children. It was in terms of the spinning-wheel that Gandhi addressed himself to the millions.

The swadeshi part of the Gandhi programme met with its greatest successes in the Punjab and Bombay, although no part of India proved itself irresponsive to the charka in at least some degree. Gandhi assured me that India had produced over $5,000,000 worth of handspun, handwoven cloth in the first year of the experiment at reviving this ancient cottage industry. But the economics behind the spinning-wheel is obviously not of the modern world, and I came across few intellectual Indians, with the exception of the Congress workers, who were willing, no matter how ardent their Nationalist sentiments, to support in either theory or practice the swadeshi movement. Gandhi's genius as a politician, however, lay in devising different appeals to different sections of the community, and by indissolubly identifying swadeshi with swaraj, he forced swadeshi upon India as the most visible emblem of non-cooperation.

I remember visiting the *Burrabazar* of Calcutta, the principal cloth market, a very few days after landing in India, and in spite of the fact that the Calcutta *marwaris,* who are the great merchant importers and the handlers of cotton piece-goods in India, are naturally opposed to the whole swadeshi programme, I saw plenty of evidence of the success scored by the Gandhiists even in this conservative centre. Stacks of Gandhi caps and of *khaddar* cloth were ostentatiously on display in the various booths lining the covered passages of the bazar. After first dissipating hostility by saying that I was an American, I asked a shopkeeper sitting cross-legged in the middle of piles of white fabric, whether people were actually willing to pay the higher prices asked for coarse homespun, in preference to buying the cheaper and finer imported goods. He informed me that swadeshi cloth wore so much better than imported cotton that in the end it could not be considered more expensive, and that people were buying it in large quantities. Whether the proximity of two or three volunteer picketers had anything to do with his remarks I do not know. The bazar was at that time filled with picketers, who were requesting merchants to sign a swadeshi pledge agreeing to import no more yarn or cloth for a year. Where merchants refused, the picketers established themselves outside their shops and kept up constant cries of 'Please do not buy from this shop' or 'The Manchester cloth and yarns are full of sin'. I talked with two or three of these picketers, and they all said they were students who had withdrawn from Calcutta technical and higher educational institutions.

Undoubtedly the pressure of general sentiment in support of Gandhi cost merchants with large stocks of imported goods on their hands an appreciable sum, but some time later I happened to meet one who had a different story to tell. I had begun talking with him about the political situation, but he had announced bluntly that he had no interest, in it. When I asked him, instead, how the boycott of foreign cloth had affected his own business, he became unexpectedly communicative. It had affected his business very well, he said. He had simply cut off the 'Made in Manchester' stamp from all his cloth, restamped it as 'Swadeshi Goods' and had been able to put a handsome profit into his pocket.

It was recognized from the start that, although most avenues of active participation in the Nationalist Movement were more or less closed to women, on grounds of social custom, the swadeshi programme provided them with an ample opportunity to assume a full share in the work. Eager workers, most of them the wives of Congress leaders, set about stimulating interest among the women of India. Sarola Devi, Tagore's niece, Basanti Devi, wife of C.R. Das, Anusuyabai, daughter of a wealthy mill-owner in Ahmedabad, Mrs. Sarojini Naidu, the fiery poetess, are perhaps the leading women in India who have identified themselves with the Gandhi movement.

I went one day with an ardent Gandhi feminist and a conservative YWCA secretary to visit the Calcutta slums. It was an unusual opportunity to penetrate behind the *purdah,* for even here in the midst of indescribable squalor and poverty there are plenty of women, both Moslem and Hindu, who never go outside their narrow courtyards. My Gandhi friend was wearing a coarse white *sari* with a border stenciled in black. Her hair hung in a long braid down her back. She was barefoot, except for sandals. She wore neither bangles nor rings. But in contrast to her Indian appearance, she had excessively free manners betokening an English education, and I was not surprised to learn that she spoke English better than Hindustani. She carried a notebook and made notes in a professional manner as we went from house to house. After being with her some hours I had somehow the impression of a beautiful lily with a snapped stem, adrift on strange currents. Rather shyly the women let us in. I must have been the first foreigner that most of them had ever entertained, but I was far less an object of curiosity to them than the Indian girl escorting me. They eyed her askance, and when she asked them why they did not learn to make their own *saris* instead of buying them at the bazars, they gave her evasive answers. One neat little Moslem woman replied tartly that she had enough to do to take care of her house and children, and she thought on the whole that her visitor would do better to stay at home and mind hers. An old woman, whom we talked with in one of the narrow alleys told us that she was a Christian and that she considered Gandhi a trouble-maker. But a fragile girl with a baby astride her hip and mournful, beautiful eyes said, with suppressed passion in her voice, that the Mahatma was surely going to save India. I came away that morning with the distinct feeling that most of the women of the masses had as yet no individual sense of responsibility in the matter of swaraj.

Another day I visited a spinning and weaving school for women, run by the sister of C.R. Das, where twenty aristocratic young Indian girls had been brought together and were devoting all their time to spinning on the charka and teaching poor women from the neighbourhood to make yarn and khaddar. But in spite of manifest sincerity and earnestness on the part of these women, there was a certain artificiality about their work. It reminded one of the short-lived war-knitting craze. Even these women kept telling me how hot and unpleasant, in contrast to cool silks, swadeshi saris were. There is no convenient badge, like the Gandhi cap, that may be worn comfortably by the women. Nor can the women half adopt swadeshi, like the Sikh driver of a taxi I was once riding in, and his assistant. Observing that both men were dressed in khaki, I asked the friend who was with me to find out why they did not wear swadeshi clothes. They at once refuted the imputation I had cast, one of them by unbuttoning his coat and displaying a khaddar shirt, worn like a talisman out of sight, and the other by holding up the end of a handwoven neck-scarf.

My own servant, a Bengali Mahommedan, was once caught in an amusing predicament regarding the matter of his dress, and he hypocritically lied his way out of the difficulty. On the occasion in Delhi when I first sent him with a note to Gandhi, he reported on his return that Gandhi had asked him why he was not wearing swadeshi clothing. 'I told him I buy tonight,' Abdul boasted, appreciating his own cleverness in evading an awkward situation. For Abdul was a 'die-hard', who had no use for Gandhi or any of his ways, and he knew that I knew he had not the slightest intention of buying any swadeshi clothing. He reckoned a little in advance, however. Fate decreed that he should carry a note to Gandhi in another city, not long after, and to his consternation, Gandhi sternly demanded why, when he had made a definite promise, he had not kept his word. Abdul hastened to tell him that the very day we returned to Calcutta he would most certainly adopt an entire swadeshi outfit. But weeks later, after we had travelled to Kashmir, back to Calcutta, south to Madras, west to Mysore and Malabar, north to Bombay and on up to Ahmedabad, where I was to see Gandhi for a second time, Abdul was still wearing his execrable black and white checks, left him as a legacy from some sporting Englishman of days gone by.

The second phase of the swadeshi movement, the boycotting and burning of English goods, stirred up an immense amount of bitter feeling in India. From this source, more smoke was written across the skies of Bombay than any other place, perhaps because the Bombay mill-owners soon discovered that the bonfires and the boycott materially helped the home industry. Wherever possible, after the Congress and Khilafat committees had organized the collection of a huge pile of cloth to be burned as a demonstration, Gandhi was invited to touch the pile off.

I did not happen to be present at any of these bonfires, but the newspapers frequently described them in vivid terms. Among my clippings I find the following, from the *Servant of India,* 14 October: 'At the bonfire near the Elphinstone Mills on Sunday night the crowd was as large as on the last occasion. It could be counted only in *lakhs* [100,000s]. The enthusiasm of the people was very great. From early afternoon people were moving toward Elphinstone Bridge, clothed in Khaddar and later in the evening it was impossible to pass along the Elphinstone Bridge and its precincts. . . . In the middle of the arena a large platform was erected for the leaders and near it the foreign clothes which had been collected during the past few days were arranged in the shape of a pyramid. All sorts of clothes of foreign make were there—costly silks, costly coats, shirts, hats and in fact everything that was considered necessary up to this time, was there thrown in a heap all well arranged, soaked in kerosene and mixed with crackers. . . . Mahatma Gandhi, whose speech was full of pathos, moved his hearers very much and he spoke with a great deal of feeling of sorrow. Some tears were to be seen in his eyes, so moved he was by sorrow at the failure on the part of the people in doing their duty towards their country. . . . The Mahatma lighted the heap of foreign clothing. The sight was extremely impressive; the vast audience, the burning clothes, and the passionate speakers, under God's sky in the growing night.' With even a remote understanding of impressionable Indian psychology, and of the incalculable power of Gandhi's personality, it is easy to perceive the far-reaching influence of meetings such as the one described, which took place in Bombay.

From the practical point of view, one may cite a few figures to show the adverse effects upon the English cotton market of the Indian boycott, combined with other circumstances attendant upon the general situation. The normal annual import of manufactured cotton may be put down at something over £50,000,000 sterling. Before the war, India was the largest consumer of the Lancashire cotton products, buying 45 per cent of the total production. This percentage dropped to 22 in 1919 but rose again to 31 in 1920. Now comes the report that shipments of cotton cloth from Great Britain in 1921 are the smallest in a period of over 50 years. But it is unfair to attribute the full, or even the largest, measure of this marked falling off of imports to the Gandhi movement, because the great rise in prices since the war, together with increased taxation to meet the deficit of 19 crores in the National Budget last year, must reflect itself in the purchasing power of the people.

It was not until after the arrest in September of the Ali brothers, the two men most instrumental in fanning the smoldering Moslem resentment at the Turkish peace terms into an active conflagration, that Gandhi decided the time had now come to recommend a serious step, hitherto reserved, in his campaign against the government. On October 6 a manifesto was published in *Young India,* which declared it to be 'the duty of every Indian soldier and civilian to sever his connection with the government and find some other means of livelihood'. The first signature was that of M.K. Gandhi, and the 46 others that followed were those of leading Nationalists representing all parts of India. After the Ali brothers had been tried and convicted at Karachi, at the end of October, and sentenced to two years' imprisonment, a resolution was passed by the Karachi Khilafat Conference approving the position taken in the manifesto. Obviously the situation was becoming critical, and when the All-India Congress Committee, which met in Delhi the first week in November, authorized each province on its own responsibility to undertake qualified civil disobedience, including the non-payment of taxes, it was agreed that the climax of the movement had now been reached. To add to the well-grounded apprehension felt on every side, the Prince was expected to arrive in Bombay in a few days, and it was impossible to foretell what disastrous outbreak his visit might precipitate.

In reviewing the development of the non-cooperation movement up to this time, one must draw attention to the fact that for more than a year the government had been following a policy very largely of non-interference. The Chelmsford government, which preceded Lord Reading's, had definitely avowed this policy at the beginning of the non-cooperation movement. When Lord Reading arrived in India to take up the duties of viceroy, in April 1921, he showed every inclination to treat with imaginative sympathy the natural aspirations toward liberty of the Indian people, and six months later, by his continuance of the non-interference policy, he had aroused the antagonism of all the conservative and bureaucratic element in India.

I had the privilege of interviewing the Viceroy at the Residency in Delhi on the afternoon of November 16. At that time, in spite of the passing of resolutions to put into almost immediate effect the most drastic measures of the non-cooperation programme, Lord Reading displayed a statesmanlike breadth of vision and a keen desire to devote all his own energies toward helping India attain her ultimate goal of self-government and self-realization. On the same afternoon, I had previously been received by Lord Rawlinson, commander-in-chief of the Indian Army. The difference between the military and administrative points of view, as represented to me by the two highest authorites in India, was most marked. And yet within 24 hours something had happened, to bring about a radical change in the policy of the government. That night the Viceroy and the Commander-in-Chief left Delhi on a special train for Bombay, to welcome the Prince of Wales on his arrival in India the following day. They did not return, as expected, the next night, because the arrival of the Prince was the occasion of a violent outbreak of rioting in the streets of Bombay, which lasted for four days, with a toll of 58 deaths and 400 wounded. Non-violent non-cooperation had suddenly become violent, in spite of all Gandhi's exhortations.

A week later the Governor of Bengal was the first to declare that the time had now arrived when men must come down on one side of the fence or the other. 'Those who are not on the side of law and order are on the side of revolution; and revolution means anarchy,' he said. The Government of Bengal issued drastic orders for the suppression of the activities of the Congress volunteers, and this declaration was soon followed by a similar one from Lord Reading on behalf of the Government of India. By independent provincial enactments, public meetings and demonstrations by

'SWARAJ' FUND AND 'CHARKA' POSTER
Gandhi and Shaukat Ali with leading non-cooperators,
Lajpat Rai, Mrs. Naidu, V.R. Charya, M. Joslin, C.R. Das

the non-cooperators were forbidden in most areas of British India, the organization of the Congress volunteers was declared void and illegal, and all offenders against the new order of things were promptly arrested and tried and most of them sentenced to short-term imprisonments of two months, the leaders getting sentences ranging from six months to two years. Thus the end of November 1921, marked the phenomenal success of the programme of non-cooperation in the sense that it had now forced the government to take active measures for its suppression. It also marked the inauguration of a new phase of the revolution, for there was an indication that Gandhi's banner of soul-force might at any moment be torn from his hands and dyed red, by the ignorant and violent masses he had stirred up to a point beyond his control.

Although for a time there was an effort to persuade the world at large and more particularly the English at home that the tour of the Prince through India was attended with marks of the greatest homage and respect from loyal subjects, now that he has left India the truth is no longer disguised. If the tour was planned to draw out an expression of loyalty on the part of Indians, it was a dismal failure. Why it was undertaken at this particular time is still a matter of conjecture. Nine months before, the non-cooperators had declared their intention of boycotting the Prince, should he come to India, and it is doubtful whether even the Native Princes, who had been placed under heavy financial strain in connection with the visit of the Duke of Connaught, just a short time before, welcomed a fresh burden of obligation in the matter of hospitality, lavish as their reputation for hospitality generally is. The visit was peculiarly irritating to India, and was in some measure responsible for the wholesale arrests which have netted thousands of political prisoners within the past few months.

In Bombay the rioting that followed the Prince's arrival grew out of the desire of the Parsis, a small, wealthy group of Indians, originally of Persian extraction and followers of Zoroaster, to present an address of welcome on behalf of their community to the Prince. Non-cooperators objected and vented their animosity by attacking in the streets Parsis, Christians and Jews who were returning from welcoming the Prince. The police, who attempted to interfere, were stoned. Tram-cars were set on fire, carriages and motor-cars stopped, shop windows broken, Parsi temples burned and persons wearing European clothes assaulted in the streets. Out of the death toll of 58, four Englishmen and one American were killed, the latter a young engineer who happened to be walking along the street and was so unfortunate as to meet a mob who turned on him and savagely beat him to death with sticks. Altogether, property to the amount of a quarter of a million sterling was destroyed.

Gandhi was at the time in Bombay, and with other leaders tirelessly spent himself in trying to quiet the disorder. On 19 November he issued a strange letter to the press. It began: 'It is not possible to describe the agony I have suffered during the past two days. I am writing this now at 3:30 a.m. in perfect peace. After two hours' prayer and meditation I have found it. I must refuse to eat or drink anything but water till the Hindus and Mahommedans of Bombay have made peace with the Parsis, Christians and Jews and till non-cooperators have made peace with the cooperators. The swaraj that I have witnessed in the last two days has stunk in my nostrils. . . . The non-violence of the non-cooperators has been more than the violence of the cooperators, for with non-violence on our lips we have terrorized those who have differed from us, and in so doing we have denied our God.' He also issued an urgent appeal to the 'Hooligans of Bombay' to desist from their destructive work. He publicly assumed personal responsibility for the disgraceful episode of the riots. 'I am more instrumental than any other in bringing into being the spirit of revolt,' he wrote. 'I find myself not fully capable of controlling and disciplining that spirit. I must now do penance for it.'

It is in utterances of this sort that Gandhi reveals himself most truly. It required high moral courage and the utmost integrity in his professed ideals to denounce, at a moment like this, those acts for which his movement was directly responsible. Fasting and prayer are obsolete in the West, but in India they are an ancient and accepted institution. To Indians, Gandhi's fasts are proof of his saintliness. However weak his political wisdom may seem to us, his ideals and spiritual vision are genuine. One reads with astonishment at the obtuseness of the point of view criticisms of Gandhi like that offered by Sir Michael O'Dwyer in a recent number of the *Fortnightly Review:* 'The ascetic pose of this unctuous hypocrite is nauseating to honest men, many of whom have for years seen through his gospel of mixed humbug and racehatred.' I have talked with Gandhi, and I have also talked with Sir Michael O'Dwyer. Sir Michael is as honest in his convictions as Gandhi, but Gandhi has greater insight into the eternal verities.

The day of the Prince's arrival, 17 November, had been declared the occasion for a general hartal, or closing of shops and cessation of all work throughout India. The hartal was carried out with varying degrees of thoroughness, but in Calcutta it was attended by almost complete success. Traffic was entirely stopped, clerks prevented from attending their work by bands of volunteers, in case they showed any inclination not to observe the hartal, and some 150,000 shops closed down their shutters. I happened to be in Agra on the day of the hartal. Except that most of the shops in the bazar district were closed, the life of the city was tranquil and undisturbed. From Agra I went on to Jaipur, and here I learned that two days before five Gandhiists had actually dared to close their shops under the painted walls of the Maharaja's Palace. Jaipur, as part of a Native State, is supposed to be immune from the influence of the non-cooperation movement. The attitude of the Maharaja may best be inferred from the fact that, when he was informed of what had happened, he hastily sent for his British adviser and asked his advice on which of four methods of native punishment he should adopt: have the offenders trampled to death under mad elephants, drop them from the walls of the fort and let them be dashed to pieces on the rocks below, blow them from the mouth of a cannon, or, if I remember correctly, chop off their hands and feet. The Englishman persuaded His Highness to adopt a very mild corrective as substitute.

The Prince was, of course, received with elaborate welcome by the rulers of all the Native States he visited. Tiger hunts were arranged for his amusement, pageants were held in which strings of gorgeously caparisoned State elephants were paraded before him, and *durbars* of feudal splendour painted for the son of the King-Emperor ineffaceable pictures. But even where there was no outward accident to mar the reception of the Prince, as in Bombay and Madras and Peshawar, the non-cooperators made it clear that India did not welcome him. His visits to Aligarh in the United Provinces and to Amritsar in the Punjab had definitely to be abandoned because of threatened outbreaks. In Allahabad he rode through five miles of deserted streets—the inhabitants having retired behind closed doors or marched away to a point outside the city where a Nationalist demonstration took place. When the Prince finally left India, sailing from Karachi in March, it must have been a great relief to every one concerned, including himself.

The government, by suddenly clinching with the situation and embarking on a policy of wholesale arrests, gave new strength to the non-cooperation movement. Gandhi urged that non-cooperators should court arrest by every possible means. There was no dearth of people offering themselves for imprisonment. Meetings were held in spite of the laws against them and enlistment of Congress volunteers went on, in spite of orders forbidding it. The government had to make good its position or acknowledge itself beaten. The papers each morning were filled with brief and ugly reports of wholesale arrests carried on in all the chief centres of non-cooperation—Bombay, Lahore, Delhi, Lucknow, Allahabad, Calcutta and Madras. Within a few weeks between three and four thousand persons were arrested in Calcutta, eighteen hundred in Allahabad, and an enormous number in the Punjab. Altogether, since November, there has been an appalling number of arrests and imprisonments. Most of the offenders are given short sentences of two months, but many of them are rearrested on fresh offenses almost at once. When I saw Gandhi in December, he wrote down for me a list of those whom he considered the real leaders of the Nationalist Movement in India. There were twenty-one names. 'I will put a "P" in front of all those who are now in prison,' he said, when he had finished writing the names, and he wrote ten 'P's' down the page. At least three more should now be added to bring the list up to date, and Gandhi's own name, with a 'P' before it, inserted at the top.

The government had committed itself, and it has since shown no signs of relenting. The Reading administration, in carrying out the Chelmsford policy, had based its position on the assumption that moderate opinion in India would be able to check the growth of the irreconcilables. It had done nothing of the sort, and after the change of government policy, it even exhibited a tendency to go over to the side of the Extremists. Resolutions were passed denouncing the excessively repressive measures of the government in handling the situation, and the legislatures were flooded with expressions of dissent and disapproval. In a debate in the National Assembly in Delhi, the motion of censure upon the action of government in indulging in an orgy of arrests was defeated by the none too generous margin of 53 votes against 33.

For a brief space it seemed that some possible solution of the trouble might be arrived at by a round-table conference, to be called by the Viceroy but the Viceroy emphatically refused to consider the proposition unless the non-cooperators first agreed to suspend their illegal activities. A preliminary non-official conference was finally called in Bombay on 15 January, at the instigation of Pandit Malaviya of the Benares Hindu University, and representatives of different shades of political opinion assembled to discuss the impasse, under the chairmanship of Sir Sankaran Nair, a prominent Indian Liberal. Gandhi attended the conference, but while declaring his unwillingness to suspend any of the Congress activities, at the same time insisted that the government should prove its 'change of heart' and create a favourable atmosphere for a possible round-table conference, by immediately releasing all political prisoners. He also dictated that the government must guarantee the immediate evacuation of Syria by the French and of Egypt by the British, the settlement of the Khilafat question in a way satisfactory to the Indian Moslems, and swaraj. The absurdity of Gandhi's position, in dragging in the Syrian and other questions over which the Government of India could have no possible control, rendered the Bombay conference a farce. Sir Sankaran Nair left the hall and the next day published an open letter in the press, stating that in his present mood Mr. Gandhi was a public menace, and that there was nothing to be hoped for from any conference with him. Undoubtedly Gandhi's position on this occasion lost for him much of the recently won sympathy of the Moderates, but it was accepted with favour by the Nationalists themselves, many of whom were now straining at Gandhi's non-violent doctrines and openly looking forward to the substitution of violence.

Civil disobedience was to have been first inaugurated in the middle of January, but was postponed to 31 January pending the possibility of a round-table conference. When that failed, mass civil disobedience was declared in two districts, Bardoli, a sub-district in Surat, and Amand, a sub-district in Kaira, which were deemed by Gandhi to have fulfilled all the preliminary conditions outlined in Delhi early in November. The government did not feel that it could postpone Gandhi's arrest any longer, undesirable as it considered the move to be. 'We must spread disaffection openly and systematically until it pleases the government to arrest us,' Gandhi wrote in *Young India*. The government was not pleased, but it saw no other way out of its difficulty. Mr. Montagu, then secretary of State for India, told the House of Commons on 14 February that some time previously the Government of India had been informed that it would have the Imperial government support, should it consider the arrest of Gandhi necessary. The official order for his arrest was actually issued the first week in February. But suddenly a dramatic incident occurred to change the situation. Gandhi revoked the order for civil disobedience, and the government decided to postpone his arrest.

At Chauri Chaura, in the United Provinces, a mob turned against the native police, forced them to take refuge in the police station and then set fire to the station, burning twenty-one of the policemen alive. This ghastly display of mob violence set an abrupt check upon the programme of civil disobedience just being inaugurated. A meeting was held at Bardoli, and Gandhi insisted that mass civil disobedience should be suspended until the wave of violent feeling had passed. Against Gandhi's express wishes, however, certain of the local Congress committees sanctioned civil disobedience, impatient with their leader's further temporizing.

On 10 March Gandhi was arrested at the Satyagrah Ashram, where he lived on the outskirts of Ahmedabad. Gandhi pleaded guilty to the charges made against him of openly spreading disaffection and of attempting systematically to render government impossible and to bring about an overthrow of the Government of India. He was sentenced to six years' imprisonment.

'Gandhi's arrest will be the sign for a general rising in India,' Mrs. Sarojini Naidu once said to me.

'But Gandhi believes that the people of India understand his doctrine of non-violence. He told me that in the event of violence there would be no alternative for him but to die in prison, by declaring a perpetual fast,' I said.

Mrs. Naidu looked at me with revealing fire in her eyes. 'Mahatma Gandhi is a great man,' she said soberly, 'too great to understand the frailty of ordinary human nature. Mahatma Gandhi does not know what violence really means.'

And there were other prophets who declared that India would rise as one man within twenty-four hours of Gandhi's arrest.

The general quiet that has prevailed means either that the masses are, as Gandhi judged them, genuinely affected by the doctrine of non-violence, or that they are indifferent, or that, without leaders, they have found themselves unprepared to enter upon violent warfare against a government that is notably equipped with a trained, efficient army.

Potential danger is inherent, however, in the agrarian and industrial unrest which continues to manifest itself in many places in India. The 9 million industrial workers represent as yet but a negligible figure compared with India's total population of 319 millions, but already within the past few years a million and a half of these workmen have been organized into powerful trade unions. In Madras as many as twenty-seven different unions have been organized. Where wages range from fifteen cents a day, as in the case of the Assam tea coolies, to thirty, which is the amount earned by the Bombay cotton-mill weavers, an economic situation lies ready at hand for exploitation by the first man who becomes a little more articulate than his fellows. Gandhi never hesitated to make use of industrial unrest for indirect political ends. Invariably, and genuinely, he sided with the oppressed mill-hand, the exploited tea coolie, the indigo cultivator. But in promoting strikes for higher wages and shorter hours, and for reduction of tax assessments in community cultivation, he gave impetus to the growing sense of mass resistance to established control.

The agrarian situation gives cause for considerable worry. There have been numerous small scattered riots and clashes, particularly in the United Provinces. Since the massacre of the police at Chauri Chaura, a movement known as the *Eka* movement has spread through several districts of the province. A former watchman and convict is said to have sent, the *gaupat,* or call to arms, through the villages. The Eka oath demands that the *ryots* refuse to leave the fields when illegally ejected; that they pay only the recorded rent and receive receipts; and that they do no forced labour. It also advocates the preaching of the Eka doctrine in the villages, and this clause has been transformed into a campaign of virulent oratory against the government and all forms of authority. The local government applied to the Legislative Council of the province for permission to raise 2,200 additional armed police. The men are now armed with rifles borrowed from the fort of Allahabad, and a service has been established for transporting them quickly to centres of trouble.

A section of the Bhils, a half-wild tribe, numbering upwards of a million, scattered over a large part of the country but chiefly centred in the hills of central India, has recently revolted and formed itself into an outlaw army wandering over the countryside, armed with knives, swords, bows and arrows. Local agrarian troubles, fanned by Gandhi's agitation, are the cause of the revolt. The Bhil uprising is less serious than that of the Moplahs last year, but similar to it.

In the Punjab, the situation among the Sikhs has produced the most serious of all the present difficulties. The Sikhs have lately endeavoured to reestablish their supremacy in the Punjab, and a political military organization, the *Akali Fauj,* armed with battle-axes, clubs and guns, is offering resistance to British military authority. The Punjab, as always, seems to be in a truculent mood. Owing to the wild border tribes along the north-west Frontier and the Khilafat agitation, there have been evidences of unusual restlessness in the northern part of the province, aggravated and brought to the surface during the time of the Prince's visit. The Punjab is the Mahommedan stronghold of India, and it was largely the necessity felt by the government of placating this bellicose element, by an official restatement of the Mahommedan Indian's position, that resulted in the recent resignation of Mr. Montagu.

The question of the loyalty of the army is, of course, of the utmost significance from the point of view of maintaining order in India. With what success the non-cooperators have been able to pursue their tactics of attempting to seduce the *sepoy* has hitherto been kept secret.

Bands of Congress volunteers have been perambulating the Punjab, armed with iron-shod staves, distributing leaflets which urge the sepoy to mutiny, and subjecting both the sepoys on leave and their families to various indignities from which the British have been unable to protect them. Recently a danger signal has been flown, insignificant in itself, in the news coming to light of small breaches in discipline among two regiments with distinguished war records, the Fourteenth Sikhs and the Nineteenth Punjabis.

In connection with the general situation in the Punjab, the most recent news is contained in the issuing of a manifesto by 51 prominent public men, not non-cooperators, protesting against the attitude and the policy of the Punjab government in handling the situation. Coincident with the departure of the Prince of Wales, wholesale arrests have been effected. It has been reported that between the middle of March and the end of April, from 2,000 to 2,500 arrests have been made, of which 60 per cent are Sikhs. It is maintained that many of these arrests have been made in connection with participation in purely religious meetings. The Punjab lawyers have issued an independent protest declaring the government guilty of 'irregular and illegal arrests, followed by hasty and questionable convictions'.

Lord Rawlinson views the general situation very gravely, as may be evidenced by his blunt statements in connection with the decision of the National Legislative Assembly not to vote certain proposed taxation, as a means of cutting down the military expenditure. Lord Rawlinson declares that the internal state of India gives cause for serious anxiety. He insists it will be many generations before India can dispense with the British garrison, numbering some 75,000. Troops are being called out almost every day to aid the police in maintaining order. The ability of the government to maintain law and order is likely to be put to a serious test in the not distant future. According to the view of the commander-in-chief of the Army in India, the ensuing months may be the most critical time known for 60 years, or since the Indian Mutiny.

But if the condition in India is grave from the military point of view, the determination recently expressed by an influential group of Indians to substitute for Gandhi's policy of non-violent non-cooperation one of responsive cooperation, is a hopeful sign. The leaders of the non-cooperation movement are, for the moment, in prison, and it is not likely that any one of Gandhi's outstanding influence will appear, to dominate the Congress and direct its further activities. Gandhi himself has, at the last moment, sheathed his mightiest weapon, that of mass civil disobedience, though local Congress committees have in some places disregarded his earnest warning against indulging in mass disobedience at this time, when the danger of violent outbreaks has proved itself a potent one. Still bitterly opposed by the National Congress, constructive opinion in India nevertheless seems on the point of rallying around the position of Pandit Malaviya, upon whom the mantle of Gandhi, in the sense of a recognized leader, now seems to have fallen. It is he who is responsible for a new programme laid down by the Liberal Federation which it is proposed shall be substituted for that of non-cooperation. It discards obsolete parts of the non-cooperation programme and the purely negative and boycott items. It supports the swadeshi movement, but includes Indian mills in the field of development as well as hand industry. It proposes the wide establishment of national schools, but urges that until these have been realized, students shall be encouraged to make the best of the opportunities now afforded them. It offers constructive suggestions for extending the present irrigation projects as a form of economic relief, and for carrying on much-needed medical work. It advocates an improvement of the condition of the backward classes. It believes the speedy Indianization of the army essential to any ideal of self-realization. It encourages vigilant and active support of all constitutional means for redressing the present grievances of Indians and advancing India on the path to full self-government as an equal partner in the British Commonwealth. Whether this constructive attitude will be able to counteract the destructive tendencies that have come in the wake of the non-cooperation movement, is still a matter of conjecture.

Gandhi has, I believe, done his work. He has made India self-conscious. He has given India a new sense of self-respect and has convinced her that she has her own message to contribute to the world. He has also equipped India with the will to assume her rightful place among nations. His programme has been characterized by many negative features; in some respects it has worked disaster, the reverberating influence of which is still to be calculated and paid for. It has never put forward even a suggestive outline of the government it would substitute for the one it would tear down. Gandhi's solitary definition of swaraj is 'the right to make one's own mistakes and one's duty to correct them'—a swaraj that scarcely offers a workable machinery of government. But Gandhi has given a moral basis and a spiritual standing to India's revolution. It is a strange commentary on the relation existing between the rulers and the ruled, that no way has been found to use Gandhi's passionate idealism and deeply religious concept of life, except to arrest and imprison him. When Gandhi dies, and I do not believe he will survive his prison sentence, India will revere him even more passionately than she does today.

For the present, the Nationalist idea of a purely self-contained Asiatic India is in the ascendant, but it will pass. It is an idea bred of the Western nations' irritating sense of their own superiority. The time has come, not when England can arrogantly impose her will as of old upon India, but when she must resolutely set about persuading India that full and equal partnership in the British Commonwealth will be of real value to India. Otherwise India will shortly choose, not merely self-government, but independence, and England will be powerless to resist India's will in the matter. 'If physical force is to be the solution, we may take it for certain that the Eastern empires of Western men will pass from the scene. The Western nations will find neither the money nor the men needed to cope with the passive resistance or active rebellion of the multitudes of the East. Even if positive disaster is avoided, the task will be given up in weariness and despair.' This is a sound pronouncement, emanating from the *Manchester Guardian,* and it may well serve as a text for government policy. The West must learn greater humility, greater generosity and greater wisdom, if it is to hold its place before the rising tide of Eastern nationalism.

CHAPTER 9

Overcrowded India

Harold Cox

IT IS IMPOSSIBLE TO UNDERSTAND anything about India unless one begins by realizing that India is totally unlike either Europe or the United States. The fact that the Indian Empire forms a political unit under the British Crown creates in the minds of untravelled persons—at any rate of untravelled Englishmen—a vague impression that India is a single country like England or France, a little larger perhaps, and inhabited by brown-skinned instead of white-skinned people, but otherwise comparable with any one of the European nations. As a matter of fact, India is larger than the whole of Europe, if Russia be excluded, and contains greater varieties of race, language and creed than the whole of Europe, even including Russia, can show. Compared with the United States, India has a smaller area and a much larger population. The area of India, including the semi-independent Indian States, is less than two-thirds of the area of the United States; but the population is three times as large.

The racial differences to be seen in India are apparent at once to the least-experienced eye. No one could confuse the sturdy little smiling Gurkha (pronounced Goorkha), whose head barely reaches to the shoulder of an English soldier, with the tall, thin Sikh (Seek) or with the fierce Pathan

***ASIA*, August 1922. Harold Cox (1859-1936) was a liberal MP, an eminent scholar and journalist. He spent two years in India teaching at Aligarh Muslim University.

(Put-haan); nor could he confuse the proud Rajput (Raaj-poot) with the somewhat servile Bengali (Bengawly). These are a few of the more obvious racial types. There are many other quite distinct races, much further removed from one another than the Englishman from the Spaniard, or the Frenchman from the German.

There are also distinctions of social habit. Take for example the question of dress. Over the greater part of Europe, as over the greater part of the United States, one finds everybody, rich or poor, wearing the same general type of clothing. In India you can seldom walk a few yards without meeting people whose dress is absolutely different. You may meet, for example, a dignified Mahommedan gentleman, more than amply clad in voluminous garments; then a Bengali government man wearing a garment somewhat like a woman's skirt, called a *dhoti;* then a Parsi shopkeeper with his peculiar head-dress, rather suggestive of the ancient Jews; and then a coolie wearing nothing at all from head to foot, except a narrow loin-cloth. A few yards farther on you may meet a holy beggar, his long hair hanging down his shoulders and matted with lime, his whole body smeared with mud, holding out his begging-bowl and asking for alms in the name of religion. In the same way with the women: some wear skirts with a tiny bodice across the breasts, leaving the stomach quite bare; others wear trousers tight round the calves and loose round the hips; others again wear a single garment about thirty yards long, which is ingeniously twisted between and round the legs so as to convey the impression of a pair of baggy knickerbockers, and then carried up across the shoulders and over the head, and so arranged that it can be used as a veil.

Many volumes have been written upon the numerous languages of India, which have been grouped according to general types or families. The actual number of languages spoken in India varies according to different estimates of what ought to be called a difference of language and what is merely a difference of dialect. The census report gives 220 as the 'number of languages spoken', adding a footnote that this figure includes 38 minor dialects. It may be said with safety that there are more than 100 separate languages in India, differing from one another at least as much as English from French, or say French from Italian, and in many cases differing very much more. For the languages of western Europe all belong to one family and all use the same script; whereas the languages of India are divided among different families which have no point of contact with one another. Some languages of course are much more widely spoken than others. Thus the language known as Hindustani is more or less a *lingua franca* over a considerable part of northern India, though very little known in the south. But even with Hindustani an awkward difficulty arises; for Mahommedans in writing use the Persian script, which flows at an easy slope from right to left, and Hindus use the Hindi script, which is square and upright and passes from left to right. The individual letters have not even the remotest similarity to one another. When I was teaching in India, I had among my pupils two boys who spoke Hindustani and were great friends, but since one was a Hindu and the other a Mahommedan, when they were on their holidays, they could correspond only in English. It is hardly necessary to add that English is the only medium through which the educated classes among the various peoples of India can communicate with one another.

The religious differences in India are as great as the linguistic, and from the social and political point of view far more important. The masses of the population are either Hindus or Moslems. In addition there are many Buddhists, Jains, Sikhs, Parsis and Christians. Finally there are numbers of primitive tribes whose crude superstitions are even older than Hinduism; for lack of a better name they are labelled Animists. Hinduism itself embraces almost every form of belief. I remember years ago having a conversation with a charming old Brahman, who explained to me, then newly arrived in India, that Hinduism was a question not of creed but of conduct. To quote his words, which impressed themselves on my mind: 'You can believe in one God or in three Gods or in thirty-three thousand Gods; you can believe that there is no God, or you can believe that God is in everything, and with all these different beliefs you can be a good Hindu, provided you follow the rules of your caste.'

That one word 'caste' is the essence of Hinduism. The Hindus, who enormously outnumber all the rest of the population of India, are divided up into a multitude of castes, religiously separated from one another. Into whatever caste a man is born, in that caste he remains until he dies. At the head of the whole system is the priestly caste of Brahmans. But the Brahmans themselves are divided into a number of subcastes, all keeping their respective rank, which is determined not by wealth but by birth. One of my best pupils in India was a very high-caste Brahman boy. So high was his caste that he could not find any one in the neighbourhood sufficiently sacred to be permitted to cook his food. He had to import an uncle, who lived with him in a hut in the college compound and prepared the meals while the boy was attending classes in mathematics and English literature. Similar barriers run right through Hinduism. The lowest castes are in fact known as the 'Untouchables' because merely to touch them pollutes a Hindu of a higher caste. I have myself seen an Indian servant, when asked by his English mistress to fetch a shawl for the baby, toss the shawl to the baby's nurse instead of handing it to her, because she, being of a lower caste, would have polluted him if she had touched the shawl before he had parted with it. In parts of southern India, where the caste system is even more rigid than in the north, the Untouchables are forbidden to walk on certain roads, lest higher castes should be polluted merely by seeing them. Thus Hinduism is essentially and rigidly aristocratic or theocratic in organization.

On the other hand, Mahommedanism, or Islam, is in theory, at any rate, and to a large extent in practice, the most democratic religion in the world. All true believers are equal in the sight of God, and no barriers of race or colour divide them into classes. Being strict monotheists, the Mahommedans are bitterly opposed to the mass of fantastic beliefs and quaint practices that characterize Hinduism, and periodically there is fierce fighting between the adherents of these two religions—as recently in Malabar, where a peculiarly warlike sect of Mahommedans set to work to convert their Hindu neighbours to Islam with the aid of the sword. Many hundreds of Hindus were killed and many were forcibly circumcised to make sure of their permanent conversion to Islam.

A chronic cause of quarrel between Hindus and Mahommedans is over the question of cow-killing. Mahommedans are meat-eaters and like to eat beef. Hindus are mostly vegetarians and all of them regard the cow as a sacred animal; in their eyes to kill a cow is a deadly sin. I remember once asking a Brahman friend whether it was a greater sin to kill a cow or to kill a Brahman. He replied that that was a very difficult question to answer: there were considerations on both sides. So I altered my question and asked him whether it was a greater sin to kill a cow or to kill an ordinary man. Without a moment's hesitation he answered that it was a far greater sin to kill a cow.

A less constant, but nevertheless a periodically recurring cause of conflict between Hindus and Mahommedans is the clashing of their respective religious celebrations. The Hindus base their calendar, as does the Western world, on the sun; the Mahommedans base theirs on the moon. Consequently the Mahommedan months are always travelling round the year, and it takes about 30 years to complete the full circle. In the month of Muharram all true Mahommedans publicly mourn with elaborate processions and other ostentations of grief the death of Hasan and Hosain. The mourning lasts several days. Every 30 years these days of mourning coincide with a Hindu festival of exuberant jollity, known as Ramlillah (pronounced Raamleela). Then there is pretty sure to be trouble, unless a sufficient number of English soldiers are present in the neighbourhood to keep the mourners and the joy-makers well apart.

The other religions of India are numerically less important. The Buddhists are a survival. For a time the simple faith that Buddha taught, 500 years before Christ, swept over India, destroying as it seemed the power of the Brahmans. But gradually the Brahman theocracy reasserted itself, and Buddhism was driven out of the greater part of India—south to Ceylon, east to Burma and China, north to Tibet. The Jains are a survival of a reform movement almost as old as the Buddhist movement, and somewhat similar in character. The Sikhs are relatively a modern development. In the fifteenth century after Christ, an enthusiastic reformer in northern India deliberately devised a new religion in which some of the features of Islam were grafted on to Hinduism. The new religion spread with considerable rapidity in the Punjab, where most of the Sikhs are still to be found. They possess a well-marked racial type and constitute in effect a distinct nationality. As regards the Christians in India, the most notable point is their steady growth in numbers. This is largely due to the appeal which the Christians, and especially the Roman Catholics, are able to make to the downtrodden classes. The lower castes find themselves lifted to a somewhat higher social plane by becoming Christians. The Parsis are a small body of highly intelligent, and for the most part extremely prosperous, people. They are the descendants of the old fire-worshippers of Persia—hence their name—who took refuge in India when the Arabs invaded Persia and forcibly converted the inhabitants to the faith of Mahomet. Most of the Parsis live in Bombay, but representatives of the race and creed are to be found engaged in business in all the principal towns of India.

The population of India according to religions as recorded in 1911 and 1921 was as follows:

	1911	*1921*
Hindus	217,587,000	216,734,000
Mahommedans	66,647,000	68,735,000
Buddhists	10,721,000	11,571,000
Animists	10,295,000	9,775,000
Christians	3,876,000	4,754,000
Sikhs	3,014,000	3,239,000
Jains	1,248,000	1,179,000
Parsis	100,000	102,000
Others	21,000	22,000
Sundry	1,647,000	2,831,000
TOTAL POPULATION	315,156,000	318,942,000

It will be seen that the number of Hindus actually declined in the last decade, and the figures for earlier years show that for some time past Hindus have increased less rapidly than the followers of other religions. The causes which give rise to the relative decline of Hinduism lie at the root of the whole population problem in India.

The dominating cause is the practice of child marriage. Hindu girls are often married long before they have reached the age of puberty; to delay the marriage of a daughter beyond that age is considered a disgrace to the family. The natural result is that a very large number of Hindu girls are called upon to face the strain of motherhood at too early an age and die in childbirth. In the words of a Hindu writer, 'They pass from the marriage couch to the funeral pyre.' A more subtle consequence of the practice of child marriage arises from the Hindu prohibition of widow remarriage.

That prohibition is not universal, but it is very widespread. Consequently if a little Hindu girl becomes married to a much older man, as very often happens, he may die even before she is old enough for the consummation of the marriage; but in most parts of India she will be forbidden to remarry. In former days many a Hindu widow, encouraged by her relatives, used to throw herself on the fire that burnt her husband's body, but the practice has long been forbidden by English law and now very rarely occurs, perhaps not oftener than once a year. These marriage customs alone account for the less rapid increase of the Hindus as compared with the followers of other religions, who, though they marry early, as judged by European standards, generally marry later than Hindus.

Precise figures are given in an extremely interesting little book on *The Problem of Population in India,* published in 1916 by P. K. Wattal, the assistant accountant-general of the province of Bombay. Mr. Wattal deduces from the census figures that of Hindu girls under five years of age no less than 18 per thousand are married, while the corresponding figure for Mahommedan girls is only 5 per thousand; between the ages of five and ten the Hindu proportion of married girls is 132 per thousand, while the Mahommedan figure is only 65. He goes on to say that, 'owing to the greater mortality consequent on child marriage and to the depletion of numbers through the prohibition of widow remarriage', the Mahommedans have a larger proportion of married females at the reproductive age period. He adds: 'This is a significant fact for the student of population, as he will herein find an explanation of the relatively greater prolificness of the Mahommedan as compared with the Hindu population.'

From the point of view of expansion of numbers, Hinduism is also at a disadvantage because Hindus cannot make converts. A Hindu is born, not made. On the other hand, Mahommedans are constantly winning recruits from Hinduism. For example, if a Mahommedan falls in love with a Hindu prostitute, he will marry her and she will become a Mahommedan. The reverse could not happen. Nor do poor Mahommedans abandon their faith for worldly advantages as lower-caste Hindus not infrequently do. On the other hand, primitive tribes, whose religious practices approximate to those of the Hindus, from time to time come to be classified as Hindus rather than as Animists in faith.

The practice of child marriage not only affects the relative rate of growth of the different religions in India, but it also affects the problem of population in India as a whole, as compared with corresponding problems among Western peoples. As the figures above quoted show, though child marriage is specially prevalent among Hindus, it also prevails to a considerable extent among Mahommedans, as indeed it does among all the peoples of India as compared with the peoples of Europe and the United States. This is one of the principal causes of the high infantile mortality that prevails

DEATHS OF CHILDREN UNDER ONE YEAR
PER 1,000 BIRTHS AVERAGE—1902-11

European peoples		*Indian provinces*	
Sweden	84	Madras	199
Scotland	116	Bengal	270
England and Wales	127	Behar and Orissa	304
France	132	Punjab	306
Germany	186	Bombay	320
Hungary	207	United Provinces	352

throughout India. The following comparison between certain European countries and some of the principal provinces of India is instructive. The figures are taken from Mr. Wattal's book (p. 20) above referred to.

On these figures Mr. Wattal comments in words which, coming from an Indian writer, are specially deserving of reproduction:

When Nature wants a school of fish she spawns a million. When she wants a few rabbits she produces large families at intervals of a few weeks, of which perhaps 10 per cent survive. To make certain of 100 Kafirs she produces 200. This is Nature playing with life in her own merciless manner, when there is nobody to thwart her wishes. She plays similar havoc in this country under very similar circumstances.

Another important contrast between India and Europe is the relative deficiency of women among most of the Indian peoples and castes. Throughout Europe there is generally to be found an excess of females over males, an excess which is specially marked in the case of England. In India the males are in the majority. Taking India as a whole the census figures—so far as they can be relied upon—show that in 1921 there were 945 females to every 1,000 males and in 1911 there were 954 females to every 1,000 males. The corresponding figure in 1901 was 963. The census authorities discuss at considerable length in their report for 1911 the predominant causes that explain the indisputable deficiency of females, after allowance has been made for possibilities of error in enumeration. As above indicated, one cause is early marriage. The child wife is killed in giving birth to another child, itself doomed to die before it has learnt to live. A minor cause is the practice of female infanticide, which still exists to some small extent in spite of the efforts of the government to stamp it out.

In former generations this practice was extremely common among some of the peoples of India, especially among the Rajputs. In their case the practice was stimulated by the custom known as hypergamy, which requires a woman to marry a man above her in rank. Clearly this could not be generally possible, unless the number of females was restricted. Consequently among the Rajputs, though a first daughter and possibly even a second would be allowed to live, the rest would be killed. Again, female infanticide was common among the Todas, because they practised polyandry, and therefore required very few women. In many other cases where female infanticide was common, there appears to have been no explanation except the general consideration that a male child was more valuable than a female. A bill was passed through the Indian legislature, in 1870, authorizing special measures to stamp out the crime. The minister in charge of the measure quoted, in introducing it, much striking evidence. For example, one investigator reported that he had visited 308 villages in the Benares division and in 62 of these he had found not a single female child under the age of six. To avoid detection, the parents, instead of suffocating the child at once, would often allow it to die a lingering death. There is reason to believe that this practice still continues and that unwanted female infants, though not directly killed, are often permitted to die of neglect.

A more extensive cause of high female mortality is to be found in the conditions under which Indian women generally live. These conditions render them more liable to plague, malaria and other infections. The situation is very clearly explained by the census authorities:

> Women spend much more time than men in their houses, in which they sit most of the day. They generally go barefooted. They sweep the floors and handle the grain for threshing or grinding. They nurse persons suffering from plague; and when death occurs in a house, they assemble there for purposes of mourning and sit round the corpse. They are thus much more exposed to infection through the rat flea, which attacks human beings when its natural host dies, and is not generally recognized as the medium by which bubonic plague is chiefly spread. A similar explanation would account for a greater mortality of women from malaria, such as occurred in the epidemic of 1908 in the United Provinces. . . . The mosquitoes which carry the germs of the disease are found chiefly in the dark corners of houses; and the women, who are most confined to them, would thus naturally be more frequently bitten.

It is worth while to add a word about a custom which exists among certain tribes in different parts of the world. Though rare in India, it is to be found there among a few of the more primitive races. This custom, known as the 'couvade', prescribes that when a woman bears a child, her husband shall go through the pretense that he has borne it, while she goes about her ordinary work as if nothing had happened. The census report just quoted describes how the custom affects certain tribes and castes in India:

> In Madras, when a Korava woman feels the birth pains, her husband puts on some of her clothes, makes a woman's mark on his forehead and retires to bed in a dark room. As soon as the child is born, it is washed and placed beside its father, who is carefully tended and dosed with various drugs. The woman meanwhile is left alone in an outhouse.

In Baroda when a woman of the Pomla is delivered of a child she at once leaves the house and is not allowed to return to it for five days. During this period the husband lies confined and undergoes the treatment which is usually given to females on such occasions. It is claimed that he actually feels the pains of childbirth. A similar custom prevails among the Dombars and Lambanis of the Bombay Karnatik; after the birth of a child the husband is oiled and fed, and remains at home, while the wife goes about her work as usual.

In addition to the unlikenesses of race, religion and social custom which so markedly differentiate the peoples of India from the peoples of Europe, there is the further outstanding fact of the greater dependence of the population of India upon agriculture. It is true that manufacturing industries are now well-established in some of the towns of India, and notably in Calcutta and Bombay, but the overwhelming majority of the population is engaged in agriculture. Even men employed as factory workers in the towns not infrequently still retain connection with their rural homes and at intervals some of them go back for weeks or months at a time to work on the land.

Dependence upon agriculture means dependence upon climate. If the monsoon is delayed, ruin and starvation may be the result. The extension of railways has in recent years to some extent diminished the terrors of famine, and the government is always prepared in advance with schemes for the maintenance and employment of the peasants whose crops have failed and whose industry has ceased. Nevertheless the failure of the rains periodically destroys the whole agricultural life of large districts, involving much inevitable suffering and generally causing a heavy increase in mortality.

In some parts of India the danger of a delayed or insufficient rainfall is to a considerable extent obviated by irrigating the land with water either from wells or from irrigation canals. The practice of digging wells must be almost as old as the art of ploughing; the construction of irrigation canals has also been a feature of hot countries from time immemorial. But the widely extended system of irrigation canals now to be found in India is a comparatively recent development and is due to the action of the British government. How far it is possible still further to extend irrigation by means of canals is a question much debated by engineering authorities; but there is a general agreement that the limits of extension are already in sight. Moreover, canal water is not a pure boon to the land to which it is supplied. It often brings to the surface injurious salts, thus rendering permanently barren large areas of land that were before highly productive whenever the rainfall was satisfactory.

Consequently it remains broadly true that population over the greater part of India is dominated by the rainfall. It is the rain that determines how many people the land will carry. If more are produced than the rain will allow the land to bear, they must die. But with rare exceptions the peasants of India, like the slum-dwellers of Europe, go on producing children without any thought as to the means of their future maintenance. It is only among the few who are relatively prosperous that any evidence is to be found of parental prudence.

The way in which prosperity dictates prudence in India as elsewhere is illustrated in an extremely interesting report on the conditions of life in a Deccan village, prepared by the Principal and the students of the Poona Agricultural College. This report divides the householders of a typical south Indian village into three groups. The first is a small group of eight families, who are in a thoroughly good position. They have enough land for their needs and relatively few children. The second group consists of 28 families, who are slightly less prosperous than the first group, but still fairly well-to-do, because they also have small families. The third and largest group 'consists of those who cannot pay their way and live according to the village standard'. These have large families.

Prudence in reproduction is rare in India. Everywhere the people tend to breed up to the limits of subsistence. In parts of the Ganges Valley, where the soil is fertile and the rainfall fairly well assured, people are thick on the ground, even 800 or 900 to the square mile. On the other hand, the mountainous region of Baluchistan, with its sunburnt soil, has a population of about 6 or 7 to the square mile.

The result of this constant pressure against the means of subsistence is a low vitality. People with no margin of subsistence have no margin of strength; at the first onset of disease they succumb and die. It is estimated that the influenza epidemic of 1918 killed no fewer than 6,000,000 people in British India and in the Feudatory Indian States. The epidemic was followed, as famine also is generally followed, by a temporary reduction in the birth rate. Thus both in 1918 and in 1919 the births were fewer than the deaths. As a result partly of this great influenza epidemic, partly of plague, which was virulent in 1915, 1917 and 1918, partly of cholera, which raged in 1919, and partly of the suffering caused by the widespread failure of the rains in 1918, the population in many parts of India declined. The increase recorded for the whole of India during the decade ending in 1921 was less than 4,000,000, namely from 315,152,000 to 318,942,000, representing a rate of increase of only 1.1 per cent.

It may reasonably be inferred that India is already overfull of human beings. Yet social custom and religious creed still impose upon Indian parents the duty of begetting children, regardless of the means available for their maintenance, with the result that children are poured into the world even more rapidly than in Europe and in the United States. Roughly, one in four of the infants thus brought into being dies before it has ceased to be an infant. Others die in early youth or early manhood. The average duration of life in India is far below the average of Western Europe or America. Beyond this is the final fact that the whole standard of life is lowered, because the resources of the country do not suffice for the adequate maintenance of the millions who are striving to live.

CHAPTER 10

Self-Government for India

E.S. Montagu

THE PROBLEMS OF THE HISTORY OF British effort in India, of India's position today and of the hazardous future, are so complicated and must be painted on so vast a canvas that it is almost impossible to attempt to describe them in the circumscribed space of a short article.

A century and a half of British effort had led, by August 1917, to this result. India had been given, by the devoted service of Englishmen and by the development of her own peoples, security from external invasion, peace and order within her frontiers. Much effort had been devoted to promoting among the innumerable races and sects recognition of the fact that they are citizens of a great empire. All the products of Western science and of civilization had been introduced to the improvement of India's material welfare. Education on Western lines had been slowly filtering through the mass by strenuous teachers, taught at our universities and in their own, from British textbooks and British classics; and Indians had been increasingly associated with the government of the country by appointment to some of the highest offices in the State.

I write these generalizations, and yet I remember that each statement has its exception: that the frontiers of India have been the scenes of warfare; that riot and disorder must constantly occur in a country which is three-quarters the size of Europe; and that, notwithstanding all the educational

**ASIA*, March 1922. E.S. Montague (1879-1924) was secretary of State for India, famous for Montague-Chelmsford Reforms, 1919.

work that has been done, the funds of a country inhabited by poor people did not enable it to be widespread, and only 10 per cent of the population of British India can read and write. There is to be found in India, as one of my greatest predecessors—the man from whom I first learned to study the problems of India—Lord Morley, so well said, every stage of development from the first century to the twentieth. There are the worshipers of inanimate objects on the one hand; there are men who can hold their own with the best mathematicians, scientists and writers in the world on the other. There is the jungle man with his bows and arrows, living, often, on lizards and snakes; there is Rabindranath Tagore, the poet and philosopher, whose name is well known in America; or the great lawyer who has become a member of the House of Lords after serving in the highest executive appointments in India and being a member of the British government—Lord Sinha.

But, with all these contrasts and difficulties arising out of the diversity of population and the diversity of the degree of civilization, British India consisted in 1917, from the political point of view, of nine great provinces, the population of some of which was as large as the population of Great Britain and Ireland, each with a governor and a government appointed for a term of years, and each with a legislature, which, however, was a deliberative assembly without control over the government. Over all presided the Viceroy, who was responsible to and bound to accept the orders of the Secretary of State, with an Executive Council, on which there was one Indian, and a legislature, the majority of which was composed of officials of the government, who controlled the decisions of the body.

What was to be the future development of such a system and in such a population? Surely in these days there could be no doubt as to the logical and theoretical mission of any empire-partnership.

All the effort for the material advancement and the creation of a big nation was useless; all the effort for the dissemination of Western civilization was of no avail; all the gradual training of Indians in affairs and the opportunities given them to share in the government were sterile if the ultimate message was to be permanent subordination.

It is a fine conception—the British Empire as a partnership of nations (each completely free) associated together by a common ideal of freedom, irrespective of race, religion or colour. The ideal had gone some distance. The French in Canada, the Dutch in South Africa had achieved, not without hardship and travail, partnership in the Anglo-Saxon community. It had long been a growing ideal of a section of our countrymen with regard to Ireland. How much anxious horror would have been spared if it could earlier have been the ideal of the whole British population. It seemed to my colleagues and myself that the time had now come to declare a similar ideal with regard to India. It seemed to us that, unless we attempted this goal, the hopes that had been raised by the trend of British effort through more than a century—hopes that had been enlivened by the experiences of the great war, by the messages given to humanity by the statesmen of the world, headed by President Wilson—would receive no answer. It was, therefore, with this intention declared that I visited India to confer with its government; with the result that I proposed to Parliament, and Parliament accepted, a measure of self-government for India, which contained within its compass the method of development until complete self-government had been reached, contingent only on the success of each stage.

Will it Succeed?

I can only say that, if it fails to produce self-government in some form or other for India, and not by any means necessarily by an imitation of Western institutions, not only must there inevitably be a growing discontent in India with the British connection, which will eventually jeopardize the continued existence of the empire, but we shall be faced with the alternative that no future political development is possible and subordination must be continued indefinitely. I do not believe that the permanent subordination, irrespective of development and capacity, of one country to another can possibly be achieved. For success the first necessity is consistency and sincerity in the effort. A paper constitution and scrupulous attention to the details of the constitution cannot be successful unless the spirit of partnership grows in and pervades the whole of our relationship with India. For instance, it is inconsistent with the spirit of partnership that there should be any sphere or branch of activity for which a man or woman is disqualified because he or she is an Indian. A suitable or fitting Indian must be as welcome as a suitable or fitting Englishman to any position in the Indian Commonwealth. It was for this reason that I appointed, with the King's willing approval, Lord Sinha to be the first Indian under-secretary of state in the British government, and subsequently I appointed him to be the first Indian governor of an Indian province. Before the war and during a large part of the war, the message that England gave to India was this: 'Send us your fighting-men. We will avail ourselves of their services as privates and non-commissioned officers in the Indian army; but whatever gifts of leadership are developed, whatever gallantry is shown on the field of battle, for the commissioned ranks of the army of India, paid for by Indian money and recruited for the defence of India, we will have none but Englishmen.' That message was not in harmony with partnership; it implied a race restriction which was inconsistent with the declared goal; and my colleagues and I decided to open the ranks of the commissioned officers of the Indian army to suitable Indians. It seems to me absolutely essential for success that, wherever there still exist prohibitions or limitations of Indian effort because of race, those limitations must be removed. We must demonstrate that we are sincere in our offer of partnership; but, on the other hand, much is wanted of the Indians, too. They must not forget the extraordinary difficulty of devising a self-governing constitution for a country so vast as India, inhabited by so many different kinds of races and of creeds, and of such diverse development and civilization. The worst enemy of India is the man who would so hasten progress that failure might result. Impatience, the refusal to acknowledge difficulties, the demand for progress based, not on performance, which was at the root of the whole scheme, but on claims and demands only, coupled with furious denunciation of their British partners, must delay and cannot hasten.

It cannot be too often said that in almost any problem with which statesmen are faced reaction and revolution are the great enemies of progress and of success. Too much speed is hardly less dangerous than too much hesitation. Reaction, shrinking from the logical application of accepted principles, and insincerity in the execution of avowed objects, produce in themselves lack of faith, impatience and insurrection, and lack of faith and impatience in themselves produce apprehension, stubbornness, reaction. If success is to be achieved, both dangers, and their reciprocal effect, must be avoided. Indians have a right to expect from Great Britain steadfastness of purpose and sincerity; the avowal of the object was a national gift to which all parties subscribed. Political changes at home can have no effect on imperial policy. On the other hand, if this essential be granted, peace and order must be enforced; when the common purpose is declared, no excuse should remain for disaffection.

It has been said that democracy is foreign to oriental countries, and that the British government has set itself an impossible task in trying to implant it in the soil of India. This criticism, to my mind, if it has any force at all, comes essentially too late. In the Report which Lord Chelmsford wrote in India in the years 1917-18 the whole history of the matter is set out.

Over 120 years ago Sir Thomas Munro, who will always be recognized as one of the great builders of the Indian Empire, wrote: 'What is to be the final result of the arrangements on the character of the people? Is it to be raised or to be lowered? Are we to be satisfied with merely securing power and protecting the inhabitants, or are we to endeavour to raise their character, to make them worthy of filling higher positions in the management of the country and devising plans for its improvement? . . . We should look on India not as a temporary possession but as one which is to be maintained permanently until the natives shall in some future age have abandoned most of their superstitions and prejudices and become sufficiently enlightened to frame a regular government for themselves, and to conduct and preserve it.'

His Majesty the King Emperor, when the Government of India Act had been given the royal assent made a Royal Proclamation, from which I quote the following:

The Acts of 1773 and 1784 were designed to establish a regular system of administration and justice under the honourable East India Company. The Act of 1833 opened the doors for Indians to public office and employment. The Act of 1858 transferred the administration from the Company to the Crown and laid the foundations of public life which prevail in India today. The Act of 1861 sowed the seed of representative institutions, and the seed was quickened into life by the Act of 1909. The Act which has now become law entrusts elected representatives of the people with a *de facto* share in government, and points the way to full representative government hereafter.

This extract shows as concisely as possible the main acts of Parliament which have traced the course of the growth of democracy in India. Side by side with these steps, there has been a steady growth in the machinery of local self-government. The ultimate goal had often been disclaimed in despatch, but, notwithstanding that, the seed was sown; franchises were introduced and extended, the principles of election found acknowledgement, and the announcement which it was my privilege to make on 20 August 1917, in language carefully drafted in the Cabinet, was the logical and inevitable outcome of the whole trend of British policy in India for a century and a half. The policy was finally and authoritatively declared and subsequently accepted by both houses of Parliament and incorporated in the Preamble of the Act of 1919—a policy of the increasing association of Indians in every branch of the administration, and the gradual development of self-governing institutions with a view to the progressive realization of responsible government in India as an integral part of the British Empire.

Even if the suitability of democracy to India is denied, the desire and a right to self-government, to the management of their own affairs, cannot be regarded as unnatural or any more foreign to India than to any other country, and such a desire can only have been stimulated by recent world events and by the natural evolution of thought in any part of the world. It would be impossible for a country like Britain to contemplate the grant of self-government in the form of autocracy or bureaucracy. Any government not responsible to the representatives of the peoples of India must be responsible to representatives of the people of England, and that would be the negation of self-government. It seems to me, therefore, that democracy was not only the logical outcome of the whole of British policy in India, but was the only form that self-government could take at the hands of the British people. I say this without pretending to foresee what the ultimate form of government in India will be, or whether democracy is the last word in political science. The ultimate constitution of India will take shape in India, and not in London; it will possibly adapt Western institutions to Indian needs rather than imitate them without qualification. But we have taken the step of devising the machinery by which the wishes of India can be ascertained through its elected representatives, and have instituted a franchise which is designed to be extended as the years go on, and to become more and more representative. In the provinces we have given the elected representatives parliamentary control of the administration of certain functions of government; we have designed machinery whereby all the functions of government may gradually, in the light of the experience which is gained, be similarly treated; we have given the provincial governments control of purely provincial affairs; we have laid the foundation of a quasi-federal system of great self-governing countries, united by the Government of India, which will in future deal only with all-Indian affairs. The evolution of the future can be left to the future, which depends, in truth, only on the capacity and responsibility of those who have been entrusted with the final stages of this great experiment in self-government.

It is next said that India is a continent inhabited by many races and cannot become a nation. The people of the United States would be the last to say that a vast area is an insuperable obstacle to nationality. Without dogmatizing, however, we may safely assume that the nationality of India must be built on quasi-federal lines, and that the provinces—either the existing provinces or provinces rearranged on a more natural and more ethnological basis—will be the unit of self-government in the India of the future. That is why the autonomy of the existing provinces was the cardinal principle the Act of 1919 and the rules and regulations made under it.

The unity of these provinces and their relations with one another are safeguarded by their common interests, by the existence of the Government of India as the supreme quasi-federal government, and by their common contribution to international affairs and to the civilization of the world. The birth-pangs of a great nation must be severe; delays, doubts and disappointments are inevitable; but I think it may be said that the track of events is in the right direction. Indian princes and Indian gentlemen sat in the Imperial War Cabinet and on the Imperial Peace Delegation in Paris. India is now represented on the governing body of the International Labour Organization, which sits from time to time under the egis of the League of Nations. India is a member of the League of Nations. All these events must tend towards nationality, must lead Indians to think of India as a corporate entity, regarded as such by other countries and giving, as India, its contribution to civilization. It will not be the first time that a nation of mixed races has been welded together by the common efforts of its citizens; the most vigorous nations of the world have been welded together from different races. Race and nationality are by no means the same thing, and the backward or undeveloped races in India can look with confidence to their more developed sister races to lead them forward to the advantages and opportunities of better education and better social organization for the honour of their country or their nation.

I do not forget that approximately one-third of the geographical area of India is occupied by the Native States, which are not, technically speaking, part of British India at all. Speaking generally—and in the small space at my disposal it is impossible to do other than speak generally—the relations of these Native States to the British Empire are governed by treaties which, in the main, were negotiated by the Crown or their predecessors, the East India Company. By these treaties the States are guaranteed security from without; the paramount Power acts for them in relation to foreign Powers and other States, and it intervenes when the internal peace of their territories is seriously threatened. The States' relations to foreign Powers are those of the paramount Power. They share the obligation for the common defence, and they are under a general responsibility for the good government and welfare of their territories. The war has brought the ruling princes into closer relationship with the Government of India. The services of these princes and of their subjects were a profound surprise and disappointment to the enemy and a cause of delight and pride to those who saw beforehand the princes' devotion to the Crown and person of the King Emperor. With one accord the rulers of the Native States in India rallied to the fight for the empire when war was declared. They have shown that our quarrel is their quarrel, and they have both learned and taught the lesson of their own indissoluble connection with the empire and their immense value as part of the policy of India.

The place of the Native States of India in the India of the future must be determined by their concourse and consent as time goes on. Their own internal affairs will develop in accordance with their history and their own needs, let us see and trust, without any interference from outside. The prominence of the democratic forces of the world knows no geographical limits, and those forces have reached the Indian states, where, in varying degrees, the princes are wisely building for their people the early stages of representative institutions. At the same time as we submitted to Parliament the Government of India Act of 1919, we formed a Council for the discussion of matters common to the Native States and arranged for collective conference between them and the Viceroy and his government on matters, such as defence which affected them as much as British India.

It is sometimes objected that, even if it is admitted that the principle of self-government was right, and that self-government, and possibly democracy, was inevitable, it was premature. It is said that it is ridiculous to talk of self-government when nine-tenths of the population could neither read nor write and had no political interests or instincts at all. There are many answers to this criticism. It is a common device of those who oppose a policy to admit grudgingly the inherent merits of its principle but to find fault with the content chosen for its application. If one waits until even the opponents of a measure are agreed as to its opportuneness one will wait forever.

Of course, in one sense it was inopportune that the foundations of the new scheme were laid during the war. I had only recently left the Ministry of Munitions, where I had been a Member of the War Committee of the British Cabinet and in daily contact with those who were actually fighting. I left for India in October 1917, with the purpose of advancing political reform in India.

The winter of 1917-18 was a strenuous one. Lord Chelmsford and I travelled throughout the Indian Empire, conferring, consulting, receiving every section of the Indian people and of the local governments, and many experienced officers brought forward their schemes and suggestions. Deputations were received, individuals discussed with us their plans, Indian princes came and suggested many alterations in their relations with the Government of India, which we were glad to accept almost in their entirety. The announcement of 20 August had been widely welcomed; hopes were high, and we hammered out the scheme which, after modification and substantial extension in Parliament, was finally adopted. It was work which must have aroused the enthusiasm of even the least imaginative of politicians—watching a constitution growing, seeing the creation of the destiny of a vast territory. It was a fascinating and absorbing work, to which all other interests were sacrificed, save only one. I can confidently say, not only of Lord Chelmsford and of his government and of his officers, but also of the India Office, that we never allowed the preoccupations of the reforms to interfere with the supreme necessity of focusing India's efforts into the maximum possible contribution to the winning of the war. Looking back on those years now, I am quite convinced that the inception of the reforms substantially helped the war effort of India. India saw that the conclusion of the war would be succeeded by a new era for them—the passing, gradually (perhaps too slowly) of the era of domination and the dawn of the era of partnership, and this had a stimulating effect on her willingness and readiness to help the empire in its greatest needs. Certainly when I took office in 1917, I found that all concerned with the Government of India had already decided that an announcement such as we then made was urgently necessary, notwithstanding the fact that we were at war, and I have never had any reason since then to doubt that they were right.

It is always better, moreover, to be a little in advance of time than to wait too long, particularly when waiting means holding back the advanced part of a population, shattering their hopes and disappointing the aspirations which they have legitimately developed, until everybody is equally ready for advancement. I maintain that a political sense can only be developed, political wisdom can only be achieved, by the exercise of political rights. If a population denied all political responsibility does not take an interest in politics, is it surprising? If a population is asked to exercise political responsibility, political sense will certainly develop. Mistakes will of course occur; political mistakes often lead to political wisdom, and it cannot be said with confidence that even a most enlightened electorate always avoids political mistakes, while it can be said with greater certainty that every extension of the franchise in every country has enfranchised people who had hitherto taken no interest in political questions.

I pass over with just a word those who fear that political liberty will endanger the imperial connection. I should have thought it was obvious that, in the twentieth century at any rate, an imperial solidarity which rests on force or subordination is far more precarious than an imperial solidarity which rests on partnership and consent, particularly when the dominant partner is a democracy such as the democracy of Great Britain. The history of the British Empire, of recent years at any rate, has shown that it is strengthened by the spread of liberty and weakened by the denial of liberty.

I come now to a far more serious criticism, one which has got to be faced and which discloses a difficulty which has got to be surmounted. The development of India has only been achieved by the devotion of the men who have manned the Civil Service of India, a service of administrators who have left England to spend their lives in India and whose record is one of devotions and selfless and successful work for which it is difficult to find too much praise. The Indian Civil Service has been much criticized for opposition to reform. It would be only natural if men were reluctant to accept changes which fundamentally altered the conditions under which they have worked, but my experience has not been that I have found obstruction or opposition among serving members of the Indian Civil Service. On the contrary, the inception of a complicated measure of reform would have been impossible without the splendid assistance which they rendered. Opposition came far more from men who had retired, who were spending the declining years of their lives vainly regretting that India could not be crystallized as it was when they left it.

But, as political life in India develops, Indian civil servants who have today to fulfil the function of the executive instrument on the one hand and a part of the government machine on the other are in the sphere of political controversy. As time goes on, the Indian Civil Service must become less of a governing body and more comparable to the civil services, the executive instrument of government, of other countries. And when self-government is finally attained, although I believe that India will often look to England for executive assistance, the executive instrument of government will be, in the main, Indian, and chosen from the population of a self-governing India. The time of transition presents problems which make it almost a platitude to say that if ever India stood in need of the best men who are willing to go from England to help, she stands in need of them today. Will they be forthcoming? Some alterations in the conditions of service will undoubtedly be necessary, but I cannot believe that if these are forthcoming the men will be lacking. The period will be difficult; disappointments will occur, difficult situations will arise, a growing feeling of nationality will require tact and sympathy; but those who helped India to its present position were not daunted by difficulties and disappointments. If it was a great work to govern India, it will be a greater work to help India to govern itself, and the object is undoubtedly so great a one that I feel confident there will be an adequate supply of men fired with the importance of its success who will devote themselves with enthusiasm to furthering it.

I do not hide from myself, and I will not hide from those who have read what I have written, sources of anxiety which have added to the difficulties of the inception of our reforms and which have caused grave apprehension as to the future. The wave of unrest which has spread from one end of the world to the other, as an outcome of the effort and fatigue of the great war, has not missed India. There is, as is well known, centred in Moscow an organization which is the enemy of civilization, which battens on and ferments, of set purpose, discontent and insurrection, which seeks the overthrow of settled government, and which, working through the turbulent countries of the north-west of India, has caused anxiety in India. I believe this danger is passing as the world is becoming better and better informed of the horrible consequences to Russia of the uncontrolled application of Bolshevism to its unfortunate people, and certainly communism sovietism and prolonged disorder are not attractive to the Indian mind.

Far worse than this has been the effect on the peace of India of the unfortunate Treaty of Sèvres and the attitude taken by British statesmen towards Turkey. There are some eighty million Mahommedans in India, a large number of whom regarded the Sultan of Turkey, the Caliph, with veneration as their leader. Mahommedans fought valiantly in the war, but their leaders never dreamed that as a consequence of the war not only would the Turkish empire over the Arab countries cease to exist but that an effort would be made with Great Britain playing a leading part, to dismember Turkey and to deprive the Government of Constantinople of all liberty. As the painful controversy dragged along, during which the Government of India and I, their spokesman, never failed to represent the views of India, the Mahommedans of India became more and more estranged, and it was difficult to convince them that Great Britain was not becoming anti-Islamic, despite the fact that it contained within its wide empire more Mahommedans than any other Power. The estrangement, moreover, spread outside those of the Mahommedan faith, by reason of the fact that the controversy sometimes took the form of the East against the West, and an attempt to confine the Turk, because he was an Oriental, to Asia. It became an Asiatic struggle. I can only hope that the attempts which are now being made to put the matter right, and the realization that the errors of policy were not the work of the people of Great Britain but only of one government which has now ceased to exist, and a realization of the efforts made on their behalf by their own government will dissipate these tragic effects. But we have paid heavily for our mistakes in India and in our relationship with Afghanistan and indeed every Moslem country. It was largely because of the importance which I attached to these views that I deliberately authorized the publication by the Government of India of the views that they had expressed in this matter, and from that time forward there has been an improvement in India, based on the knowledge that the Government of India was striving for a possible and equitable peace.

Another disturbing factor was the outbreak of disorder in the Punjab in 1919 and the revelation of the methods which had been adopted to deal with it. I have always hoped that these incidents were not misunderstood in America. Through these difficult times these few instances of race ferocity on the one side or the other stand out in amazing contrast to the patience shown by our officers in difficult circumstances throughout India. It was more than necessary for the reputation of the British army and for the good name and the canons of British justice that incidents which were not in conformity with the accepted ideas of government should be fearlessly stigmatized. But the passions aroused on one side or the other have a long-abiding effect and have awakened controversy which will take years to die down. These incidents led to a determination on the part of extremist organizations in India to have nothing to do with the new reforms. By their action in this direction they have delayed progress, and it is with great satisfaction I notice that there are now signs on their part of wiser decisions, and that in the approaching elections they will probably take their part. Men of extreme views are surely better inside representative institutions than when holding aloof from them.

But time in part and wiser counsels in part will affect these untoward factors which can disturb and hinder, but cannot of themselves defeat, the principles on which the reforms were founded. I do not underrate the difficulties; nor do I overrate the possibilities. I remain confident of the future. I believe that Great Britain and India are each essential to the complete well-being of the other. I believe that their connection can be strengthened by the acceptance of the principle of partnership, if pursued with sincerity, with determination and with patience. I cannot contemplate failure, for I do not believe that the subjection of one country to another, however benevolent, is the last word in international political science, and I feel confident that the successful help of Britons in the building of an Indian nation will win a real and valuable crown for British effort in India. Success will mean success in the highest plane of empire building; failure would mean, if failure were thinkable, a real impoverishment of the ideals of the civilized world.

CHAPTER 11

This is India

Gertrude Emerson

THE SKY WAS MONOTONOUSLY EMPTY of clouds and as devoid of colour as though all the blue had been burnt out of it; the round, flat mirror of the sea returned its intolerable stare; and somewhere between the two floated, unanchored, a gray mist.

'That is India,' remarked someone, in a matter-of-fact tone of voice.

Nobody denied the incredible statement, and the steamer continued to move on quietly toward the barrier that had risen to put an end to limitless space. Imperceptibly the mist hardened into a shore-line and then divided to form the two banks of a river, up which we were sucked with a swift-running tide. Mud-flats gave way to anemic foliage. Ruined fortifications rose here and there, tombstones of Company days. Occasionally substantial houses, built in European fashion, thrust themselves forward into line with the river. Instead of silence and solitude, there was now the bustle of many boats hurrying on appointed errands, and these boats were propelled by choruses of black-skinned men, silhouetted darkly with their sweeps against a glitter of sun-smitten water. They might have been a tracery in granite from ancient Egypt, so archaic and unreal they looked. Suddenly my eyes were drawn downward to the deck immediately below the rail where I leaned. Here a sharp-featured man was in the act of prodding to life a half-dead bear. The bear got up, sobbing and whining, and began to dance. Then an agile monkey turned somersaults, and a long-haired goat was enticed into gathering its four feet on to an unsteady wooden cylinder. The three

**ASIA*, March 1923.

animals salaamed respectfully, while the obsequious Indian waited for *bakshish*. I was reminded of the juggler with his animals carved on the walls of the Bayon at Angkor, still doing tricks these thousand years, though the jungle has long since marched in and taken the royal city; reminded of the Brunos and the Jocks in the purlieus of my own childhood. But already Calcutta was in sight and I could distinguish the expressions of curiosity on the faces of the many-coloured throng at the dock.

'I am Kim. This is the great world,' my heart began to sing; but the words changed quickly and the rhythm broke: 'This is the great world of India, and I am not even Kim. What is India? Shall I, alien as I am, ever understand?'

Calcutta is a city of over a million inhabitants. Yet it is not only possible but inevitable that here, as elsewhere in India, the white man should live peculiarly to himself. I-tsing, the Chinese Buddhist pilgrim who travelled in India toward the end of the seventh century, made a humble note in his *Records:* 'If we come to India in Chinese garments, they laugh at us; we get much ashamed in our hearts, and we tear our garments. . . .' But I-tsing went to Buddhist India as a pilgrim, and the Englishman came as conqueror of the Hindus. There is a difference. The white man considers his caste as above that of the Brahman. Unashamed, he continues to wear his own style of clothes and for the most part takes refuge from the Indian sun and the Indian people in the sanctuaries of his home, his hotel, his club, his office, his graveyard. And it is not easy for the stranger to find India in Calcutta.

When I think back to impressions of my first weeks there, I remember chiefly the outward appearance of things, such as the unexpected reversal of what my eyes were accustomed to, in the dark skins of the men and the white garments they wore; their sharp features and deep-set, restless eyes, contrasting unpleasantly, I could not help thinking, with the gentler type of the Malay face; the incredibly thin legs of the sweepers in the streets, and always their manner of beaten dogs. But the sound of bare feet padding incessantly along the pavements was soothing to the ear and the grace of the women in gay *saris* and clinking silver jewellery was a solace to the eye. The painted horns and glass necklaces of the oxen, like the strangely painted foreheads of the Hindus, came to be an integral part of the picture. So did the gray-throated crows, which thought nothing of swooping down and making off with a piece of bread from one of the tables on the balcony of the Great Eastern Hotel, and the sacred cows, which sauntered along the sidewalks, helping themselves to greens from the shops and holding up traffic very successfully. Elephants and tigers were curiously absent, but jackals, I was told, ran about at night, and once, as I emerged from a bank, I saw standing in front of me a white *ghari*-horse, fantastically painted over with large, round, orange spots. Out of the bank came a respectable Bengali gentleman, wearing a pith helmet and a white linen suit. He disappeared behind the black shutters of the ghari, the *syce* on the box gave a smart slap of the reins and the painted, wooden rocking-horse trotted off down Clive Street, apparently without attracting the attention of any one in the world except myself.

All day the heat beat down mercilessly from above, with intent to kill, and clouds of dust rose chokingly from below. At last came the night, with its breath of coolness. The colour ebbed out of the streets, the confused turmoil subsided; and European society woke to life. At five we had tea. At nine we went to dine at Firpo's. From there we drifted to the Grand Hotel to dance. We felt that life was a pleasurable experience and we were sorry for the people at home, who knew only how to work and make money. And when our parties broke up after midnight, and we returned through the empty streets, we scarcely noticed the corpselike figures of Indians sleeping in the dust underfoot.

I caught only glimpses, now and then, behind this obvious and exterior aspect of India's greatest commercial city of something that disconcerted, of something certainly not ticketed and on display for me to see, that had its origin in a world of thought essentially different from mine. One day, for instance, I saw an old woman prostrating herself ecstatically in the road in front of a cow, afterwards seizing its tail and touching it to her forehead, by way of worship. I remember a man slowly pulling up a load of bricks to the top of a new building and singing as he worked. I asked Abdul Aziz, the sad-faced Bengali who became my 'bearer' the day I arrived in India, what the words meant. He answered: 'It is a song about God. He told God not to let the rope break.' Once, early in the morning, I went riding on the Maidan. The friend whose horse I rode took me around by the river, where steps led down to the water; and here both men and women, with their garments on, were bathing for purposes of religious purification, according to their practice. On the steps was a sacred *tulsi*-plant, which each person watered with a few drops from his fingertips. Presently all the people filled little brass jars with water from the Hugli—for the Hugli is one of the many mouths of the sacred Ganges—and, forming into a compact band, marched off together singing a *mantram* for the god of their sect, whose V-shaped symbol was painted in lines of red and white on their foreheads. On still another occasion, I watched a Mahommedan saying his evening prayers, with curious dignity, in the midst of a noisy crowd waiting for a ferry-boat. He stood, as required, with his hands folded on his stomach: then bowed, his hands resting on his knees, and knelt, with his hands placed flat on the ground and his forehead pressed to earth. Three times he went through the ceremonies of his prayer, while his face gradually lighted up in the sunset. Then, with the others, he scrambled and pushed for a place on the boat.

But most vividly I remember the *Durga-puja,* the great annual religious festival of Bengal, held in honour of the goddess Durga, or Kali, from whom

Calcutta has taken its name. For ten days business was at a standstill. The *sahibs* cheerfully hurried off on shooting-trips, while Hindus of all sects and castes crowded into the narrow lanes and streets leading to the Kalighat temple. Here I saw for the first time 'holy men', naked except for a loin-cloth, their bodies and faces smeared with ashes, their hair matted and dyed a rusty red. They were lying on beds of spikes under umbrellas, but I noticed, a little cynically, that the spikes appeared quite blunt. Gaudily painted clay images stood in rows in front of the image-makers, who were at work within the entrances of their dwellings. Cheap prints of Kali, made in Germany, were everywhere offered for sale. A Hindu was leading about a cow, with a fifth leg growing out of her back, which he permitted the superstitious to touch in order to receive some ill-defined blessing in return for a very clearly defined number of *pice.* Down the middle of one of the narrow turnings sat a double row of maimed, deformed and horrible creatures, degenerates, who, in the name of religion, practised beggary and traded upon the ignorance of the devotees. Little Hindu boys, some of them with wheedling smiles and coaxing, laughing eyes, ran after us, patting their stomachs suggestively. All along the way were scattered images and monstrous symbols of the gods, such as the *lingam* of Siva's worship, sometimes with Devi in the form of a snake wound around its base, of Krishna with his flute, of Ganesh with his elephant's trunk painted red, of the half-divine monkey Hanuman, of a goddess to avert cholera and a god to promote fertility. Sometimes worship was paid with a little incense, sometimes with flowers, sometimes with libations of water, but almost always a Brahman priest, another and more sinister type of beggar, was intrenched near the scene, to separate the superstitious worshippers from such few miserable coins as they still had left. I saw two women, obviously frightened, backed into a corner by one of these priests. It needed no understanding of Hindustani or Bengali to interpret what was taking place.

The temple of Kali itself proved frightful beyond words. The courtyard of a very ordinary mud-and-plaster structure, with none of the dignity of the fine old temples to be found elsewhere in India, was swarming with warm, half-naked humanity. Everywhere were black bodies glistening with oil and perspiration. At one side goats were being slaughtered, as many as a thousand a day, I was told, and the stone flagging was red with blood. The air was torn with the agonized bleatings of the victims. I saw a great knife flashing, a crimson jet, a head dropping to the pavement. The man who had made the offering received a wet, red mark on his forehead. Then he gathered up the carcass, for the lower castes of Hindus do not scorn to eat meat, as do the higher castes, and carried it off. At the other side of the temple, the image of Kali was being displayed. The expression on the faces of the crowds surging up the step and fighting for entrance to the temple is something I shall never forget. It was my first sight of Indian hysteria, of the religious madness which lies ready to wake at almost any provocation in the masses of the Hindu people.

And the goddess whose festival was inspiring this orgy of slaughter and frenzied religious passions? One can read, in books, philosophic analyses of the Sakta cult, which grew up around the wife of Siva, as the divine mother, as the genetic principle of activity, the force, creative and recreating, expressing the universal spirit or Absolute, as manifested in all things. Behind the temple sat a holy man, who may have contemplated such intangible mysteries, as he fumbled his rosary with his right hand inside a heavy bag, while a stream of people came up humbly and paid him reverence. He was it seems, a graduate of the University of Calcutta. His face was keenly intelligent and his eyes quietly wise, though the expression made me wonder suddenly whether he were not under the influence of some narcotic. I do not know what Kali meant to him, but when I squeezed through a narrow passage, the priests momentarily holding the way clear for me I saw a horrible and fantastic vision of a thing with a dark face, three eyes, four arms holding aloft symbols of blood, and a red, insatiate tongue hanging down to the bottom of the lighted window, through which I gazed. It was surprisingly little, this picture-image, not more than fifteen inches high. But I believe that the Hindu masses, who came from the sacrifice of goats, verily saw Kali as a living reality, with monstrous attributes and superhuman energies, and baneful, yet worshipful, power.

After a nightmare, one wakes with a sense of intense relief to find that the indeterminate darkness, a moment before potential with alarm, is now, by the light of reason, rendered absurdly innocuous. One is grateful for the safety of four walls, for the quick recognition of humdrum objects falling into ordered places. In Indian imagination, the coloured cosmos flowers growing at Darjeeling may well have been Parvati herself, even one with Durga, while the great snowy crests of the Himalayas stood mysteriously metamorphosed into the god Siva. To me they were sufficiently lovely, as flowers, and marvellous, as mountains. After the incomprehensible plainsfolk I had seen, the laughing, ruddy-faced hill people, whose drunken singing echoed of October nights across the folds of the still mountainside, where lights gleamed, brought relaxation of spirit and abatement of distress. And often, in the weeks that followed, I fell back, for comfort, on the sheer beauty of the Indian land as I came to know it: the wide sun-burned plains, the great rivers, the palm-fringed coast of Malabar, the mighty barrier-ranges of the Himalayas, hiding away the Happy Valley of Kashmir.

From the West I had brought with me a singularly glamorous tradition, as I soon found out, of the material riches and magnificence of India. This tradition had its beginning, I suppose, in the time of the Roman traders, but it must have received great stimulus during the crusades of the Middle

Ages, when Western Europe first came into close contact with the East. It was the wealth of India that Columbus originally set out to find and that inspired his contemporary, Vasco da Gama, to a similar enterprise. But it remained for the adventurous European chroniclers of Mogul court days, followed by the stream of English merchants who amassed very considerable personal fortunes out of the early British-Indian trade of the nineteenth century, to popularize the conception of oriental splendours to be found in India. The fact that the chief articles of trade brought from India were always articles of luxury, as far as the West was concerned, set fire to Western imagination. Merchants brought back with them fine cottons and linens, incomparable weavings like the shawls of Kashmir, embroidered silks, carved ivory, sandalwood, pearls, silver and gold work, and the spices which, in the days before ice, were eagerly sought after for preserving food. We who send to the East our sober freight of 'Tyne coal, road-rails, pig-lead', not to mention 'cheap tin trays', find a strange romance in the thought of 'a cargo of ivory, and apes and peacocks'.

In Delhi and Agra and Lahore, I at last came upon evidence of the brilliant days of India's history; for here were lavishly scattered the great red sandstone forts and gates of Akbar, the marble palaces and 'pearl' mosques of Jahangir, Shah Jahan and Aurangzeb and the magnificent tombs they constructed. Very marvellous were the traceries of the marble screens, pierced like lace; the graceful writing in stone of Persian poems and texts from the Koran; the ornamental panels and borders, made by inlays of carnelian, amber, jade and all the precious materials of Asia, exquisitely cut to the shape of petal, leaf and stem. But my footsteps had a way of echoing oddly on the marble floors of palaces eternally empty, and occasionally, when I met Indians, they, too, were strangers, wandering about, idly curious.

I sat alone for a long time once at the top of one of the four minarets surrounding the Taj Mahal. It was a night of a full November moon, and silver mists clung to the Jumna, flowing silently past the great marble platform from which the Taj rises with ineffable grace. I had had my first view of this far-famed 'Crown of Palaces' from the Jasmine Tower at Agra, whence Shah Jahan, an old man and a prisoner, fallen upon evil days, must often have looked out mournfully at the beautiful mausoleum he had erected many years before, in honour of Mumtaz Mahal, his queen. Its dome had appeared to me, then, glancing white against a sky of swirling dust. Afterwards I had seen it gray, as snowflakes sometimes are, against a white sky; and I had seen it a thing so shadowy and faint that it dissolved in space, a bubble blown. At sunset, called in India the 'hour of cow-dust', it had gathered to itself all the lotus radiance of the upper air, where it had glowed in splendour long after darkness had fallen on the city. Tonight, I found it symbolic of infinite tenderness and beauty. Suddenly, in the moonlight, it was like the breast of a lovely woman.

The sentinel cypresses stood guard below, along the Persian water-course leading from the outer gate to the entrance of the Taj. An everlasting hush seemed to have enfolded the universe, while I sat weighing, one against the other, the beauty of love, the anguish of death, which had fashioned this strangely perfect tomb. Then three young men came sauntering around the far side of the Taj, laughing and talking in loud voices and singing songs in some unknown Indian tongue. Once more the alien present was upon me, and the past receded yet a little farther down the corridor of time. I descended the dark, winding stairs of the minaret. I took off my shoes and followed the two turbaned guardians, carrying their lighted lantern that sent the shadows scuttling in sudden panic, first into the lofty hall where the false tombstones repose, and then down the incline to the chamber beneath, where Mumtaz Mahal and Shah Jahan lie buried with stateliness, side by side. Even before I had entered the vault, the guardians were hastily clinking silver coins down on the tombstones of the mighty dead. I could hope only that the sleep of the dead is sound, that their dust knows no trouble of insult, nor smoldering anger.

What shall I say of the old magnificence of despotic rulers in India, except that it has passed, or is rapidly passing? Splendour, assuredly, is not of the India of today. Go a little way into the country, and every trace of it is gone. Where is even the bright stream of oriental colour, in thousands of mud villages scattered from Bengal to Bombay, from Kashmir to Travancore? Between walls of caked mud, half washed down by last season's rains, the road is laid. A few bony cattle and dogs lie about on the bare, dusty ground. A few women are gathered at the village well, filling their earthen jars with water. Perhaps a half-dozen monkeys sit sedately, like a conference of elders, under a tree that casts a kindly shade over the niche where the village god resides, in becoming poverty. Outside the door of some hut a stringed bedstead presents almost the solitary evidence of the ancient institution of property. A painting of fighting elephants or of gods, or an incident from the *Ramayana,* traced in white on a wall, is the sole visible proof that here are human beings raised a little above the level of the dust they tread. Some dreadful calamity, you feel, must recently have passed this way. But there has been no famine, no devastating epidemic of any sort. Except for the arrival of a moneylender in the community, there has been no particularly calamitous happening that any one can point to. It is merely that the millions of India subsist, like this, without any margin at all. The placid centuries have gone on sifting down their seasons in due order. Now the summer rains are over and the harvesting is done. Once again begins the slow withering up of the plains, under a sun that is inexorable and pitiless.

These millions in India have always been poor. They are likely never to be anything else.

The East is wiser in many ways than the West. The East, in its early contacts, looked to India, not for material greatness, but for spiritual enlightenment. Because I had happened to live for two years in China and Japan I had grown familiar with the quiet face of the Buddha, lost in these outposts of his realm. More recently I had seen something of Buddhism as a living religion, in Burma and Siam. I had grown to think of India as having it all, the fountainhead of Asiatic religious inspiration. But when I came to India, I made the belated discovery that here Buddhism had already been dead a thousand years.

So I saw no yellow-robed priests, no shrines and nothing other than ruins; and it was to the modern museums that I had to go to find the last vestiges of the greatness of the Buddha. One of these is at Sarnath, on the side of the famous Deer Park near Benares, where the Enlightened had first 'turned the Wheel of the Law', or began to expound the doctrine of *karma* and the eightfold-path of deliverance. Archeologists have been very diligent in their excavations at Sarnath. There is a vast area covered with debris, inside which the stone foundations of several monasteries and shrines have been successfully cleared. A number of invaluable and beautiful sculptures, including the great lion-capital of Asokan pillar and many Buddhist statues, the finest of the period, have been recovered and placed on exhibitions at museum. But the desolation that can be wrought thus I have never felt as I felt it among all that meaningless marbled ruin and scarred waste, where only the broken sculpture of Asoka's pillar still stood, and the mounds of one or two crumbling stupas. Even Akbar's Tower, on the crest of its spot seemed to have shared in the general destruction. It is as though it no longer sustained the boastful ambition set forth in an Arabic inscription above the doorway: 'As Humayun, king of the Seven Climes, now residing in paradise, deigned to come and sit here one day, thereby increasing the splendour of he sun, so Akbar, his son and humble servant, resolved to build on this spot a lofty tower reaching to the blue sky.'

But I have the brighter memory of Ajanta, which I would not willingly relinquish. It is impossible to imagine anything stranger than this remote retreat of an early Buddhist brotherhood. Here the hermit tradition, fascinating to India ever since the days of the forest philosophers 3,000 years ago, manifests itself in perfection. For 900 years, from the second century BC to the seventh of our era, communities of monks dwelt in this inaccessible spot, far removed from the world that they, like the Great Solitary, had put behind them. What manner of men were they? One stands awestruck at the thought of the gigantic labour involved in carving the living rock, century after century, into temple rooms and great monastic halls. Here is no hired workmanship, but unquenchable fervour and religious zeal. The countless stone pillars supporting the roofs of the caves are all elaborately carved, and the rock walls from beginning to end are painstakingly and beautifully sculptured in relief, or adorned with darkened frescoes depicting the life-story of the Buddha. It was not Gautama's idea that he, who denied the existence of God, should be worshipped in after ages. But his followers were able to find no more perfect expression of the ideals inculcated in Buddhist philosophy, of moral responsibility, of charity and gentle compassion that should exclude from its warmth not one living thing, of humility, of renunciation, than in the representation of the Buddha himself and the scenes of his long life. The personality of this wistful seeker after peace still pervades the world like a subtle perfume, after 25 centuries. It inspired the men of his own time, and those who were closer to him than we are, with warm human devotion and a very great love.

The present is not an age of visible temple-building. For an expression of the meaning of that which is actual one must look to social institutions, to the economic order and to ceremonial practices. But the Indian continent is so vast, the racial groups are so confused, their customs and religious beliefs so varied, that it seems impossible to point to any common impulse. Even the most distinctive aspects of Indian life, such as polytheistic worship, the disciplinary caste system, the position of inferiority assigned to women, the social ostracism of widows, child marriages, the sacredness in which animal life is held, the practice of religious mendicancy and asceticism, are not easy to study from personal experience or close observation. Indian life flows by, turbid, repelling, wrapped in its own inscrutable mysteries.

The Hindu caste system is the most distinctive institution of India, but the average Westerner, who is as much outside the pale as the fifty million 'untouchables' in India, in practice knows very little about it. The laws of caste, however, not only dominate every relationship of Indian society, but they have come to regulate practically every act in Hindu life. The Hindu belongs essentially to a crystallized social order. He was predestined before birth to become a member of the caste to which his ancestors have always belonged, and he can no more change his caste than he can change the dark colour of his skin. Infringement of caste law means expulsion from caste, and the terrible fate of becoming 'untouchable'. Hinduism itself consists as much in obeying the ceremonial laws of caste as it does in the worship of Vishnu or Siva or Devi or Ganesh or any of the gods.

Caste laws or customs in India have originated primarily from a conception of defilement and purification not easily comprehensible to the Western mind. What we have made clean with soap and water, we are apt to look upon as ceremonially clean, in so far as we are at all sensitive to ritual purity. But what the caste Hindu regards as ceremonially unclean, he does not think capable of being cleansed by any process of sterilization or any sanitary measure whatsoever. It has been the tendency of all religions in India to regard life as essentially sacred, and acceptance of such philosophic doctrines as metempsychosis and karma, the cumulative power of good or evil to work itself out to an ultimate moral conclusion through a series of connected lives, has in India minimized that difference in evaluation of animal and human life characteristic of a Western attitude of mind. Anything associated with death, the antithesis of life, becomes 'unclean' in the mind of the Hindu. No orthodox Hindu will touch meat, particularly beef, since Hinduism has deified the cow, or anything known to contain the germ of life, even an egg; his feeling for our beefsteaks, our leather shoes and gloves, which we accept without compunction, is one of profound abhorrence. He has branded with the name of pariah, from *parai,* a drum, that degraded class of Hindus among whom there are some willing to defile themselves by beating the drum, made from the skin of a dead animal, at funerals and other ceremonies. Because of a similar prejudice, the strings of the *vina,* a musical instrument popular with high-caste Hindus, are always made from metal, instead of gut.

The caste Hindu, who is scrupulous in his observance of ceremonial cleanliness, also finds the body itself, in many ways, capable of conveying defilement. Nothing is farther from cleanliness, to his way of thinking, than our bathtubs, handkerchiefs, bristle toothbrushes, made to do repeated service, table silver, that has suffered pollution by being used even once, and in fact all our habits with regard to food and all the promiscuous contacts forced upon us by our way of living. Wind instruments are actually taboo, or have been until recently, to the high-caste Hindu, so extremely sensitive is he to the idea of defilement from the mouth. The rigid separation of the castes in India comes from the belief that those who do not observe the same laws in regard to cleanliness carry with them their own contamination, atmospheric as well as physical. Outcastes—and there are fifty million of them—are not permitted to enter certain precincts of Hindu temples; they must draw water from their own wells and live in their own villages or districts; even their shadows may constitute serious defilement. Yet, at the same time, no simplest religious ceremony can be performed in any orthodox Hindu household without first 'purifying' the floor by an application of cow-dung, and otherwise violating our soap-and-water standards of decency.

Caste works incomparable hardship upon millions, who suffer from its exclusiveness, but it is caste that has hitherto held together in rigid discipline the many divergent elements of Indian society. Now it is slowly but surely beginning to break down, and the rate of speed must increase as time goes on. Western institutions, which do not permit caste practice in extreme form, have already gone a long way toward destroying the significance of caste itself. Railroads are now an inextricable part of Indian economic life. British law does not take into consideration the caste customs of a criminal when it sends him to prison. Factories and mills, which are just beginning to be established in India, draw recruits, like the army, from every caste. But caste so far remains the great controlling force in the Indian social order, and no one who understands India, I believe, wants it to disappear too rapidly, especially when political and economic conditions are undergoing tremendous changes and upheaval, as they are at this time. Until there is some stabilizing influence to substitute for it, it must be accepted as securing the framework of Indian society.

Without the past, what is India's present? More and more, as one tries to understand India, the conviction grows that nothing in India is haphazard; nothing is without an explanation to be found in an inexorable tradition, rooted in dead centuries. And this tradition is an embodiment of an essentially religious attitude toward life. Long before Buddhism flowered and died on the stem, men in India were reciting hymns of praise to the great forces of nature defied as gods of fire and rain, wind and sun and sky, hymns which represent the earliest literature of the Aryan people from which we ourselves are sprung. Still today, in spite if of all the later developments of a Hindu pantheon, the rise and fall of dynasties, the political changes inherent in foreign invasions, these identical hymns are recited by countless thousands of Hindus. India's fundamental unity lies in an unbroken recognition of a spiritual order in the universe, outlasting worldly phenomena; in the aspiration manifest in all Indian philosophic thought toward an identification of the self with spiritual forces; in the emphasis in Indian social thought on obedience to a system of moral law. Out of the answers that have been found and discarded and found again, in India's quest for knowledge of the supreme truth, Indian civilization has slowly been built up.

India has produced many great philosophers, but it is not to the philosophers, after all, that one must turn for an appreciation of the essential quality of Indian life. Only the fused experience of millions can reveal that; and against the millions, I was one, and alien. At the bathing-*ghats* of Benares, I saw, as every one may see, countless multitudes of Hindus gathered to be healed of sickness, to be cleansed of sin and defilement, to die, that in their last immersion in the sacred river, they might come forth in purity, as they believed, and enter straight into heaven. Slowly I was poled up and down the Ganges. I saw the funeral pyres being lighted and smoke curling lazily upward. I saw attendants bringing bodies, wrapped like mummies and laid on stretchers, down the steps of the burning-ghats; dipping them into the water; letting them rest with the feet immersed and the face cloth thrown back: for the dead are fortunate, they think, who have their last look on the sacred river. A little farther down the stream, the living were standing up to their waists in the water, or resting after their ablutions under the great woven umbrellas, like pavilions, scattered along the ghats, or casting orange marigolds, one by one, as offerings upon the surface of the muddy river. What the Nile was, and is no more, to Egypt, the Ganges still is to India today. But temperament alone decides, perhaps, whether one shall see the bright rays of the rising sun illuminating the red stone palace of the Maharaja of Benares and gilding the domes of the many temples, the fluttering doves, the crowds, the colour, the motion, the life; or whether one shall remember chiefly the superstition and degradation and filth, the unsanitary mingling of the dead and the living; or most marvel that here, as perhaps in no other place in the world, men clasp their hands in worship to the rising sun and a great river, and repeat prayers to them as gods.

India is the saddest land I have ever seen. Yet I am not sure that the material wealth of my own country, nor a philosophy synonymous with 'all modern conveniences', has produced much fundamental happiness for us of the West, nor peace of mind. Multiplicity of comforts does not answer the need of the soul for significant beauty, nor teach adjustment to life, unconditioned by material resources. In our eagerness to produce, we have found little time to possess our souls. In spite of India's failures to meet the tests by which we commonly measure a given state of civilization, meaning material civilization, India has a perception of life that is spiritually significant. It is the saint and the ascetic, after all, who are the living ideal of India's millions. What other country patiently supports, as India, over a million *sadhus,* who have 'renounced' life as a great illusion? What country, except India, would have allowed Gandhi, with his preaching of self-discipline, of non-violence, of fasting and prayer, to become the national leader? The masses of India are rich in their unconquerable love of the marvellous, out of which they fashion the ceaseless miracles of their gods. They have hallowed their own land with the beauty of imagination. Everywhere are the sacred spots about which myth and legend cling, and the humblest peasant in India may, and does, become a pilgrim to the sacred shrines of his inheritance. Through the objective expression of religious feeling in past ages, art is closely interwoven with the threads of all life in India. The Indian villager is not shut in by the mud walls of his hut. Very little is his house, and very wide his universe. Without is the forever dominant and ruthless nature of the tropics, enlarging the world of his individual experience beyond the limits of the horizon. He is the plaything of great forces, such as torrential rains and a merciless sun. For months in the wet season, he cannot work; he becomes the possessor of infinite time. He is rich beyond the mighty of the earth. From below, as from above, Indian thought slowly converges and takes form: not accomplishment, not progress, not happiness, is the purpose of life, but the working out of a conscious relationship with spiritual truth. Out of narrow circumstance, the illiterate Indian finds escape in his mystic heart, where dwell the gods whom he worships.

The educated leaders in India today are uniting in an effort to reform many institutions that have grown out of debased Hinduism and a rigid form of society. They are borrowing from the West the Christian ideal of social service and are losing something of their old sense of isolated individualism. But not all change is progress, and Indian philosophy has so far wisely been unwilling to forego its vision of an ideal peace and order. The greatest minds of India believe that no product of Western energy, and no expression of our mechanistic genius, will solve the problem of the old questing for spiritual wisdom.

Is it the inspiration of this ideal, or merely an attachment to what has become familiar through dusty centuries, that makes Indians strangely loyal to their land? I remember this incident of a visit to Rabindranath Tagore's school at Bolpur, called *Santiniketan,* Abode of Peace—a cluster of plain buildings, in an insignificant grove, set down in the centre of a wide, treeless plain. I had spent two interesting hours with Dr. Tagore. Afterwards, accompanied by a young Indian teacher of science, who had just returned to India from a year or two of study in Germany, I was walking slowly back again to the house in which I had courteously been invited to spend the night. Moonlight was beginning to silver the dark earth, but the fires of sunset smoldered still in the west. The night was warm and intensely quiet. Far out on the plain we heard the jackals calling, and a cart that we could not see lumbered creakingly along some hidden road. He was talking of politics and sundry things, as we picked our way along a faintly discernible path, a white thread guiding our feet in the darkness. He broke off his discussion abruptly.

'Is it not beautiful, all this?' he said reverently, and his voice thrilled with inexplicable emotion. . . . And then again, 'It is all so marvelously beautiful!'

I knew that he meant to include more than the remnant of the sunset. I knew that 'all this' was India.

CHAPTER 12

Indian Miniature Painting

Percy Brown

IT IS NOW FAIRLY WELL ESTABLISHED that the miniature painting of India resolves itself into two broad divisions or schools. On the one hand there is the indigenous painting of the country—religious, domestic and mystic—commonly classified as Rajput, because it is associated with the chief cities of Rajputana and the Hill States of the Punjab. On the other hand there is the art of the Mogul emperors—in temper and intention entirely different from the foregoing. It is materialistic, eclectic and aristocratic, yet connected with the indigenous school in a peculiar way. For although it is fundamentally an art of the country, blended with it is a strong Persian element brought over by the Mogul emperors to India from their ancestral home beyond the Oxus. On this account such pictures are referred to as Indo-Persian or Mogul.

The Rajput art, since it is in many respects older and more profound than the Mogul, may be described first. Although a period of several centuries separates Rajput painting from the wonderful mural frescoes of the early Indian Buddhists, there is little doubt that the Hindu art took its origin from that source. It has been truly said that what the early Italian frescoes were to the art of Europe the paintings of Ajanta in India were to the Buddhist art of Asia. These mural decorations, executed on the living

**ASIA*, March 1923. Percy Brown (1872–1955) was Principal of the Government School of Art in Calcutta. He believed that Indian artists should find inspiration in their own art rather than that of the West.

THE TORI 'RAGNI', OR MELODY OF TORI

rock in the first centuries of the Christian era, are only the meagre remnants of a great classical school of painting which flourished in India with the growth of the Buddhist religion. The influence of that school may be seen in all the painting of Asia, from the recently discovered frescoes in Eastern Turkestan, the temple banners, or *tankas,* of Tibet, and the Buddhist art of China, to the temple of Horyu-ji in Japan, the eighth-century frescoes of which recall in the strong outline of their figures the grandeur of the Ajanta compositions and the feeling for life and character which these reveal. Centuries after, we get a distant echo of this art in the miniature painting of the Rajputs, but the intervening space is a blank and a difficult one to fill—very few concrete records of painting emerge between the decline of Buddhist painting with the decay of the Buddhist religion towards the seventh century and the revival of the art in the sixteenth century under the Moguls. For the course that Indian painting followed during this period of nine centuries we are mainly dependent on written records. Intelligent travellers to India in the Middle Ages have not failed to relate how lavishly the Hindu temples were painted with figures and ornament. That the art continued with the revival of the Hindu religion, after the fall of Buddhism, is plainly discernible. But practically nothing which can be regarded as belonging to this long interval now remains, and the hiatus is almost complete. For, from a variety of causes, most of the buildings themselves perished, and, where they survived, the paintings, as the centuries progressed, were not executed in fresco, but in the less permanent form of tempera, so that time and the climate have caused their entire decay.

If, however, these evidences of the art disappeared, the actual craftsmanship still lived, eager for any noble incentive. Encouragement came with the stable rule of the Moguls in the sixteenth century. The patronage which the Mogul emperors gave to the Indian painters and which eventually produced the Mogul School, a brilliant episode of a hundred years or so in the annals of Indian art, reacted on the art of the Rajputs, revitalized it and gave it another period of activity. But it ceased to be a mural art; for, imitating the prevailing methods originally derived from Persia, it became an art of miniature and also largely of illustration. The epics of the Hindus lend themselves to a graphic form of narration, continued through a long series of pictures, and it is not uncommon to find groups of miniatures, each depicting an event or incident, and illustrating, when combined, the main story of these mythical poems.

As we have seen, the same imperial influence that stimulated the Rajput art to a fresh lease of life was responsible for the creation of the corresponding school of painting, that of the Moguls. These Moguls were an offshoot of the Mongols of Central Asia. They carried with them to Hindustan a Persian culture, the impact of which may be seen in the language, literature, writing, architecture and arts of northern India even to the present day. And one of the activities of the people in which the Mogul dynasty took a keen personal interest was painting. The Emperor Akbar, who was the first to establish a settled administration in the new territory in India, during the latter part of the sixteenth century, early realized the inherent gifts of the Indian artist in this direction. But he soon saw that an infusion of new blood was required to give the indigenous art a new life. Several Persian artists therefore came over to the court of the 'Great Mogul' and were engaged to carry out the Emperor's orders for pictures. It is not necessary here to describe the state of painting in Central Asia at this period, except in briefest terms. The actual culmination of the Persian school had been reached, the great masters of Herat, Samarkand and Shiraz, such as Behzad, Mirak and Sultan Mahommed, had passed away, but the traditions of their magnificent art still lived. And it was these traditions which were brought over to Hindustan by Persian artists engaged by the Emperor Akbar. The names of three of these precursors of the Mogul School are known to us. They are Mir Sayyid Ali of Tabriz, Khajah Abdu Samad from Shiraz and Farrukh Beg, the Kalmuck. The work of these men had a profound influence on the character of the rising school. The first two named were closely associated with the school of Behzad. In fact, Abdu Samad's father, a very distinguished painter of Herat, was a contemporary of this 'Raphael of the East'. The Mogul School was therefore a continuation of the Behzad tradition, but under other conditions and a changed environment it developed into a very different art.

Much of the dissimilar character which Mogul painting assumed began when, under the advice of the Emperor Akbar, the Indian painters undertook to copy examples of Persian pictures. They did this under the supervision of the three artists named above. Sometimes they copied them literally; at other times they translated them into their own artistic language, until gradually the Indo-Persian or Mogul style came into being. The work of the artists at Akbar's court was therefore of a mixed character. Some of it is purely Persian some purely Rajput-Hindu, and some a combination of the two styles, but so loosely incorporated as to be easily resolved into its component parts.

This mixed art became really fused into a fixed style of painting under the regime of Akbar's son and successor, Jahangir, who mounted the throne of the Moguls in 1605. The esthetic temperament of this monarch was undoubtedly largely responsible for the consummation of the Mogul School. The political conditions that prevailed during his reign also helped much. He found himself ruler of a great empire in which all the hard work had been done for him. And this state of affairs gave him leisure to indulge in the inherent enjoyments of a wealthy dilettante. Among these none gave him a greater pleasure than the art of painting. Under his intelligent patronage the work of the painters matured, and the best miniatures of the school were executed during his reign. But even at this stage it did not become quite independent of its parent school in Persia, for two artists from Samarkand joined the ranks of Jahangir's court painters and did much to strengthen the style at this particular time.

Probably the only fault to be found with Jahangir's patronage is that it was so enthusiastic as to monopolize the art. He retained in his service a fairly large staff of artists, whom he employed in executing pictures of all subjects that pleased his fancy. Many such depict him seated in state, holding court under the most gorgeous conditions, and surrounded by brilliantly attired members of his suite. Some of these miniatures illustrate incidents that took place while this sumptuous potentate was travelling over his dominions—a duty in which he spent much of his time; others show him hunting or engaged in the various occupations that made up his daily life. Jahangir was also interested in gardens, flowers and natural history. These formed subjects for his artists, so that flowers in bloom, trees bearing fruit, and all sorts of birds and animals were painted at his command. A survey of Mogul art readily proves that the pictures of this period which have survived are almost entirely the personal expression of this esthetic emperor. In his days Indian painting was essentially an imperial art, an art of the court—it had no vogue outside the royal circle.

But under the rule of his successor, Shah Jahan, Mogul painting took on a slightly different aspect. This monarch, who ascended the throne in 1627, had not that interest in painting which characterized his father, Jahangir. Not that Shah Jahan's nature was lacking in appreciation of beauty—one glance at his portrait, as painted by his own artists, shows us the most refined and sensitive features. But his own personal feelings lay more in the direction of architecture, and it was this form of expression which flourished with such vigour during his great and glorious reign. The splendid palace-fort at Delhi and that pearl of oriental architecture, the Taj Mahal at Agra, are proofs of his energies in this respect. And so Mogul painting ceased to be the monopoly of the court and began therefore to find favour with the people—not the common people, but the princes and nobles, chiefs and officials who constituted the aristocracy of Hindustan. Each personage of any repute kept his own painter as part of his establishment. It was during this period, before the middle of the seventeenth century, that the great body of Mogul painting was produced, and probably nine-tenths of the miniatures of a good type that are now in public and private collections date from Shah Jahan's reign. In character, in technique and in their artistic qualities generally, they are representative examples of this art; yet they do not quite display the ingenuousness and spontaneity of the pictures painted in the earlier reigns. There is an indescribable sense of overripenness in many of these productions, the colours are overelaborated, the drawing less restrained—in a word, there is the first note of a decline.

This initial step of deterioration was followed by a further decay under the Emperor Aurangzeb, who succeeded Shah Jahan in 1659. And just as the finest efforts of the art were due to the personal character of one of the earlier Mogul emperors, so its degradation may be traced to the puritanical mentality of a later member of the same dynasty. Aurangzeb, a man of high ideals, had many excellent qualities, but he had no sympathy with the arts. For lack of support, the artists—once the favourites of the court—became dispersed over different parts of the peninsula. Many of the families either took up other crafts of a more popular character or gradually became extinct. Others carried on their art in a desultory way in the cities of Rajputana and Bengal and even as far south as Mysore and Tanjore, where painting of a certain kind is practised to the present day. The Mogul School of miniature painting, which had dawned with Akbar, reached its meridian with Jahangir and its rich sunset during the splendid reign of Shah Jahan, and it now faded out in the inauspicious days of the Emperor Aurangzeb.

A comparison of the Rajput and Mogul schools may best be made by means of examples. Plate given on page 162 is an illustration of what is known in India as the *Rag Mela,* or art of 'picture music', an indigenous form of expression which enabled the artist to paint from a melody and the musician to play from a picture. The particular musical mode here depicted is that known as the *Tori Ragni,* or melody of Tori, a musical divinity who attracted to her side the deer in the desert by the seductive strains of her *vina.* This ragni is played before sunrise during the hot season. The scene is replete with symbolism and mysticism, gently pulsating with a sense of quiet, yet deep, emotion. And over the whole broods an atmosphere of a religious rite, something from the creed of the country which is present in every aspect of Hindu art. When all this is understood, it is not difficult to realize that the picture is of the Rajput School. There is no sentiment, no religious significance, about this miniature; it is a representation of a very realistic historical episode. This picture is Mogual. The two miniatures here selected are no doubt extreme examples, but the same principles may be applied to all specimens of the two schools.

And, furthermore, the Mogul artists specialized in that very realistic form of painting, the portrait. While the Rajput occasionally indulged in likenesses of specific individuals, the Mogul painter made them the keynote of his art. Mogul miniatures are therefore mainly portraits, not only pictures of single persons, but often groups of people taking part in some ceremony or entertainment. There are several examples of single portraits by Mogul artists. A feature of pictures, which bear the seal of the Emperor Jahangir, is their border. This shows what an elaborate and sumptuous work of art the miniature became when the Mogul dynasty was at the height of its magnificence. Such are the brief outlines of these two aspects of Indian painting. The resemblances between them are, to the more practised eye, largely superficial. Both Rajput and Mogul pictures are paintings in miniature, and both are essentially Indian in their subject matter. These are obvious evidences of similarity, but the divergence in the two schools at once begins. Rajput miniatures express entirely the sentiments of the Hindu; Mogul miniatures speak of the thoughts of the Mahommedan. And just as much as these two religions are fundamentally dissimilar, so the productions of these two schools differ in temper, intention, subject and character. The Rajput picture has sentiment, religion, domesticity, mysticism or some similar characteristic. The Mogul has none of these—it is a plain statement of fact. But it is doubtful whether the painter of any other country or period ever excelled the Mogul miniaturist in the richness of his pictorial effects.

CHAPTER 13

A Way Out for Rural India

Daniel Swamidoss

ON SUNDAY MORNING, AT HALF PAST eleven or so, when I begin to talk to a strange audience about the rural work of the YMCA among Indian Christians, as I have done so often during my visit to America, I see with the intensity of vision granted only to the inner eye my Indian villages, deep-shadowed, for it is half past nine in the evening there, and silent, unless some dog bays the moon. It is doubly night in those villages; there is the darkness of intellectual and spiritual unenlightenment and there are other demons as well—debt, dirt and drunkenness, for example—which handicap the depressed classes, to which most of the Christians belong, even more than the caste people.

Frequently the village Christians fall short, pitifully, amusingly short, in their attempts to practise the religion into which they have been baptized. And the tenets of the faith they grasp still less readily than its virtues. Into the school-house—a mud-walled, thatched hut 20 ft. long by 15 ft. wide at the utmost—they crowd to listen to sermons that they cannot understand. Hours before the time for a service they assemble—sweepers, leather-workers, watchmen—some two hundred inhabitants of the Outcaste quarters that lie a half-mile or a mile from the village proper. Patiently they wait or restlessly come and go while the teacher-pastor is collecting missing members of his flock. At last, when it has grown intolerably hot, both inside

**ASIA*, March 1923. Daniel Swamidoss was the Secretary of Rural Work of the National Council of the YMCA in India.

LEATHER-WORKERS AND THEIR MAHOMMEDAN EMPLOYER
Leather-workers belonging to a cooperative society are learning how to buy leather and to sell saddles, buckets and shoes through this organization.

and outside the hut, the service begins. The preacher preaches and preaches. Bodies are reeking; minds drowsy. Half the men fall asleep. The babies cry. The women gossip with one another. After the sermon the congregation sing—possibly something about how 'Jesus paid it all', or some other song equally puzzling to those chronically in debt—and one or two may go out to try to steal some grain or a stray chicken or bullock.

Starvation, like repletion, is a foe to righteousness, and the Outcastes are almost always hungry. As the hereditary servants of the village they are paid in various ways for their labour, and when the crops are harvested, they are entitled to measures of grain from the landholders. They have received from the British government a portion of the *inam* lands for their service to the village, and occasionally they have acquired a little land by purchase or have obtained tiny plots through the influence of missionaries or others interested in their welfare. But between their trivial holdings and their huge indebtedness they are hard put to it to live.

As a symbol of the suffering that the Outcastes of a village may endure in the lean years, I often think of the bare mud walls of a now ruined hut in a village in the Nizam's dominions which I visited once with an American YMCA secretary. The tragedy had happened during a season of famine and influenza, when a pair of cattle sold for $3, fine babies went for $1 apiece and men and women lived or died on a diet of grass-seed gruel. The Outcaste man and woman and three children who lived in the hut left home and for three days wandered about, looking for something to eat. At last on the fourth day, a kind-hearted man gave them a meal. They would not eat it till they had washed. They tied the food carefully in a piece of cloth, brought it home and left it in their hut while they went to the well. Then, having made themselves clean, they came home with joyful faces, to break their long fast. During their absence, however, the roof had caught fire and the house burned. Immediately, as was natural for Indians, they thought that they had incurred the displeasure of God. Thereafter life could have no meaning for them. In despair the man led his wife and children back to the well. First he threw the children in, one at a time, and then his wife, and finally he himself jumped in. So there remain only the crumbling mud walls of the hut to remind the villagers of this family who could starve but could not endure the curse of God.

Even in normal times Indian villages swarm with the hungry. When I was in boarding-school as a boy, my roommate and I cooked our own food. The poor in the neighbourhood, knowing that the school housed a hundred boys who had enough to eat, used to come in procession, one after another, begging us for food. A morsel here, a morsel there, and soon we had given away all that we had prepared for ourselves and had to cook more or go unfed.

Small wonder is it if certain of the Outcastes discover that cattle-lifting, highway robbery and other questionable modes of livelihood yield swifter and less meagre returns than begging. Unhappily, Christians as well as non-Christians succumb to temptation, and such names as 'Abraham', 'Moses' and 'David' appear among the known depredators or 'KDs' in the police registers. Outcastes are sometimes involved in feuds that disturb the peace for generations. I remember that, in a certain village where the Outcastes had offended the caste people, the latter showed their displeasure by burying a dead cow outside the village instead of giving it to the Outcastes, as custom decreed. On the second day the Outcastes dug up the carcass and made a hearty meal of it. What end need there be to the vengeful quarrel thus started? Hostility between two caste families is also likely to involve the Outcastes. For instance a landowner who wishes an enemy out of the way will hire Outcaste bravos to kill him. He offers one of these wretched folk Rs. 50, a fortune to a man so poor, or promises to take care of the culprit's family if he has to go to jail. The Outcaste feels he is getting a gilt-edged insurance policy. So he yields and becomes, as it were, the mercenary soldier of the big landlord. I was present once at the trial of a case involving two rival families among high-caste landlords in Cuddapah, south India. The feud had led to a pitched battle in the daylight, in which the sweepers and leather-workers were employed. While the enemy landlords were in hiding, the Outcaste retainers of the aggressor, armed with clubs, axes and swords, advanced upon the Outcaste quarters of the village of the other family. About a dozen lives were lost in the encounter. Of course the police came after the fight was over and led a batch of the belligerents before the district judge for trial. It is heartbreaking to the Indian Christian social worker to find fellow-Christians involved in such scrapes and humiliating to hear it said, as he goes about among them, 'This also is one of them.' And yet in a sense that is true. He knows better than any one from outside can know the sorrows of his people and their needs and the temptations that beset them.

Yes, it is heartbreaking, heartbreaking and humorous, to see what shifts and turns the Christian Outcastes try in order to exist, and to discover how literally, out of their bodily hunger, they sometimes interpret the offer of the bread of life. In a certain village in the Telugu country lived one of these naive Christians. He was a teacher-pastor named Timothy, a weak brother among the great number of able and honourable Christian leaders. He taught school six days in the week, led a Bible class on Sunday morning and preached twice on Sunday for his congregation. He had a wife and six children and he received a salary of $2 a month from the mission. The mission would not increase his salary because he had studied only up to the fourth standard, the end of the primary course. Timothy felt that he must have more money. He had a real economic problem. Because of his status in the village, he could not resort to begging. He was too poor to borrow. The only alternative was to steal. But he was too old to steal. So he organized the young men of his Bible class for a plundering expedition. They scoured the neighbouring villages and brought home a stray cow. The animal was slaughtered, the meat was apportioned among the young men and the skin given to the teacher-pastor, who sold it to the skin merchant for $3 or $4. Thereafter a similar raid was conducted each Saturday evening while Timothy was preparing his sermon. Four trips a month brought him $12 to $16. One day a rather recent acquaintance, seeing that Timothy's wife was attractively dressed and not without jewels and that his children were growing fat asked him, 'How is it that you seem to be prospering on $2 a month?' The teacher-pastor, with a happy smile, answered calmly, 'Ah, the Lord is mindful of his own.' Three or four days later, this friend, who had heard some of the village gossip and had come to know the truth, said to him, 'Timothy, how *can* a man who does the sort of thing you do be a preacher and teacher and talk to these poor people about God's love?' Then Timothy said contentedly: 'Well, sir, if I cannot testify to God's love, who can? I have done this for ten years, and the good Lord has never once handed me over to the police.'

Poor Outcastes! If they reject suborners' bribes or other ill-got gains, they are seldom enough able to refuse loans. And the devil is generally at hand in the guise of a professional moneylender or a rich landlord. In the effort to keep in his clutches those who have been for centuries the hewers of wood and drawers of water for the caste people, the rich landlord lends them money from time to time at exorbitant rates of interest. The normal minimum rates are 12 per cent in south India and 18 per cent in north India. The rates are higher for small sums and for money lent on personal security. On mortagages with or without possession the usual rate is 12 per cent, with a time limit for repayment. If a man borrows Rs. 1,000 at 12 per cent, it is generally stipulated that the whole amount shall be repaid in three years. In default of that, a new bond is executed for three years, for a fresh sum, including the unpaid interest. The usual result is that on account of a bad season or two or sickness, the loan is never repaid, and one day the man finds that the court has issued a decree authorizing the sale of his land. If the land is worth Rs. 5,000, the moneylender lets the debt mount up to perhaps Rs. 4,000 and then makes a profit by bidding the land in or commissioning some friend to bid it in for that amount, as can easily be done, since people are afraid to bid against him or his agent.

The professional moneylender is less willing than the rich landlord to saddle himself with realty problems. He prefers to lend money on grain and produce. He may lend to a farmer who needs cash with which to purchase seed or to tide himself over until his crop is ripe and harvested. A loan of this sort represents practically a mortgage on the standing crop, which is appraised at a minimum value. When the wretched debtor is unable to pay his loan, the moneylender takes over the crop at the low price agreed upon and holds it until the market is at its height. Also he preempts at the lowest wages the labour of those who owe money to him, instead of leaving them free to sell their services in the open market. In fact, he takes also the labour of the wife and children of a debtor and repays them perhaps with a meal a day and a trivial present, and if the man possesses a manure-pit, he thinks he has a right to that, too. Of course matters of this sort are not mentioned in the note, and if the rate of interest happens to be 36 per cent, it is decorously set down at 12, to save the moneylender's face. Thus chronic indebtedness becomes the greatest disability of Indian farmers. This is true of both Christians and non-Christians, Outcastes and caste people. There are for all classes not only the heavy rates of interest, but the concomitant evils of free labour, low wages and serfdom.

From the point of view of dealing with such conditions, the courts seem strangely inefficient. I have in mind two brothers, who inherited from their father sixteen acres of land. Being ignorant and without foresight and proud of keeping their little patrimony intact, as they had received it from their father, they did not divide their land. Then at a time of need the elder brother obtained a loan by mortgaging his portion. He was unable to pay the debt, the interest accumulated, the moneylender foreclosed and the court passed a decree for the sale of the land. Not only the elder brother's portion but the whole property of sixteen acres was put up at auction. I went to court in the interest of the wretched younger brother, but I was not permitted to plead because I was not a lawyer. The poor man was overwhelmed with expenses in connection with a protracted case, which could and should have been settled with summary justice as a purely village affair.

If the masses of the rural population were literate, the struggle with those who oppress the poor would be a less unequal contest. The borrower could read the rate of interest set down in a note and he would not be pitiably fooled by a pretended receipt for money paid; nor would he quake as he now does in the presence of petty officialdom. But the percentage of literacy in India is very low. Even if one includes the cities and towns, only 6 per cent of the men and 1 per cent of the women are literate, and in the villages scarcely one in a hundred is able to read and write, especially in the Outcaste quarters. And how sorely the one who knows a little is tempted to cheat the many who know even less, who can say? I remember the case of a native pastor who was particularly clever in making use of his superior knowledge. It was the year for taking the census, and the government was glad to have some one who could read and write volunteer to check up the preliminary list of names of the inhabitants of a village to see that no mistakes had been made. This pastor went before the villagers and said: 'I have come to tell you that the government is going to give land to all those whose names are on this list but not to anybody whose name is omitted. I have been at great pains and expense to obtain this benefit for you and to make sure that all the names are included, and I should be very grateful if each of you would give me 2 rupees or 3 rupees to reimburse me for what I have spent.' The people of the village said: 'Ah, yes, you are our spiritual father, and now you are kind to us as a temporal father. We will gladly give what you ask.' And so they took up a collection, and their pastor made off with his swag. But when the truth was known, his fellow-pastors lost no time in having him dismissed.

If even their Christian pastor will take advantage of these poor people and prey upon them in this fashion, it is not surprising that non-Christian subordinate officials have far too few scruples. The village accountant can collect a little more than the due assessment. The sub-engineers and overseers of the irrigation department have their share of annual graft. The Indian police have also certain perquisites, and the *vakils* (lawyers), the underpaid government clerks in the collectorate and the *taluk,* or county, officers come in for their quota. When the collector goes his rounds through the district and stops at the different rest-houses to receive the various taluk officers and their staffs who come to do business with him, he travels about with an immense entourage that gives the impression of a moving camp. He has a government allowance for the expenses of the journey and he himself pays the proper funds into the hands of his butler and his cook and his other servants, but they pocket the money and then go foraging among the people of the countryside and take their chickens and their grains and their fruits or commandeer their labour and pay them nothing.

As a result of these handicaps of a poverty that sometimes drives them to crime, indebtedness that often reduces them to serfdom and illiteracy that makes them the prey of the unscrupulous, the village Christians are in a parlous state. They number five million and the majority of them are from the depressed classes. In the mind of the average Indian who is not a Christian, Christianity seems to be just a change of label. The people are still poor and ignorant, he reasons, and no wonder: Christianity is the religion of Outcastes. It would appear, however, to an impartial observer, that the depressed classes are hastening to embrace the new faith for the very reason that they hope through it to be no longer Outcastes. The missions, and America, which generously supports them, look upon mass conversion as the triumph of the Gospel. But without any denial of the many cases of intense personal conviction, it may be admitted that hope of release from the social degradation imposed by Hinduism is largely at work in what are known as mass movements toward Christianity. In recent times these movements have taken place on a scale so huge that the missions have lacked men and money to enable them to minister to the spiritual needs of these people and they have frequently had to refuse to receive them.

The missions are trying to meet the situation as far as they can through their schools and industrial institutions. Indian Christians are likely to disapprove of this type of service because they think it encourages an influx into the church of those who would not have entered it without some bait and who will not be a credit to it in the eyes of the non-Christian world. Of course many of the older school of missionaries who feel that beyond everything else the heathen must be converted, are not interested in social service for its own sake. I share the view of the younger school of missionaries, who believe that social service is a very real part of the Gospel. It is in fact what the Indian masses chiefly need. They are quite incapable of profiting by metaphysical or theological theory. It is unfortunate that in America there is still so much theological discussion and in some cases so pronounced a cleavage in faith and policy between the older and the younger generation of missionaries as to hinder a concerted programme of social service and to retard the social redemption that the slow centuries have yet to accomplish in India.

Nine years ago the YMCA in India was invited by the missions to share in this great work by undertaking useful offices on behalf of the village Christians. Happily the YMCA, which had already proved its genius to meet the peculiar needs of students, the business class and the army, received this summons to new activity just at the time when K. T. Paul, an Indian well versed in the needs of Indian villages, became national general secretary. The organization was therefore in a position to respond to the call, and accordingly at the January 1914, business meeting, the National Council created the Rural Department, with a budget of Rs. 4,000.

Paul had plans for rural amelioration but no staff to put them into effect; so he asked three of us who were all south Indians to become his first helpers. I had long known Paul and I was already familiar with YMCA ideas and ideals. And, too, I was a son of the soil. My people were originally farmers of the Sudra caste, worshippers of Siva. I had known hardship and had seen my mother suffer. Partly for that very reason, perhaps, I found it difficult to turn my back on a government career to become a YMCA rural secretary. Indeed my friends and kindred were opposed to my doing so, but during the long month in which I debated the problem with them and with myself, I thought much of what had been in the heart of my mother, who was a Christian, in all the years since she named me and set me apart, not to be served, but to serve. And at last, timidly, I made my choice. It is strange to remember now those weeks of doubt.

Since one of the main activities of the staff of the Rural Department of the YMCA was to be the organization of cooperative banks, the Government of India, which had already taken the initiative in enterprises of this sort, though not specially among the Outcastes, kindly offered to give us three months' training for our work. At the end of this period we were assigned to different areas of south India and began to make surveys of the villages.

In America a programme to meet the social conditions I have already described would no doubt involve boards of directors and committees and dinners. In India it means indigenous methods. When I enter a village with the idea of starting the cooperative work, I have first of all to win the confidence of the people; for they wonder what ulterior motive I have in coming to them. They have been cheated so much that they hardly believe that anybody can bring them a gift. Perhaps begin by quoting Gandhi. 'Mahatma Gandhi has said to you,' tell them, 'that your salvation lies with yourselves.' 'Ah,' say those who are not Christians, 'this fellow is a Christian but he respects Mahatma Gandhi,' and they are not unwilling to listen. 'But,' I go on, 'the only way you can begin to help yourselves is to help one another.' 'Ah, sir,' they say, puzzled, 'I have so many troubles of my own that I cannot take upon me the additional burden of my neighbour's misfortunes.' Then I must tell them stories. Or I say to them: 'What do you do when you see a neighbour's house on fire? Do you stand with arms folded and say, "It is not my house; let it burn!"? No, you get a water-jar and go to the tank and get water and help put out the fire.' 'Ah, sir,' they answer, 'but a spark from the fire may fall on the roof of my own house and consume it.' 'Even so,' I say, 'with this fire of debt,' for one can play on these two words in the Indian tongue. 'It scorched one neighbour yesterday. Today it shrivels another. Tomorrow it may consume you.' They see the point.

Then I tell them my scheme for the cooperative bank. I make it clear that I could not negotiate with each one of them, for I have many villages to visit. But I am willing to deal with them as a group, provided they consent to be individually and collectively responsible. I explain that if I lend the village Rs. 1,000, I can collect that sum from all of them, or from any one, if the others do not keep to their agreement. 'But, sir,' they say in alarm, 'there are many fellows that are not honest.' 'Exactly,' I answer; 'then you must pick out those that you trust and take only such persons into this enterprise.'

Though we can start a bank for as few as ten members, we may try for forty. But the forty will have dwindled to thirty within a week, for people are suspicious and the weak-kneed drop out. If we get thirty who believe our words, we first collect the membership fee and the share capital. Each member pays a small admission fee (4 cents to 8 cents, or 2 *annas*) and buys a share (1 rupee, or 32 cents) or more up to a limit of 20 shares. We take in perhaps something like 45 rupees on that first day.

Then we say: 'Thirty men cannot run a bank. Please let us have five who will be your elders, your *panchayet,* and manage it for you.' The people are used to this idea and agree. We explain that these men must be able to keep watch over the affairs of the bank, to judge character, to do things on time, etc. They listen attentively, and then they say: 'Sir, I understand. I think I am the man.' So thirty hands go up. 'Sir, make my father president'; 'Sir, choose my brother,' they entreat, thinking, as men do the world over, that it is an advantage to have a relative on the board of directors. Finally we get five fellows. The one who serves as president and treasurer is generally a man of property. He must be able to read and write. Since only members can be officers, sometimes the schoolmaster employed by the mission is persuaded to become a stockholder, so that he can serve as president and keep the books. But he must not be too clever.

I borrowed Rs. 400 at 7½ per cent interest from a friend to start the first bank. As village banks multiplied, it became evident that a strong central organization was needed. In the course of time 'Christian Central Cooperative' banks were established at Madras, Lucknow and Lahore. They are like any other banking corporations except that they do business only with the village banks. They lend money to the village banks at 7½ to 8½ per cent and the village banks lend to their own members at 12½ per cent. The difference between the 7½ per cent charged by the central bank and the 12½ per cent charged by the village bank goes into a reserve fund. The money saved in this way is deposited and becomes an additional security to the financing bank. The hope is that this reserve fund will in time be large enough to become the working capital, so that the village cooperative banking system may be self-sustaining and loans from the central banks may be unnecessary.

Since the village bank does business with the central bank through the medium of the post-office, no village bank building, no office with counters and wicketed windows and vaults and safes is needed. If you happen about seven in the morning to wander into one of the countless groves of trees that shelter the thousands of villages scattered over the plains of India, you may chance to come upon a meeting of the board of directors of the bank. In the very centre of the village is a big, shady tree, with a little square platform two or three feet high built round the trunk. There sit the elders of the village, each wrapped in a sheet, each with a twig toothbrush in his mouth, talking village politics for an hour or two before dispersing for the work of the day. Possibly a villager who wishes to borrow money paid a visit to the house of the president the night before and obtained a promise that the matter should be further discussed in the morning. If he has gone off now to hunt up a missing director or two, the other remain comfortably on the platform, cross-legged or with feet resting on the ground, chewing betel-nut, perhaps, or smoking and polishing their teeth with the toothbrushes and discussing among other things the character and prospects of applicants for loans. If a man's grandfather has been in jail, or he himself has ever fallen foul of the police, or if his wife has quarrelled with the wife of one of the directors, those facts are take into account.

Though non-members may deposit money in the bank, only persons who live in the village and belong to the cooperative society may borrow. A man who wishes to obtain a loan must bring two sureties and sometimes in addition must put up his land as collateral security. He must borrow for productive purposes and no more than he needs. If he says he wants Rs. 100 for a cow, one of the elders may ask: 'Can't you buy a cow for 75 or 80 rupees? Last month my uncle's cousin bought a cow for 60 rupees.' The board, unlike the moneylender, encourages him to borrow economically, and it would also help him buy the cow, so that the seller cannot cheat him.

A particularly valuable phase of the work of the bank is what it does with the assistance of the YMCA secretary to set the people free from their bondage to the moneylender. In one village where the people were nearly all indebted to local moneylenders, I lent a big sum to pay off this indebtedness. First I sent for the village servant to announce a day for settlement with the Outcastes. So he went about beating his tom-tom to attract attention and then chanting his announcement: 'All who have lent money to So-and-so and So-and-so and So-and-so are invited to meet the YMCA Secretary and the Board of Directors of the Cooperative Bank in the school building after dinner tonight.' Then he would go a little farther on and beat his tom-tom once more and repeat the invitation. When the moneylenders came to the schoolhouse, I said to them something like this: 'Is there any hope of recovering the money lent to these poor Christians? Can they even pay the interest? Here is a fellow who borrowed 100 rupees, which, with the accumulated interest now amounts to 200 rupees. He can never pay more than 10 or 20 rupees. We will pay you a lump sum if you will agree to cancel the debt.' So I might bring the debt down to Rs. 125 or Rs. 150 and settle for that amount. By this method I have saved as much as Rs. 200 to Rs. 300 in one day. Of course the board of directors takes no risks and unless it is sure that with its guidance the debtor will become solvent, it does not attempt to finance him. The cooperative bank is a business corporation, not a charity enterprise.

Many moneylenders, seeing the people slipping out of their clutches, say: 'We will reduce our rate of interest; borrow from us.' But the people reply: 'No, you may reduce your rates, but here we are our own bankers. We prefer to manage our own affairs.' The cooperative banks offer their members further advantages besides lower rates of interest. They encourage part payments and charge interest only on the balance still unpaid. Also they enter every transaction and, unlike the moneylender, give a receipt—and an honest one.

Besides making cheap money accessible, the Rural Department of the YMCA undertakes to teach the people how to use the money wisely; in particular how to secure better crops and a higher return on the seed and labour they invest. Their own time-honoured methods of farming are labourious. Yet the farmer thinks himself a past master of the art of farming and would not believe that a YMCA secretary could teach him anything. What he sees, he believes, however, and here and there, sometimes quite unexpectedly, we are able to make him see. Once, for instance, I had bought a plow as a sample for a village. The people came and looked at it and said: 'We don't want it. We have never used anything like it and we do not wish to take risks. It's so heavy and it costs so much. You say you paid 10 rupees for it, but it's not our custom to pay more than 1 rupee 8 annas.' So they would have none of it, and when the July rains arrived and the plowing season began, every one in the village secured a country plow and went to work. But there was one fellow who could not get a plow anywhere. He did not want to lose time while the ground was wet; so as a last resort he took my plow and prepared his field. His neighbours laughed at him and he joined in heartily. Five months later the real difference began to show. The crop on his field was sorghum. It was six feet high, but similar crops on the neighbouring fields were only four or five feet high. So, arithmetically, we can prove to the eye of the custom-loving villager the superiority of crops grown from government seed and fertilized by scientifically tested manures.

Still, even when the Outcaste farmers are willing to adopt more modern methods of agriculture, they cannot support their families on the yield from one or two acres of land. And if they have no holdings of their own, wages are so low that they cannot live. In either case the hope lies in industry to supplement the income from the land or reduce the supply of farm labour to a point where it begins to have some commercial value. So we make it a point to encourage the cottage crafts already existing and to start others. By introducing the fly-shuttle into the old pit-looms we have made it possible for the sweeper classes, who do weaving, to make a longer cloth in a shorter time. Also we have been teaching the leather-workers how to get leather through the cooperative society and how through it to sell or barter their saddles and buckets and shoes. We take orders and buy leather wholesale when the market is low, and we save our customers the need of crying their finished wares in the streets. When a leather-worker has made a pair of shoes worth a rupee, he may 'deposit' them in the village bank—probably the house of the YMCA secretary, in this case—and receive a certain number of *annas* on account. When the shoes have been sold, the maker is paid in full.

We have also introduced cooperative buying at the weekly central market that forty or fifty villages hold perhaps every Sunday. Carts come from all directions bringing grain, rice, chillies, jaggery, pulse and salt. And the juggler comes with his tricks, and the man with a monkey and a goat, the snake-charmer, the fortuneteller, the sweetmeat-vender, the missionary and the preacher with tracts, the acrobats, cows, pigs, chickens. It is a gala day. The man who has four annas walks ten miles to spend it. In a village of a hundred families everybody goes to market and nobody earns any wages. People dispose of their wares and buy provisions and amuse themselves and are quickly gone, so that by Monday only the cart-tracks are left to prove that all the life and colour of the market existed a few hours before. Market-day gives diversion, it is true, but it is too great a luxury for the very poor. Our men saw economic loss in it. So on Friday the bank secretary asks each family of Outcastes to tell him what it needs from the market. He gives two men their wages in cash to go to market and buy for the whole village. These two men pay cash at wholesale prices for goods of first-rate quality, come back to the village and within three or four hours have distributed all their purchases. On Monday everybody must pay. The idea works and will spread, we hope, through the contact between villages.

The notion of cleanliness is as new and strange in the Outcaste quarters as that of thrift. When we try to explain the effects of impure water and dirt and foul air, the people, forgetting how many have succumbed to disease, say only: 'Sir, we have been living like this for thirty years and are not yet dead. What you say cannot be true.' Their thatched huts with mud walls and floor, a doorway, and, as a rule, no windows, contain a single room about twelve feet by ten. In the rear are earthen pots for grain and drinking-water. The fireplace, where the housewife does her cooking, is also indoors, and the fire-wood and cow-dung cakes used for fuel make a cloud of stifling smoke. The family probably has four or five or six children, and if it is fairly well-to-do for the Outcaste class, it may possess also a buffalo with a calf and half a dozen chickens and a pig or two. And at night the farmer and his wife and the six children and the buffalo and the calf and the pigs and the chickens all crowd into this one room, shut everything up tight to keep out evil spirits and sleep the sleep of innocence, perhaps, but not of common sense. Living conditions so unwholesome force us to be, in season and out of season, officers of the public health.

But even the medical and sanitary aspects of our work are not dissociated from its economic phases. We make the bank keep a small stock of medicine, such as quinine, zinc ointment, mentholatum and castor-oil, in the house of the president. Members in need of medicine can obtain it only by buying a small dose or doses. Otherwise, if it happened to be bitter or nauseous, they would not take it. But a father has a hold on his child when he can say: 'Take it, take it! I have paid half a cent for that!' Also we find that moral suasion and a little tight money work well together. The people come to recognize that a window may be the price of Rs. 10 or Rs. 20 lent, that they must be washed and combed when they ask for financial favours, and above all that they must have maintained their character for sobriety if they expect the bank directors to regard them as good risks.

Drinking seems not abnormal in so hot a country as India, where a man can get for 2 cents, through the legitimate government channels or on the sly, a refreshing draught of toddy made of the fermented juice of the coconut or of the palmyra-palm. Yet in spite of nature and custom, habitual drinkers are excluded from the bank and, if a member is caught drinking, he is punished. In a certain village, one day, a member obtained a loan from the bank with the help of two sureties. Then, overcome by temptation, he spent 10 cents for drink. It was seven in the evening and already dark. But the two sureties saw him at eight. They reported him to the directors, who met at ten in the schoolhouse. The five members were all present. There is never any want of a quorum when a meeting of the bank directors is called for. There were also fifty more persons, men, women and children, from the village; for word had gone abroad and a bank case is interesting. The discussion lasted till four in the morning. The board unanimously decided to fine the man 8 *annas*, and rather than lose his standing he paid the fine, at five in the morning. Sometimes the method of punishment is more drastic. On one occasion a man who had been drinking was tied to a tree, since he had no property and could not be fined, and each of the directors gave him four lashes. Afterwards, in talking to me, he said: 'Sir, I will not drink any more. It is not that I like drinking any less, but I do not like to be tied to a tree.' There are also, to be sure, ideal motives for abstinence. A man who has been converted and has heard the Bible story connected with his new baptismal name is sometimes moved to heroic self-restraint. 'Am I not Daniel?' he asks proudly. 'Have I not come out of the lions' den? And shall I drink?' Or perhaps, through some more inward apprehension of the faith, he may be inspired to a touching steadfastness.

The YMCA secretary, while fighting debt, dirt and drink, is also mindful of the demon of darkness, and so he awaits eagerly the moment when the people in whose village he has started a bank will say: 'Sir, you always keep the accounts. When can we do this for ourselves?' 'What,' the secretary answers, 'can't you trust us?' 'Yes,' they explain, 'but you are not always here. Should we not learn to do it for ourselves?' So the secretary says, 'If you will come to me at the schoolhouse in the evening, I will teach you.' All reply joyously that they will come. They begin to arrive at six. The schoolhouse is lighted by a thin kerosene lamp, worth half a cent, which emits a dim light and plenty of smoke. The pupils, not youths, but men much older, sit on the floor before the light and begin to spell out the words in the primers. Or they sprinkle chalk on the floor and trace letters in it, as if on a blackboard. They are so tired that in fifteen or twenty minutes they loll on the floor and presently fall flat and go to sleep. Yet the government may be able to certify, after the men have studied for a year with whatever recourses, that the secretary has been able help to them, that eighteen out of twenty have been introduced to the elementary principles of the art of reading, and so me fellow of middle age may go running fully about the village, shouting 'I am the best in the class, I am the best, the inspector says so!'

But of course the night school provides only the bare, primary techniques of reading and writing and figuring, but while furnishing ideas to an illiterate population it cannot compete with agencies as the lantern-lecture and the gramophone. Over these books the people do not fall asleep but when they see the YMCA picture-telling equipment, they lose no time in advertising the fact in both their own area and the country round about. one can be pretty sure to have an audience of about five hundred to seven hundred.

During the war, when the price of carbide was going up, I thought that I would test my idea of the possible danger of helping those to whom one brings benefits without asking anything in return. The cost of a carbide tin was only 80 cents. So I asked the forty or fifty families in a certain village to subscribe a cent each one for the carbide that would provide enough acetylene gas to give them entertainment of two hours or so. But they said: 'Sir, why do you ask us to pay?' I decided then, not to give a lecture that night. I dismissed the crowd and went to bed. Around twelve o'clock I was waked by a sudden commotion and a murmuring. Some fellow came up and called, out to me: 'get up, sir, get up; here is the money'. By half past twelve I started the machine and till half past two lectured to an assembly much larger than the one I had seen earlier. This time there was a louder commotion. The people said: 'Sir, we have got the money. How is it that you close such a sale?' But I had gained my point, and the people know they must pay for their own use.

In another very important way it began to foster the growth of ideas and visions that the people can themselves help to achieve. Once a year, after the harvest which comes between January and the end of April, and before the torrid summer, when men work no more, but wait until the rains begin in July, we get together a number of cooperative societies for a three days' conference. We sit under the trees, sleep and eat and have meetings there. The people bring their own food and put a group of men in charge of the catering department. We make reports on the progress made by the present societies during the preceding year. Sometimes a local doctor lectures on sanitation or a government agriculturist gives practical talks on farming. There is a good deal of competition for small prizes: for boys and men, empty bottles and tin cans, collected from the cities and much thought of in the villages; for girls and women, needles, thread and soap, combs and baby frocks. There are eager contests in weaving. We give a prize, a loom, perhaps, to the man who weaves most in a half-hour's time. We reward also the society that has made the best showing in cooperative work. As a prize we gave to one society a tin of kerosene and to another a Bible, with large type.

The different villages provide social diversion. At times there is a dramatic performance by the men of a village. There is music. Especially there is the *kolatam*, a musical folk-dance of the utmost grace and charm, in which villages often compete. The words sung to the melodies are songs from the ancient epics or the effusions of local poets or topical skits on village politics. So, sometimes, taking this cue in regard to matters of local interest, we compose songs embodying the cooperative rules, and the people learn them by singing them as they dance. Also to our delight, there are sports, such as running, jumping and three-legged races. Strange as it may seem, it has not been easy for us to carry out the physical part of the

YMCA programme, which is so popular in the West. I recall an evening when I was playing with the boys and the whole village came out of curiosity to see what we were doing. There was a look of displeasure on the faces of the *panchayet*. They were afraid that the boys would not respect them if I took away the feeling of awe with which they regarded an elder. Suddenly I heard one member of the board call out, 'Sir!' and I thought our game must come to an end. But when I stopped and asked what the trouble was, he scratched his head and asked, 'Sir, may I play with you?' Then the rest wanted to join in. Similarly other communities have been brought round to feeling that the secretary can be trusted, and in his absence they have done what they could to develop sports, especially for the conference.

Often, in the midst of this gay interlude in the monotonous lives of the crowds that flock to us from the country round about, I think how rural Jesus was and how well his Gospel of more abundant life answers to the need of these villagers. It is, of course, the specific function of the missions, not mine, nor that of the Rural Department of the YMCA, to look after the spiritual welfare of the village Christians. Yet we believe that we, too, are serving the cause of 'pure religion and undefiled'. And I am sure that, for secretaries and people alike, to work is to pray. I am inclined to feel, indeed, that a man capable of answering the countless questions put to him by the village elders before they lend him Rs. 10 has the spirit of thrift and self-help and cooperation that is seemly in a Christian, and for this reason, when I am asked about our church, I sometimes name, not irreverently, the cooperative bank.

CHAPTER 14

Medieval and Modern Hinduism

Ananda Coomaraswamy and *Stella Bloch*

IN THE FOLLOWING PAGES WE PROPOSE to give some account of the religion of India, mainly from the twelfth century to the present day, only neglecting the quite modern developments such as the Arya Samaj and Brahmo Samaj. If, for the sake of convenience, we discuss the matter under various headings, this method must be held to imply, not the existence of mutually exclusive tenets, but only the varied content of sectarian formulation.

As background to the theistic faiths to be described must be understood, on the popular side, all that body of beliefs and customs which is generally spoken of as folklore and includes aboriginal (pre-Aryan) elements, and on the other, the whole body of inherited tradition constituting the higher culture. Under the latter heading must be mentioned the survivals of Vedic ritual in ancestor-worship and domestic and personal ceremonies (birth, initiation, marriage, death and offerings to the dead) requiring the services of a Brahman priest, but not connected with temple worship; the fundamental philosophy of the Upanishads (salvation is attained with realization of the identity of the innermost self or soul with the Absolute Brahman); the formulation of this philosophy as the Vedanta, in the unqualified monism of Sankaracharya and the qualified monism of Rāmanuja; the doctrines of

***ASIA*, March 1923. Ananda Coomaraswamy (1877–1947) was author of many books on Oriental literature and art. His wife Stella Bloch was the author of *Dancing and Drama East and West*.

karma and *samsara* (the universe is a ceaseless becoming, determined by causal necessity); the monastic systems of Buddhism, Jainism and Hinduism; the submergence of Buddhism, both the primitive and the later, in India proper, the decline of Jainism and the substitution of theistic faiths for both Buddhism and Jainism; the general knowledge and influence of the two great epics (*Ramayana* and *Mahabharata*) with their developed mythology and clear statement of ideal social order; the universal acceptance of the *Bhagavad Gita,* in which the Upanishad doctrines, combined with the path of devotion to a personal deity and of spiritual progress through selfless fulfilment of vocation are first and fully set forth; and most important of all, for our present purpose, the rise of the ways and doctrines of *bhakti* (loving devotion to personal deities) and consequent development of Hindu theology and the connected cults of images and temple service; finally, the influence of Islam, after the twelfth century.

Thus the religion of late medieval and modern India is essentially a multifarious theism, overlying on the one hand the primitive beliefs of aboriginal tribes and connected on the other hand with a pure and profound philosophy. Accordingly, the deity is constantly described as possessing all the finite powers, qualities and activities imagined by human love or fear, and at the same time unconditioned and immanent, only indeed to be found in the worshipper's own innermost nature. Philosophy and worship are not divided; worship is recognized to be a necessary and inevitable, and therefore convenient and proper, qualification of ultimate truth as apprehended by finite consciousness. The worshipper knows well that the god whom he worships is not outside himself; and yet in spite of himself he must passionately love some for concept of god, even while, like Sankaracharya, he prays for forgiveness for the threefold error of having ventured to visualize in contemplation the form of One who is formless, of having by hymns and psalms praised One who is beyond all speech, and of seeming to limit His presence by visiting sacred shrines.

Let us then first take into consideration the nature of personal worship and the use of images, since these images and the temples built for them are to a majority of foreigners the most conspicuous features of Hindu religious practice. Worship implies an object of worship: the Absolute Brahman cannot be regarded objectively. Hence the Supreme is to be approached under some disguise or aspect. The forms of deities and of their images are determined by the relation which subsists between the worshipper and the adored divinity. That is, he is worshipped by the individual or group in the form best suited to their understanding and necessities; he takes the forms that are imagined by his worshippers. He (or she) is nevertheless ultimately One, and thus the Hindu god is never jealous of other gods, for as Sri Krishna says, 'They also who worship other gods and make offerings unto them with faith do verily make offering to me.' Hinduism is not in the Western sense a missionary religion. 'Let every man,' says *The Wishing-tree of Devotion,* 'so far as in him lieth, help the reading of the Scriptures, whether those of his own church or those of another.' Nor, on the other hand, are the Hindus likely to be converted to Christianity; for, as the Abbe Dubois confessed, 'To make a new race of the Hindus, one would have to begin by undermining the very foundations of their civilization, religion and polity.'

The essentials of the office of personal worship consist in the realization of a mental image of the deity, in accordance with a text describing his form and attributes, and the making of real or imaginary offerings (flowers, incense, water, etc.) to the image. A material image, constructed by an imager, according to the same canons, is employed in the same way, not as an end in itself, but as a means (*sadhana*) of approach to, and identification with, the deity. An image is prepared for worship by a ceremony of invitation and may be subsequently secularized by another formula—some images, indeed, are regularly made of impermanent materials and destroyed after use. There are even temples in which the principal shrine is empty, and the immediate object of worship is an 'ether image'. Material images are classed as immovable, placed in the main shrines of temples; movable, used in processions and festivals; and those used in personal worship or private chapels. The representations of the deity forming part of the external sculptural decoration of a temple illustrate his varied forms and activities, but are not the object of a daily office.

It will be seen that Indian religious figures—however we may have considered them as beautiful or otherwise—were neither designed nor used as 'works of art'; they are useful objects made by craftsmen in response to a command or demand for the clear and repeated presentation of a given form with a known significance. Precisely as in European Christian art: 'The artistic representation of sacred subjects was a science governed by fixed laws which could not be broken at the dictates of individual imagination,' and 'Through the medium of art the highest conceptions of theologian and scholar penetrated to some extent the minds of even the humblest of the people' (E. Mâle, *Religious Art of the Thirteenth Century in Europe*). There is nothing vague or mysterious in Indian religion, whether expressed in verbal or in visual imagery; for the whole *raison d'être* of religion is to express ideas in comprehensible and easily apprehended forms. From the Indian point of view, both religions and art are forms of statement and thus are nearer to modern science than to modern art.

Around the service of the image has grown up the whole system of temples, priests and temple servants. Most of the great temples are supported by endowments. The temple, as in medieval Christianity, is the house of the deity and not, as in Protestant practice, a shelter for a congregation. The individual worshipper visits and honours the deity in his temple, as the medieval Christian visited the shrines of saints. The temple priest is not a preacher or teacher (*swami* or *guru*) but a caretaker and servant of the shrine, and his position is not at all highly respected. Closely connected with temples and sacred sites (very often sacred rivers or mountains) is the system of pilgrimage, which may involve long journeys extended from the furthest north to the extreme south of India or from East to West; before the days of railways and still to a large degree, the *Wanderjahre* spent in pilgrimage, and sometimes undertaken by whole families together, have a very high educational and cultural value. A common form of charity consisted in the erection of buildings designed to shelter wandering pilgrims and other travellers, and in many cases the caretaker of such rest-houses was bound to supply free food and water to all comers, who carried, of course their own bedding and cooking-utensils.

The great powers worshipped in medieval and modern Hinduism are Siva, Vishnu and the Goddess Devi, in innumerable forms and called by innumerable names. As we have already implied, either of these to his worshipper is Isvara the Supreme Overlord, but every form is in the last analysis the manifestation of one and the same undivided energy. The forms of Indian theism being fully developed long before the twelfth century, we shall only deal with the late developments here.

A great Vaishnava devotional movement originated in India about the eleventh century, when the psalms of the Twelve Alvars were grouped together by Sri Nathamuni in the *Nalayira Prabandham.* Ramanuja at the same time put forward his interpretation of the Upanishads in a metaphysical system in which love is identified with the earlier concept of knowledge, the world is interpreted as a theophany rather than as a mere mirage, and the name of the Supreme Being is Narayana. The doctrine of *avatars,* or incarnate manifestations, characteristic of the Vaishnava systems, though not exclusive to them; ten such avatars or descents of Vishnu are usually recognized, by far the most important, from our point of view being those of Rama and Krishna. The story of Rama already presented in the Sanskrit *Ramayana;* but now the cult was more fully and definitely developed by Ramananda in the fourteenth century and by his pupil Kabir, a revolutionary and unsectarian mystic, brought up as a Mohommedan weaver, and almost as much a Sufi as a Hindu. In contrast to the sectarian form of other Vaishnava poets, his mysticism is indeterminate and universal: 'The sea and its waves are one surf—where is the difference between the sea and its waves— . . . because it has been termed a wave, shall it no longer be known as water?' In other words, does the nature of man partake any less of the nature of God because he is known to us as man? 'All the men and women of the world are his living forms.' 'More than all else do I cherish at heart that love which makes me to live a limitless life in this world.' The third great exponent of the cult of Rama is the poet Tulsi Das (1532–1623), whose vernacular version of the *Ramayana* has been rightly called the Bible of Hindustan; this is a more objective faith, laying greater stress on conduct. Many other writers made Bengali versions of the *Ramayana.*

Meanwhile Nimbarka, in the twelfth century, had put forward a system similar to Ramanuja's, but particularizing the love of God in the adoration of Krishna and Radha. The story of Krishna and the symbolism of his relations with the milkmaids of Brindaban, and particularly with Radha, are the dominant motifs of late medieval Hindu poetry, painting, music and dance in northern India, and must have, for the world at large, a greater significance and a deeper charm than any other form of sectarian Hinduism. Krishna, the incarnation of Vishnu, is brought up as a herdsman on a farm in Brindaban; beloved of all men alike, he beguiles the hearts of the milkmaids by the magical notes of his flute, so that they forget all else, and are ready to abandon their whole world, their social duties and their honour to follow him. He dances with them on moonlight nights on grassy lawns beside the Jumna; he takes their all as the price of the ferry (the 'further shore' is an ancient symbol of salvation); and only in return for the uttermost self-surrender he gives himself. This is not the relation of a historical event, say the Vaishnava writers, but an image of the relations existing, in an inner kingdom, between the Lord and the hearts of his adorers, Krishna is not a man laying down a standard of conduct to be followed by men; he is God made manifest as Love. It is characteristic of Indian experience that all the circumstances and vicissitudes of human love are recognized as natural images of this inner life. The modern *nautch* (dance), in which the technique of the Indian drama survives, is mainly concerned with the Krishna cycle, and like all other arts it is regarded as a means of attaining spiritual freedom. By setting forth the mutual relations of hero and heroine, in their esoteric meaning, and by clearly expressing the 'flavour' (a technical term of esthetic, equivalent to 'beauty'), it gives to men an understanding of life, and through that understanding come the virtues of peace and patience and the bliss of Brahma. Indian dance and music, learned in form and passionate in content, to Indian spectators are means, not of excitement or of mere *divertissement,* but of tranquillity; in Indian life it was not necessary to persuade the masses to a hard-won appreciation of the arts, because all the arts were only concerned with the essential realities of life. The practice of the arts was understood (like any other vocation) as a kind of *yoga,* the real appreciation of art as perfect experience—but an art for art's sake would have seemed as lacking in justification or value as to drink for the sake of drinking.

The great developments in Saiva theology after the classical period are found in the Saiva Siddhanta system of southern India. The Scriptures of this devotional system include the *Tevaram* (psalms of the four great Tamil hymnists), the *Tiruvachakam* of Manikka Vachakar, the mystical works of Meikanda Deva and his followers, in all, mainly from the seventh to the fourteenth century, but still a living literature. The devotional songs are to be heard every day in the great southern temples, and in the streets of the southern cathedral cities—such as Madura or Tanjore—where the life of a great capital has centred for centuries around ancient shrines, whose enclosures and towering gateways dominate the city visually as the ancient and living faith informs its life.

Siva is represented iconographically, 'non-manifest', by the *lingam,* usually established in the main shrine of a temple, and by a great variety of manifested forms, both gracious and terrible. Of all these forms, the best known and perhaps the most significant is that of Nataraja ('Lord of the Dance'), representing the cosmic activity of the deity—more particularly, the Five Activities, or Powers, of Creation, Maintenance, Destruction and the Embodiment and Release of Souls: 'Our Lord is the Dancer, who like the heat latent in firewood, diffuses his power in mind and matter and makes them dance in their turn.' The worship of the deity in this form is only truly accomplished when the cosmic dance is realized as taking place within the consciousness of the devotee himself, in accordance with the Sanskrit text, *'Devam bhutva, devam yajet'*—'Only by becoming the god, may he worship the god.' It will be seen that the two ikons, the 'non-manifest' lingam and the manifested Nataraja, represent concepts comparable with Ruysbroeck's divine theology, in which the nature of God is described as at once Eternal Rest and Eternal Work.

Associated with the Lord is his consort, 'Energy' or 'Power', known variously as Devi, Sakti, Uma, Parvati, etc. These male and female principles are often represented iconographically side by side, or the Sakti may be conceived as part of the god's form. In the same way every Hindu deity has a feminine counterpart or active power; Vishnu, for example, being associated with Lakshmi, Krishna with Radha and so on. But inasmuch as the Devi (goddess) who assumes these forms is worshiped as the Great Mother, the Supreme Power, in other words, as God, by the large class of Hindus known as Saktas, we shall refer to her cult in general rather than in specific terms.

As Supreme Brahman, the Devi is beyond all form and quality; as Mother of the Universe she has Supreme, Subtle and Material forms, in the latter of which she becomes the object of contemplation and worship. She has indeed both male and female forms, but is chiefly contemplated in the latter. In her are glorified all the power and beauty of women. She is everywhere revealed in Nature; and he who worships natural forms otherwise than as manifestations of herself, is compared to a man having in his hands a bright lamp and nevertheless falling into a fearsome pit. In no other religious system is the feminine principle exalted to such transcendent heights. If it be remembered that the gods are everywhere created in the forms of human imagination and according to human experience, it will be obvious that here, in the theology and worship of Devi, lies the answer to the uninformed criticism of the status of women in Hinduism, so prevalent in the West.

The cult of the Goddess is particularly developed in the system of metaphysics and ritual known as the Tantra, the purpose of which is to secure the emancipation of the devotee by arousing in him a consciousness of the Devi present in him in subtle form. The Tantra does not exclude, but embrace other sectarian forms of Hinduism. It is called a fifth Veda; it is a fulfilment of the Vedas. Inasmuch as the times have changed (we live now in the last and worst of the Four Ages of decreasing Righteousness), and the following of Vedic tradition is no longer possible and should not be attempted by those not qualified thereto (as none now are), the Tantra is Hindu religion in terms adapted to our age and experience to present conditions. It is not restricted to twice-born castes, but is open to all men and to women; there are Tantric forms of communion in which all caste distinctions, from the highest to the lowest, are temporarily abolished. Women may not only receive the Tantric initiation, but, inasmuch as the Devi is the supreme guru, may themselves initiate.

The guru is a religious teacher and guide, to whose direction orthodox Hindus of all sects commit themselves. A very special relation exists between the guru and the disciple until such time as the latter attains to full enlightenment. The guru, in Indian life, is honoured more implicitly than any other being, of whatever sex, rank or caste—but with this greatness goes a great responsibility, for the sins of the disciple are held to recoil upon the guru. The same relation of teacher and disciple, in only a slightly less intense form, exists as an essential factor in Indian education, where the teacher teaches only those whom he considers qualified to receive instruction.

The means by which this elaborate religious scheme becomes translatable into a foreign mode of thought is its social science (all the arts come under this heading in India). Ancestor-worship, in theory an inexplicable religious peculiarity becomes in practice the inevitable vehicle of law and order. The ceremonies to dead ancestors and to future descendants imply a responsibility and constancy in every man toward his vocation, as the son of honourable predecessors, as the true inheritor and upholder of his father's honour, and moreover as the heir to his father's tools and handicraft. So is order established and the means for its preservation contained within itself.

A man's position in the state is ordained before birth—before birth his duty awaits him and he is thus welcomed into a world prepared for all his needs. Long before the known existence of images this conception of order reigned and the first father of an ordered family was the progenitor of every atom in the large world of Hindu civilization. For the first principle of fatherhood is the bequeathing of the worldly position and goods, spiritual knowledge and character of a father to his son, thereby ordaining that every son take up the thread of his father's life, nor let it drop to oblivion.

From the establishment of family grew the distinctions that eventually became a system—the fixing of caste. It was not till the full development of the Hindu pantheon and the establishment of image-worship that the caste-system reached its zenith, at which time Hindu society branched forth into infinite intricacy. The utterance in defined terms of the epic, up to then a huge literature of legends, is the opening out of the flower of this great civilization. The epic is the fountain of life—from it each caste learns its duties, from it each craftsman learns the laws of his vocation, the laws of spiritual approach to his task and every step of execution.

The caste-system prescribes four main types: the Brahmans, who are spiritually powerful, the Kshatriyas, kings and warriors, the Vaisyas, or landowners and agriculturists, and the Sudras, who are servants. The three upper castes are called twice-born, initiation into the Vedas in early manhood being the second and significant birth in this life—the spiritual birth which renders a man responsible in all human relations. This second birth or initiation into the sacred law is inaccessible to Sudras, foreigners and women.

Women have no separate power but acquire a position in this life and the next through father or husband. A dutiful and virtuous wife is promised a union with her husband in heaven. Her virtue may even determine the salvation of her husband. Though she be a Brahmini (a daughter of the highest caste) her quality and station are indeterminate or negative till she has joined her lord; in proportion as she is a devoted and virtuous wife does she assert her quality. The perfect fulfilment of her vocation obtains for the courtesan, likewise, a life in heaven and an auspicious rebirth on earth. Women are not considered independent individuals capable of winning complete emancipation (*nirvana*) alone. But they are ever revered above all men in motherhood.

Simultaneous with the fixing of caste arise the laws that govern food and the preparation of viands. Again what might on first sight be a peculiar fastidiousness proves itself to be an essential substance of Hindu tradition. The original conception of food laws arose out of a profound instinct for sanitation, equivalent to, or better, a branch of, nature-worship—the religious organization of man's relation with nature or agriculture. The instinct toward purity here manifest is the obvious physical vehicle for the spiritual and religious content. The barbarian, the lowest servants (Sudras) and strangers are eternally barred from the table of a Hindu and the precincts of food are as guarded as the holiest shrine. The laws regarding food, though set forth in severely religious formulae, are a form of science governing health and economics.

It is the law that a man take to wife a woman of his own caste, that his children may be of pure blood and thereby most suited to their caste and vocation. The sons of a merchant become merchants in turn and the daughters are educated by their mother's precedent. Women who are lawful wives beget daughters destined to marry; courtesans, always learned and talented, bequeath to their daughters the arts in which they are skilled, besides the art of love. This rule of inherited vocation is founded on the scientific observation that the offspring is utterly true to its parentage; and all change of pattern is wrought by time and circumstances, not by human reform, rebellion or deliberately organized innovations. Conditions change and complicate with those contingencies of caste mixture which automatically occur, breaking the original law into many subdivisions, to be regarded not as concessions but as new verses conforming to one measure.

The *Bhagavad Gita* says, 'Better one's own duty, though devoid of merit, than the duty of another well discharged.' And this is the underlying theme of the whole Hindu social and religious structure. To the prince the duties of princehood are the one path of life; to the warrior the duties of his caste and vocation. The activities not ordained by caste and vocation are, however excellently performed, the gravest of sins and severely punishable by the state. In this way human conduct becomes a mode of ritual wherein no activity or thought is undefined or arbitrary and wherein every gesture against the prescribed order and harmony is regarded as a superhuman evil, not a sin against men but a transgression against the universal order of things. The active performance of duty on earth becomes the conception of salvation (except in the cases of the ascetic and the *suttee,* both choosing to leave the world for a direct and personal experience of divinity in severest solitude). So closely is duty woven into the texture of Hindu life that every man feels and thinks only in the language destined for him: no envy for the Brahman's supremacy disturbs the prince; and in turn the Brahman does not long for the magnificence that attends a leader of men. Likewise the craftsmen are suited to, and suited by, their work. All castes and vocations are regarded equally, one as important as another to the architecture of the state. That the master commands and the servant obeys are ordinances of a divine intention and therefore do servants obey and masters command without loss or gain of dignity—both acting in reverence to One Law. The living of such a life is the fulfilling of universal law and of individual type. Fulfilment in this sense is the only perfection possible in this world or any other.

CHAPTER 15

'Jadu', White and Black

Glimpses, by Way of Folklore, into the Mind and Soul of India

L. Adams Beck

IT IS THE TRUTH THAT, IF YOU WOULD know a country, you must know something of her religion and something of her literature; for the first is her soul and the second her mind, and if you know something of these two and know them sympathetically, you will not be far from that inner spirit which is a compound of both and makes the nation a living entity. Sympathy is knowledge. A greater truth was never uttered than in Wordsworth's lines:

And you must love him, ere to you
He will seem worthy of your love.

You may live in India for half a lifetime, you may 'speak with the tongues of men and of angels,' but unless you have sympathy, it profits you nothing. What follows is an attempt to record some gleanings from Kashmir and other parts of India, from people who told gladly because they knew they were gladly heard.

**ASIA*, February 1924. L. Adams Beck (1862-1931) was a prolific writer, an expert on Asia and the Buddhist Studies. Author of several books including *The Splendour of Asia* and *Way of Power, Studies in the Occult*.

There are few delights the world has to offer like camping in Kashmir. The houseboat life on the river Jhelum, where, whenever you are satiated with one loveliness, willing hands tow you to another, is so wondrous that the brain at last refuses to be further astonished, though the heart still outstretches its eager palms. The beauty of the 'Happy Valley', with the snowy rampart guarding its serene perfection, is world-famous; yet no poetry, no brush can convey the faintest impression of the real thing as it breaks upon the sight. But the 'Happy Valley' is not the place for folklore. The city is too near—Srinagar, 'City of the Sun,' which, like all towns, is an enemy to shy and secret hauntings. It is when the train of ponies is loaded with the camp-equipment, and, patriarchally riding at the head of your cavalcade, like all the explorers of the gorgeous past, you set forth to the camping up the Himalaya or the Pir Panjal—it is then you may hope to glean strange stories from the lips of Salama or Ahmed Khan as you do the day's march or sit after it by the camp-fire among the pines. Very wonderful are the campfires with their heaped logs and pine cones! In a moment the beautiful, wavering flames leap up and send their radiance over all the ghostly forest that sighs and whispers about you. It is the time for the opening of hearts, both Moslem and Hindu; for in Kashmir two faiths share the throne. I have not found the one less given to the supernatural than the other, though logically one might expect a harder realism from the Moslem.

We were camping up a river in Kashmir. One glorious morning, while I was fishing with Pir Bakhsh for snow-trout, we saw a snake curving swiftly away. I looked at the evil grace of its flight. Snakes are said not to be deadly in these heights, but I have my doubts!

I said I hoped we should have no trouble with them in the tents.

Pir Bakhsh answered unconcernedly: 'Presence, no! No snake coming in tent.'

I asked why.

He hesitated. 'Snake's governor not allow him going in tent, *Huzoor.*'

I begged to hear more—to know who this governor was.

'Huzoor, am a poor man. How should know? It is very great snake. The snake-people are obedient. The Presence need not fear.'

'But,' I said, 'a memsahib found one yesterday near her tent.'

'Presence, near, it may be, but not within! Unless the snake be touched. If touched, the snake-people will enter. They will creep even into the beds. It is an order.'

Then I reflected. It was true. I had not heard of any snake within a tent here—no doubt mere chance. But the interest is that this man's belief was a survival from the old snake-worship of Kashmir. The divine Nagas were a mighty race in days gone by. Their women were fairer than human but always had a sinister strain in their beauty—snake's blood under the satin skin! The men were kings and warriors, strong men of their hands. The

Naga kings were not, however, devils. They took their due share in reverencing the Buddha when he was made manifest on earth, and in the Ellora caves and at Ajanta they and their queens do obeisance before Vishnu and Siva. And there are great survivals of their worship in Kashmir. Nearly all the temples either stand in water or have a water-court within, with cells for devotees ranged about it. For the Naga kings and queens loved water—the crowned snake-heads never curved themselves so placidly as when mirrored in still water.

There was a temple on the rocks opposite our camp, with the Lidar River singing between on its way to join the Jhelum—a broken but lovely little temple with beautiful carved pillars, broken also. It was too small to have a water-court, but at the entrance a clear spring sent up its silver bubbles against the ruined steps where the ferns grew long and green—a pure, deep pool, gray with calm and clearness. That little temple was a haunt of snake-worship of the sort that is typical in other parts of India also.

Even in the glorious temple of Martand there is the space for a huge water-court with its cells about it, where the devotees, lost in meditation, could look into the unwavering calm of the water and submerge their souls in peace. Much might be written of water in Indian theology and legend. But the Naga gods have fallen, though Kashmir is still a land of singing or dreaming waters, and the great serpent lake—Shisha Nag—still shines, a frozen jewel in the heights of the mountains.

The next bit of folklore I gleaned from a family of Hindus. A native child in one of the *doongas*—the boats of the servants, which follow the houseboats—was very ill. It was a wasting disease, and the little creature was a piteous spectacle, a tiny framework of bone and olive skin. A memsahib was implored to help and did what she could with harmless remedies and foods and failed. A European doctor-sahib was called in at her instance, and still the child faded. Finally a native doctor, if that be not too dignified a name, was sought, and he acted with the utmost resource. He painted a black bird behind each of the child's ears, and it immediately recovered.

Was this faith-healing? But no—the child was too young for cooperation. What interested me was that this bird was the divine Garuda—the famous vehicle of Vishnu. And Vishnu is worshipped as the preserver in the Hindu trinity. What wonder that the bird should heal?

It is useless to ask Europeans about these things. They live in the heart of fairy-land, but few indeed of them know it or trouble their heads about it. I have met many who left India in blissful ignorance as to whether Siva is a god or a goddess and care nothing one way or the other. May the Blue-throated God have mercy upon their rebirths!

A few weeks after, we were camping high up the Himalaya by a little green island embraced by the river, rippling very sweetly over a pebbly bed. We called it Minnehaha there—'Laughing Water,' and the name might have been made for its delicate beauty. A half mile above, this very river falls in a tormented cascade, crashing and shattering itself into dust and spray among the huge boulders. Here the pine forests were dense about us—the friars of the solitude, whispering their eternal mystery; but all the talk by our camp-fire was not of beauty but of bears! 'Does the Presence know,' I was asked, 'that true story of why the bears sleep in winter?' The reason is very simple, but it is safer to know it.

It appears that the bears in the mountains are a very wise people. In every country they are that. 'The Old Man in the Cloak,' 'The Dog of the Gods' are known in Scandinavia as well as in India. These bears are cunning in herb-lore, and, as the cruel winter approaches, they seek for certain herbs known only to the bear-people, and, eating of these drowsy leaves, they sleep until the exquisite spring breaks with her wave of flowers upon the mountains. Once a hunter, tramping through the empty pine forests, came upon a sleeping bear with its hoard beside it, prepared for the long dream. He knew of these sleepy herbs, though he had never seen them, and he ate and slept. But Baloo had slept for only half the winter and was sore and angry at being compelled to sit up and stare at the snow and the hurtling of the auroral lights while all the other bears were sleeping, especially since he knew that many of the mountain people would rob the hoards to escape the winter. Winter is terrible in the mountains, with the hunting packs of wolves in the moonless nights and the bone-piercing cold and the bitter scarcity. So, being wise as a man and wiser, this bear in the next summer gathered poisonous sleep-herbs and laid them in his store, and when the hunter, awaking, invited others to join him in this new discovery, they ate the herbs and slept a sleep that even the glad onset of the spring could not break. And since then, though it is not uncommon for men to find the store of the bears in the autumn woods, they touch it no more.

This story was unquestioningly accepted as true. Indeed, faith in the nature knowledge of animals is universal in the mountains and in no way surprising: these pine forests, climbing steadfastly upward and dumb with snow, would force strange convictions. The beliefs of roaring western cities and of the Himalaya must needs be different, though, if the surface of things-as-they-are cracked and let the cities through, we should find that the Himalayan beliefs are not, perhaps, so nearly extinct as we fancied. There is a good deal of primitive man in us all when the right call is heard.

We passed, just after this, a small, deep pool, in which I found repulsive leeches waiting for a prey. They could be dangerous. A man half dazed with *bhang* slept not a great while ago by a damp, mossy cave, and the leeches crawled out and sucked his blood. In the morning he was like a waxen image—cold, bloodless, dead. Here is the foundation for a Naga story! One sees it growing.

We had gone higher still when I gleaned my next folk-story—one passionately and steadfastly believed in the wilds. We had crossed the great

Himalayan pass, the Zoji-la, and were in the country that is called Little Tibet. The pass is only between eleven and twelve thousand feet high and is therefore a very welcome gateway in the iron ramp of mountains dividing Kashmir proper from the higher country that runs up to Yarkand and the Roof of the World. All the grace and beauty of Kashmir are left behind at the foot of the Zoji-la, and you are in a high, bare land with arid plains and cold, gray rivers running through beds of stones and boulders. Yet not without a desolate fascination of its own! By this way the trains of yaks and *dsos* come down to Kashmir, bearing Tibetan bricks of tea and woven *namdas,* or saddle-cloths, and carpets and much strange merchandise from near the highest heights of the world.

The mountains have an ambushed look, gloomy and dangerous, and it seemed an adventure, riding, riding in the mist and lashing wind through ways as stony and lost as the Valley of Humiliation in *The Pilgrim's Progress.* Rounding one of the spurs, we came to rose-coloured rocks—a kind of crimson porphyry. I felt that the drops falling from it should be blood. It had weathered into bright purple, in places overgrown with the close-fitting scales of a little golden lichen. I never saw stone so beautiful nor so strange. But the mountains of this high world are of amazing colours as they take the light. I have seen them of a burning copper, of a wild, sunset red, of a crocus yellow, of a lapis lazuli blue. Witches' work! There is no kindly rain to soften them; for the great range intercepts the monsoon that gives Kashmir its softer beauty, and the sculptors of this land have been the frost and ice giants and the ax of the biting gales.

We came to a little hamlet lost among the mountains, and there I saw a wild peak overshadowing the way, so pinnacled, so weird in its sculpturing that I felt instinctively I should hear something of it before we went farther. And I did.

Many, many centuries ago, I was told, a Maharaja came up from India, travelling in peace, but with a royal retinue, to visit the King of Yarkand. He stopped and looked at this mountain, and its wonder drew him like the Rock of Magnets in *The Arabian Nights' Entertainments.* He said he would climb it with some of his bravest men and see the supernatural fortresses in the clouds. The few poor people implored him to think better. It was sacred to terrible Gods, they said. It would be an impiety to violate those awful heights. But he was young and presumptuous and would not hear. And as he climbed up the sheer sides with his men, a great mist gathered them up and they were seen no more; for they were all changed into gray stone and stand looking down the wild precipices to this day. I saw them—pinnacled figures like the watching statues of a Gothic porch in Chartres or Exeter.

But every Saturday at midnight the few poor Mongols below bear the rattle of the drums, and gong beaten and the cries of men and bustle of preparation for then the Maharaja wakes from his stony sleep and says,

LOOKING UPON THE JEWELLED PRETTINESS OF KASHMIR WOMEN IN THEIR BRIGHT-COLOURED TUNICS AND TROUSERS, ONE REMEMBERS THAT THE LEGENDARY INHABITANTS OF THE KASHMIR VALES WERE THE NAGAS, A SNAKE-PEOPLE, WHOSE WOMEN WERE FAIRER THAN HUMAN

'Tomorrow I will go to Yarkand', and the men half dreaming still, bestir themselves for the road. But when the earliest, coldest sunbeam touches them, they all dream into sleep again and the snow is white upon them. Yet it is known that the time will come when the Gods will have pity upon their long death, and the life will flow through their stony veins, and the sun will warm them, and they will stumble down the mountain and go bewildered to Yarkand; for they do not know that time has fallen away like

THERE ARE BEAUTIFUL WALKS AMONG THE PINE FORESTS ABOUT GULMARG—'MEADOW OF FLOWERS'. SUCH MAGIC OF PLACE AFFECTS HUMAN THOUGHT. THE WEST IS THE INHERITOR OF THE GREAT RELIGIONS AND FAIRY-TALES THAT MATURED IN THE UPLIFTED PLAINS OF INDIA, AND, IF THE SURFACE OF THINGS-AS-THEY-ARE CRACKED IN OUR ROARING WESTERN CITIES, THE HIMALAYAN BELIEFS MIGHT PROVE TO BE NOT WHOLLY EXTINCT

the sand in an hour-glass and that the King who should have welcomed them is dust. But they will find little else changed in Yarkand; for it is very far in the great distance.

The men who told me this had often heard the roar of the drums in the dark. It is so terrible to hear that your heart turns to water within you, and you shout and say a prayer for the poor souls lost in the heights. People would go up if they could, but it is impossible, for at a certain altitude fierce snow-blasts and mists swoop down upon you and icy torrents sweep you back. So the moment of release must wait the time of the Gods. Very near are the Gods in India!

I have seen two divine sages in the form of white eagles at Tirukalikundram in southern India. Their sin also, was presumption. But being pitifully enchained to bird-form, they come asking for food at the hands of men, and it never fails them. Always before noon they come, beating the air with strong wings—some say, from far-off Burma. I sat with the crowd and saw them take their portion and then fly away to rest at holy Benares and do penance there, before returning to Burma and thence again seeking their food at Tirukalikundram. It was believed; and a young Brahman with a delicate, haughty, dark face was good enough to write out for me the miracles that I might hope to see if I stayed at this most favoured and holy place.

THERE ARE FEW DELIGHTS IN THE WORLD EQUAL TO LIFE ON THE JHELUM RIVER, FOR THE EUROPEAN IN A LUXURIOUS HOUSEBOAT OR FOR HIS KASHMIRI SERVANTS IN THE HUMBLEST OF 'DOONGAS'— MERE DECKED-IN PUNTS, TOPPED BY SHACKS WITH ROOFS OF REED MATTING

It is hard in India to draw the line between folklore and religion. It is at best very misty. The malefic powers seem to be stronger than the benignant, as is the case with most of the earlier faiths. A small instance or two must suffice.

We were sitting in the uplands, on some rocks covered with the glorious plants of the wild peony. These are lovely even when the flowers are gone and only the carved leaves remain and the massive seed vessels, full of seeds of pure rose embedded in milky white. They waved about us as I listened—and heard this tale and many more.

A memsahib had to discharge a servant, and he thought he owed his discharge to the butler. Soon after, the butler complained of sores on his feet, small, raw holes, which would not get better, do what he would. At last he could not walk. The European doctor came but could not help with all his medicines, dearly as they are prized by the natives. It was clear then to the butler that this was a case for the *jadu-ghar*—the wonder-worker. He came and put ointment on the feet. No result. It was then evident that this was a true case of *jadu*—magic. All the household assembled and jadu of the strongest was made and enlightenment besought. It came. The jadughar said he must dig in the garden. Objection was made by the powers of the house, but they yielded eventually and, unhesitating, the man chose a spot and dug. And lo! a lump of sun-baked clay roughly shaped in the image of a man, and into the feet were thrust large thorns inscribed with strange characters. The butler said that the jadu was for him and that now his feet would immediately heal. They did.

I have heard of many cases like this. So Rossetti's 'Sister Helen' repeats itself in India! If this was faith-healing, I think one must also admit it was faith-harming. It raises the whole question of the power of the malignant will, which was at the bottom of all the witchcraft of Europe and New England. For myself, I incline to believe with India that the will to evil, focused spiritually like a ray of searing flame upon its subject, may do hurt that as yet we little understand, and that this may have been the grain of truth in the horrible fears of the Old World. India has much of the wisdom of age with some of its follies, and we have not yet, so it would appear, sounded the depths of the human spirit for good and for ill.

There is, for instance, the dreadful *marshakhs* belief, in the Punjab, in unholy alliance with the snake for benefits to be received and given. A man grows restless with twitching pains, lancing neuralgias, and the only cure is the bite of a venomous snake. The restoration to health is instant. Such a man is haunted by snakes wherever he goes. They crawl to his feet from the rivers and appear themselves to receive warmth and health from the contact. Is there truth in this wild story or no? At least it is believed. No doubt it, too, is a relic of the almost universal worship of the serpent-tribe. I have found in China and Japan that the crime-stained soul is often known to glide off to its haunts in the shape of a snake. I have a strange Japanese story to this effect. Dragon- or snake-worship—who knows?

But I go too far afield. How many people know that there is an Indian version of the hand of glory, that medieval horror of Europe—the dead hand of a murderer? Or that in the Night of No Moon the sanest European may be robbed by the blowing through the mosquito-nets, as he sleeps, of a strange powder that induces catalepsy, while the burning of four enchanted candles at the four corners of his bed retains him in the open-eyed slumber of the senses that sees his possessions removed but holds him in a chain of iron from speech or movement? For in the Night of No Moon strange forces of evil move in the dark, and if you know the word—if you can bring yourself into full harmony with them—their power is yours.

And these people in India and Tibet gain knowledge that is beyond explanation. Is it not a curious fact, vouched for by Europeans, that the Buddhist oracles at Lhasa long ago foretold the exact years of the coming of the British and of the Chinese war and of several other matters—prophecies that, set down as they are in black and white, cannot be denied? What do we know—where shall we set our limits? The better I know the East the less dogmatic I grow in regard to what is or is not possible.

Do you believe, for instance, that by performing what is called *yogasamyana,* one may bring one's mind to be in tune with any state of being? Impossible! Yet you will find educated Indians who say that this is common knowledge. I have known one to assert that he found himself in tune with the vibrations of plant life and could not remain in peace in a room where a plant was slowly dying of thirst. The explanation given is that all states of being are made up of certain sets of vibrations and that you have but to attune your own vibrations to the rhythm that governs any other set and for the time you will be a part of it. There are Indians who contend that this is simple, scientific fact. But consider and see how far-reaching a fact, if so it were!

I might go on forever; for in my wanderings I have collected much material on this fascinating subject. One needs, of course, the thread of knowledge of the faiths and legends involved, to string one's bits of folklore together to advantage. I think one could glean little worth having if one had not that.

If I have seemed to dwell too much on the setting, remember that it was a part of the magic—of the wonderful world in which these people live. It has made them what they are. It has given them the beliefs that in a way are kindred to our own. For we too are inheritors of the great religions and fairy-tales that matured in the hills and uplifted plains of India. As Max Müller long since pointed out, the very words of our Indo-European ancestors lie embedded like fossils in the language we use daily. In repeating the words 'Our Father,' we do but repeat the sounds uttered in prayer by our remote forefathers of the Vedic days in India. Go to the East and learn; for from it comes the Light that enlightens the world!

CHAPTER 16

A 'Pariah' in the Heavens

Rahu, by Whose Shadow the Sun is Eclipsed and the Hindu Driven to Bathe in Holy Waters

L.G. Blochman

TO A MAN USED TO THINKING IN TERMS of logarithms and Kepler's laws—not Kepler's metaphysical vagaries—the application of the Indian caste system to astronomy seems far-fetched and the influence of a solar eclipse upon the bathing-habits of a people, incredible. But to a Hindu, whose life is dominated by caste and whose astronomy is an astrology in which the heavens are peopled with conscious beings, these beings must perforce be governed by the caste system. Thus, when anything unorthodox takes place celestially, there is a corresponding hubbub on earth, and numerous rites are performed in India to straighten things out. Of all heavenly phenomena requiring earthly rectification by Hinduism, the solar eclipse calls for the most elaborate observances.

The sun is the Brahman of the heavens. His supremacy is unquestioned. He makes the white man perspire and curse; he ripens fruit and hardens bricks. Yet during an eclipse this high-caste lord is tampered with. His brilliant disk is distorted and his light is diminished. Since no one with any caste would think of meddling with him, the blame is fastened on Rahu, an Untouchable, a figure corresponding to a member of the lowest order in the Indian social system. *Candalas,* the Untouchables are called in Bengal,

**ASIA*, October 1924. L.G. Blochman (1900-75) was a journalist and novelist who spent a few years in India. Author of *Bombay Mail* and *Bengal Fire.*

Pariahs in southern India. They are scavengers, sweepers and menials at the burning-*ghats.* Contact with them renders a high-caste Hindu unclean and sends him scurrying for a bath. Should even their shadow fall upon food intended for Brahmans, the meal is polluted and cannot be eaten. Such as they are on earth is Rahu in the sky. It is said that he sprang into being on a day long ago when the gods were drinking *amrita,* an immortality-giving cream that they had churned from the ocean. As they quaffed the cream, the sun and the moon discovered in the group a demon in disguise. They told Vishnu, who promptly cut off the demon's head. This head it was that became Rahu, the Outcaste, eternally sworn to revenge. And when Rahu interferes with the beneficent functioning of the sun, even by throwing his shadow across it, the sun is contaminated.

When, during the period of an eclipse, this unclean sunlight streams down upon the earth, the world and all its inhabitants are defiled. On the day of an eclipse the Hindu follows a strict schedule to purify himself and his belongings. He may take no food nor drink during the eclipse. Any cooked food or drinking-water in his house is thrown out. Brass vessels are scoured and earthenware pots destroyed. Offerings are made to Brahmans for special purifying rites, and alms—a ransom—given to Pariahs for the unveiling of the sun by their kinsman Rahu. Personal purification must be achieved by a bath in some stream. Any flowing water will cleanse the body, but none so efficaciously as the holy rivers of India: the Ganges, the Indus, the Jumna, the Godavari, the Nerbudda, the Kaveri and the Brahmaputra.

Every holy bathing-place was thronged on the occasion of the latest eclipse. Those who could afford it made pilgrimages to the most sacred spots, the better to wash away the taint of the eclipse, and railways ran special trains to Benares, Allahabad and Hardwar. Even Calcutta was favoured with an influx of country Hindus come to bathe in the Hugli, one of the mouths of the Ganges. And modern Calcutta, the second city of the British Empire, Calcutta the occidental, with its street-cars and telephones, paved streets and electric lights, became for a day a stronghold of ultra-Orientalism.

For miles along the banks of the Hugli the bathing-ghats were swarming with humanity. Special organizations were arranged to handle the crowds, who, bent on bathing in the purifying, though muddy, river, fought for access to its waters. Long before breakfast Calcutta started for the riverside. At seven o'clock the vanguard of bathers was out in force. Venders of things to eat were fitting up, on stilts in the water, shops where waist-deep, the devout might pause for a moment to buy sweets or betel-nut. Beggars were settling in choice places outside the ghats and were being periodically ousted by marshals with important-looking badges. More marshals with more badges were stretching ropes to control the crowd and were herding early comers into their proper lanes. By eight o'clock thousands were assembled on the banks; by nine o'clock the throng contained tens of thousands; and by half past ten, at the height of the eclipse, more than a hundred thousand.

From all directions and in all manner of ways did they come to bathe. Pedestrians crossed the *maidan,* or great park, of Calcutta, in never ending streams of brown and white, with here and there a dash of red or green as female contingents shyly joined the march. Some walked in groups chanting, with upraised hands to the accompaniment of gongs and cymbals. High-caste women rode by in closed *garis* the wealthy went by in taxis and scores went hanging on the outside of trolley-cars—like bees, swarming.

Closely packed into Auckland Road, which leads to Babu's Ghat, was a yelling pushing mass of people. In and around stalled cars, through an entanglement of garis, jostling and jolting each other the perspiring crowds dealt out noisy charity to rank upon rank of beggars draw up along both sides of the road. Monstrosities, animal and human, helpless cripples and hopeless drones, the diseased and the indolent, howling infants and shrivelled ancients, religious fanatics and financiering heretics—all were wailing and moaning and grovelling in the mud. Before each mendicant was spread a dirty cloth, on which lay a pile of grain and copper coins, the offering of Hindu charity. The sacred-bull, emblem of the god Siva, was ever present. Dozens of them, born aristocrats, stood clad in gorgeous blankets of crimson

ON THE DAY OF THE ECLIPSE IT SEEMS THAT ALL THE HINDUS OF CALCUTTA ARE CONTAINED IN THE HUMAN RIVER THAT MAKES PART OF THE SACRED HUGLI FROM HOWRAH BRIDGE TO GARDEN REACH. BY SEVEN O'CLOCK, AS SOON AS THE FIRST PILGRIMS ARRIVE AT HOWRAH BRIDGE GHAT, VENDORS OF SWEETMEATS OR BETEL-NUT HAVE SET-UP SHOPS ON STILTS IN THE RIVER, WHERE THE DEVOUT MAY PAUSE, WAIST-DEEP, TO BUY

and orange, embroidered with sea-shells, their horns wrapped in cloth. A few pitiful monsters, with a fifth leg growing from the hump, were being exploited. The masters of sound animals would extend their hands and beat gongs; the masters of deformities would wave the extra leg and wail. A young girl, just out of the river, her wet garments clinging to her, walked among the beggars, distributing handfuls of corn from a brass jar. An old lady followed, giving rice from a cloth pouch.

A skeleton covered with brown parchment was standing on his head. I watched him for two minutes, and he moved not an inch. He might have been dead. But no! Some one dropped a copper before him, and one bony leg swayed ever so slightly. A leper extended a rotting, fingerless hand. A white-haired patriarch dropped an *anna* before an idiot, who rolled his eyes and gibbered. A naked boy held one hand on the idiot's head and shouted at the passing crowd with the self-assurance of an auctioneer. A *yogi*, or ascetic, with hair like rope was sitting upon the business end of a bed of spikes emerging from a plank. He was naked, except for a loin-cloth, and ghastly gray from being smeared with ashes. He wore round his neck the sacred thread of the initiated, or twice-born, Hindus of the upper castes, and therefore he received much rice and many coppers.

When I reached the river-bank, the crowd was even thicker. Some one a hundred feet away stumbled, and the wave of humanity that was set up, swept me against an iron picket-fence. People were fighting to get into the ghat, which was crowded for yards out into the river. There were more beggars and more shouts. Men were selling bright paper ornaments and things to eat. I was again pinned to the railing, and then, while bare feet walked on my shoes, was carried forward with another wave. This time the wave carried me to the ghat entrance. A man with a yellow ribbon told me I might not come in. While I was telling him there was no alternative, the wave swept me forward another yard. Then I escaped to a ferry-landing.

From the new point of vantage I could watch the acres and acres of brown, bare shoulders. The bathers stood arm to arm until they were neck-deep in the water. One could not be surprised at reports of a drowning here and there. If I had not seen the pushing, shouting mob on the banks, I should have conjectured that all of the seven hundred thousand Hindus of Calcutta were contained in that human river, which made part of the Hugli from Howrah Bridge to Garden Reach. Just as the evil shadow of Rahu was slipping from the edge of the sun, I decided to go home and take a bath myself.

CHAPTER 17

The Singing Voice of India

Elemental Song-Lore Gathered from Workers on Misty Hillsides and in Noisy Streets

Mary Lucia Bierce Fuller

I LOVE TO REMEMBER A DAY IN THE Western Ghats, in India, when I was out walking, with several pounds of rich red mud on my boots, and saw on a hillside a woman and four half-grown boys and girls transplanting in a drizzling rain from one narrow terrace to another. The broad, green valley below, and the silent, rugged mountains all about were etherealized by a fine, floating mist that veiled the ancient signs of habitation. It seemed that in all this silent world of mist and mountain were only these five weak human creatures, courageously grappling with infinite forces and making their small, brave marks on the everlasting hills. I walked down to them, and, as I went, a song met me, a high, minor chant, as elemental as the wet green earth and the mountain streams.

Martanda hung out a yellow banner from Fort Jejuri;
The wind blew a little breeze.
The maid donned a new 'sari,' the maid minced;
The wind blew a little breeze.

⋆*ASIA*, October 1924. Mary Lucia Bierce Fuller (1882-1965) was born in India of Missionary parents of note. She earned fame with her biography of *Pandita Ramabai*.

There was more of the song, but I could not recall it when I got home. Each phrase was repeated seven or eight times with varying inflection, by one and another, as their deft, quick hands planted again the brilliant, lush young stalks; and two or three together always took up the line a second time with fresh emphasis, as if it were a new thing, before going on to the next. They said the singing kept them warm. I was glad to hear it; for they were half-naked under their palm-leaf rain-hoods.

No one can be long in India and see anything of Indian life without being struck by the singing in field and street and the many sorts of work that can be done to the lilt of a song. Even the globe-trotter, who skims over the surface of things, notes the singing of the dock coolies as they pull and haul at ropes and cranes. He must think this the influence of the sea, since seamen have always sung, did he not hear the same chantey-like music from coolies hoisting huge building stones with pulley and chain:

'What load will thy bullock carry?'
intones the foreman, as his men draw breath after a pull.
'Four bags, brother, four bags,'
answer the men, as the stone mounts by rhythmic swings.
'Thy bullock is eating our field!'
protests the foreman.
'Let him eat today's day, let him eat tomorrow's day;
Day after tomorrow's day we will tie him to the black peg!'
reply the men cheerfully.
'The black peg is broken,'
laments the foreman, and,
'The mango-flowers have fallen!'
shout the men, out of breath, as the stone swings into place.

Or they may sing a charming song, popular all over the Maharashtra, even in Bombay, where it is incongruously broken in upon by clanging tram-gongs and the honk-honk of impatient motor-cars:

Oh, Rama, Rama, aye, Rama!
In Rama's garden, in Rama's garden,
Are two four-ox draw-wells, deep wells,
And two Khilari bulls, tall bulls;
Drives them the master for delight, delight.
To jasmines flows a runnel, wimpling, rippling,
While the mangoes' shade falls on the tamarinds—
And Rama's heart goes out to Sita, Sita!
Oh, Rama, Rama, aye, Rama!

Each line is sung at least twice, and by Rama and Sita are not intended the great originals of these names, which are, as here, often used conventionally, as Phyllis and Corydon, Strephon and Chloe are in English pastoral poetry.

Indian herdsmen and shepherds, too, have always whiled away their long days with song and pipe. In the country one often hears the herdsmen, even the youngsters who pasture the cattle, buffaloes, goats and sheep, singing of the simple things that make up village life. One does not need to shut one's eyes to see again a lad sprawled in the shade, crooning to himself with his staff beside him; or another, leaning against a tree, fluting on his *pova* wistful phrases as sweet as bird-calls; or a naked child, taking home his herd in the evening, perched astride the rump of a great leisurely buffalo, digging his hard little toes into her bulging black sides and singing with shrill sweetness:

My Kapila cow's udder is smooth as betel leaves;
My Kapila cow's eyes are like clouds in the sky;
My Kapila cow's teeth are like excellent boiled rice,
My Kapila cow's neck is like a wrought-iron arch.

Kapila, who is a fabulous black cow, belonging to Vishnu, fulfils all the wishes of her worshippers. In her honour there is a very great festival, called *Kapila-shashthi,* which comes only once in 60 years, since it depends on the conjunction of certain stars and planets. It is so holy a festival that to bathe in sacred rivers on that day, or, better yet, in the sea, into which all the sacred rivers flow, to worship the gods and Brahmans, to give alms and to make presents to priests are acts that free the worshipper from all his sins. There is a very long song, sung with doting fervor and enjoyment, about Kapila, in which her every feature or member—in each dwells a god—is described and adored. This Kapila was altogether black, and so all-black cows even now are named for her and accounted sacrosanct. They are of course very rare, since they must not have even a speck of other colour. Whenever one of them is found, to walk round her confers such merit that the circumambulation is called *prithvi-pradakshina;* that is, a circuit of the earth itself. There are old women who will tell you with all happy simplicity and confidence that they have in this way circumambulated the earth.

Delightful it is to hear the songs Rama sings as he drives his well-bullocks, or to sit in his 'watered garden' in the shade of a great tamarind, near the bountiful, cool, deep well, and listen to his long, singing halloos, with their abrupt pauses, and the final high note mingling with the gurgling swish and soft roar of the water as it empties from the leather *masak* into the trough or tank that feeds the irrigating runnels. Antiphons to these musical drippings and splashings come from the hidden green worlds in the gracious old trees all about, where busy birds call, twitter and coo in unending contentment: the sleepy fat bullocks grunt sometimes and naked little children play about with hilarious shouts or birdlike chirpings, while from all sides comes the fragrance of roses, oleanders, jasmine and delicious wet earth. Small wonder Rama-Adam yearns for Sita-Eve in such an Eden.

Meanwhile Sita is at home, singing at her work or crooning to the baby. Many are the songs she sings in little couplets about her own life, her Rama and her children, her work and neighbours, gods, goddesses and festivals, birth, rebirth and death. Some she makes up herself; the rest she inherits along with her savoury recipes, her manifold fears, her quaint ideas about the world, her ideals of submission and patience. The first of the songs that I set down here was given me by a little Christian Sita, very daft about her devoted Rama and very *triste* because he was away from home.

To what village has he gone? Tell me truly, Sakubai.
For nine days there has been no moon in my house.

For thy sake I would be a kite-bird in the sky:
I would put on bird's feathers and circle above thy head.

I tied a knot in a silken rope; I could not loose it:
Thy love and mine I try to break; I cannot break it.

Womankind is fond—too fond:
Men forget, forget.

My soul to his soul gave I—in vain, Sakubai:
Men are faithless; he cares not for me.

Ah, what vixen has taken thy love from me?
She has torn apart a ruby and a diamond set together.

A fish of the water cast upon thorns am I:
A third has shared the love of us two.

Ah, where is he, the heart of my heart?
Heavy are my eyes with watching and waiting.

There are many more couplets; for the Indian woman's naive, spontaneous praise of husband and children need never have an end.

A woman with children—here and there a clutter:
A barren woman's house is always tidy,

joyously she sings.

SLOWLY GRINDING THE DAY'S FLOUR, MOTHERS CROON THEIR LULLABIES OF LOVE AND CHARMING NONSENSE, OR IN SHRILLER MINOR STRAIN SING OF IDEALS OF PATIENCE AND SUBMISSION, OF GODDESSES AND FESTIVALS, OF BIRTH, DEATH AND THE WORLD THEY KNOW

Step softly, lest thou tread a thorn,
My darling beautiful with white feet of moonlight.

So fair is my daughter, so fair,
Her calves are as the white hearts of plantains.

So many suitors for my daughter, our courtyard cannot hold them;
We have built a pavilion in the road.

Her throat is slender like a fluting pipe;
Her plait hangs down her back like a swaying cobra-queen.

Master son-in-law has made my bird his own,
And far has he taken her—a mountain lies between us.

I will choose a moon of moons for son-in law,
For my darling beautiful, my gem in a casket.

Of the gods I ask only a little, little wealth,
But sons like Lahu and Akush.

How many times must I call thee, my son, my athlete?
Needst thou make thy playground in a tiger-thicket?

The god's god-seat is beautiful with flowers,
And in my womb a propitious son.

Since the babe creeps and plays, the court is become too small:
We have widened it by the veranda of the hall.

It is eveningtide; the cows and calves come home—
Play not in the path, my little son.

With creeping and playing my babe is weary,
And comes to my lap for rest.

Follow me not, sounding thy rattle;
On the road some evil eye may fall on thee.

Lakshmi [goddess of good fortune] has entered our back door:
It was the babe called her in.

The cowherd for the cow, the herdsman for the buffalo,
And God himself to watch the suckling babe.

Marathi lullabies have much in common with those of other lands. They are full of the doting fondness one always associates with such songs, the same inconsequent, charming nonsense, at times, and the same love of impossible grandeur. With slight variations the one that follows is heard in many places:

Sleep, sleep, my sandalwood babe, sleep, sleep!
Thy mother hath gone to the carpenters' lane.

'O master carpenter, O mistress carpenter,' saith she,
'Is my babe's lacquered cradle ready?'

Sleep, sleep, my velvet babe, sleep, sleep!
Thy mother hath gone to the tailors' lane.

'O master tailor, O mistress tailor,' saith she,
'Is my babe's silken bonnet ready?'

Sleep, sleep, my golden babe, sleep, sleep!
Thy mother hath gone to the goldsmiths' lane.

'O master goldsmith, O mistress goldsmith,' saith she,
'Is my babe's silver belt-chain ready?'

Once in Khandesh I got some lullabies from a beggar-girl, a very old little girl of nine, who, besides cradle-songs, sang, as well, Solomonic sermons on the follies of the man who seeks out strange women and the honestly earned troubles of him who has two wives. Here is one of her prettiest songs:

Mother, catch a scorpion for me
And make a ring of it for me.
Refrain: Never has it been so done, my human babe:
The world is of a different sort.
Thy cradle swings on the veranda,
The moon swings in the clouds—
Hush, Krishna, weep not, nor ask.

Mother, catch a snake for me
And make a whip of it for me.

Mother, catch a tiger for me
And make a Nandi bull of him, for me.

Mother, catch the earth for me
And make a mattress of it for me.

Mother, catch a cloud for me
And make an elephant of it for me.

Mother, catch the stars for me
And make parched corn of them for me.

Among the very dearest of the couplets Sita sings as she grinds the day's flour or rests on a swinging bed, if she has one, are verses about her parents and their home. Especially does she sing of her mother. Her old home is called *maher,* 'mother-house'; and *sasar* is the house of her *sasu* and *sasara,* parents-in-law, where she, her husband and children live. Maher and sasar are among the most important and poignant words in a woman's vocabulary; to a little girl, few words can be so awesome, if not actually terrifying, as 'mother-in-law.' *Sasubai,* 'madam mother-in-law,' is one of her most fearsome bogies.

But what a sweet word is 'maher'! And how lovingly it is spoken by wee, homesick brides, snubbed and harassed young wives, sad-eyed young widows and weary, patient old women who are at life's end and empty-handed. I shall always remember a young Brahman girl I saw once at the Poona station, with her mother-in-law, a hard-faced, able-looking woman. The girl was a slender little thing, about fifteen, with great fawn's eyes in an exquisite, sensitive face. When I first noticed her, she was helping to lift pudgy big bundles out of the train. Sasubai, with the thrift and energy typical of west-coast Mahrattas, would of course consider nothing so foolishly wasteful of perfectly good money as a coolie. I soon discovered that the child had an immense boil on her instep, and I ached for her as she stood pale and faint while Sasubai gave clear instructions. As soon as that stern lady turned away to the booking-office, I said, 'Do sit down!' She sank to the ground and answered in a voice quivering with pain, 'One may not sit when elders stand.' We chatted a little, and then she exclaimed with great longing, 'Ah, if I were at my mother's house, I could rest!'

And so it is that maher has come to be used figuratively for a refuge, a retreat, a place of pleasant resort, and *sasurvas* (residence at sasar), I am sorry to say, has become a synonym for all sorts of harassment and vexatious restraint. When little girls part their hair for several plaits, the right parting is called *mahervat* and the left *sasarvat*. *Vat* means way, and the right side, you see, leads home! Both maher and sasar are used in many pointed proverbs. In little girls' play-songs come lines like these:

On the way to maher is a great arched gate,
On the way to sasar are pricking thorns.

Going to maher, one feels delight,
Going to sasar, the coconut breaks!

And, alas, 'the coconut breaks' means that tears flow. Any message or visitor from maher is a thrilling happiness, and he rarely comes empty-handed.

I keep sending thee word by any who come and go—
It is a year since I saw thy face, my mother.

My mother-in-law's speech is like a bitter 'nim' leaf:
My mother's speech is like milk and sugar.

My neighbours tell of things spiteful and foolish:
When my mother speaks, her words are gold 'mohurs'.

My mother, my mother! She showed me this world;
Of her eyes she made lamps for me, of her hand a shade.

Mother, in good faith drank I thy milk,
Never will I be faithless.

In a strange land is neither mother nor aunt:
My soul is in a foreign country.

Folk's talk is but 'grain'—chaff,
My father's talk is jasmine and jessamine.

(The original has *zai* and *zui*, which are two varieties of the jasmine-flower.)

My father comes a visitor; Sasubai is all hurry and bustle.
On his golden canopy the pearls glisten and glister.

My father asks me, 'Daughter, what-like is thy sasar?'
'Like rice of mango-blossoms on a plantain leaf, my father.'

I will go to my mother's house and sit in the courtyard,
While my beautiful sisters-in-law bend to serve me.

When one goes to sasar, one keeps looking back:
One's heart is with one's mother!

When one goes to sasar, one's eyes fill with tears,
And Father says, 'My suckling!' and wipes one's eyes with his scarf.

The butcher slaughtered a cow but now:
And my father feared not to give his daughter to be a co-wife.

A good father should not give his daughter to be a co-wife;
Nor should folk bicker in the butcher's doorway for their cows.

When I go to maher, my dear, there are my mother and father,
My brothers and my sisters-in-law, all golden images.

The next couplets are about brothers—and their wives. Brothers are very fondly loved, and the festival of *Bhaubija,* when brothers either come to see their sisters or, if possible, take them home for a visit, is eagerly awaited. Indifferent brothers are a great grief, and jealous sisters-in-law a sad fly in the ointment. A cynical couplet comments dryly:

Sisters-in-law agree for a while:
In the gardener's garden the beds are planted far apart!

and another says bitterly:
In my mother's time coming and going; in my father's full right;
But in my brother's reign, I cannot claim a cupful of stale buttermilk!

But a devoted brother, a sweetly amenable sister-in-law, nephews and nieces, are among the keenest pleasures of life. An only brother, especially of several sisters, is naturally very much spoiled. Many sisters will not comb their hair on Monday, nor wash it, since their doing so might bring their brothers bad luck. Tousled heads are always very noticeable in girls' schools on Mondays. In some castes the raw, unhemmed front of a woman's bodice shows that she has a brother.

Bhairaj and *bhairaya,* or *bhauraya,* both meaning 'brother-king', or 'darling brother', are much used, as in the following couplets, as terms of endearment.

We four sisters are as sparrows in four villages.
When wilt thou come as guest, Bhauraya?

Past my door go painted carts—
Brothers taking their sisters for the Bhaubija.

Why art thou bitter, my neighbour, that I have a guest?
For Bhairaj I have sent for milk and sweetmeats.

I give his bullocks grass and grain and grated coconut:
My brother has come to visit me, sitting in a chariot.

I tie his mare with heel-ropes; she has silken reins:
My brother's father-in-law has come a guest to my house.

All the village talks of my new bodice
That Bhairaya made and gave me.

Bhairaj sews me a bodice, Vahinibai [his wife] looks askance;
And for stubbornness my brother sews on pearls.

Bhairaj sews me a bodice; Vahinibai looks askance.
What sweetness now in that bodice?

My brother says, 'Serve my sister milk and curds.'
My sister-in-law says, 'The buffalo yesterday kicked over the milk!'

Brothers and sisters-in-law have I:
My sisters-in-law are jewel-caskets, my brothers, amulets on my neck.

I make thee a vow, O god of my mother's house,
Let my brother's son come to my house!

I sweep the court; it is full of pebbles and marbles—
My brother's children great and small play here.

Very fondly, too, does Sita love her sisters, and she mourns when they live too far off for frequent meetings.

I have sent a message to my darling far away to come:
She has a cart, my sister, with green broadcloth curtains.

CHAPTER 18

Indian Snake-Charmers

Saffron-Clad Rogues Who Tame the Sacred Cobras with Their Flutes

Lily Strickland Anderson

WE ENTER THE BAZAR UNDER A cloudless Indian sky. The dusty palms stand motionless in the hot air. Gaily clad natives throng the crowded place, idling and endlessly bartering in noisy good humour. Pariah dogs nose into dustbins and rubbish piles. Nimble-footed goats and sacred cows amble unreproached along the side-walks and take toll of the baskets of *ata,* pulse and grain in the *banyas*' stalls. Crows, impudent and incurable thieves, filch dainties. A procession of cart-bullocks, urged on by the cries of the drivers, pushes its leisurely way through the congested thoroughfare.

Suddenly there comes to our ears the thin, nasal whine of a gourd flute, accompanied at intervals by the sharp rattle of a 'monkey drum'. This announces the presence of the snake-charmer, that wily opportunist who is always found where the crowd is thickest and the chances are best for gathering *pice.* With quickened interest we follow the insistent music to its source and come upon a group of dusky, impish-faced Nats in saffron rags, squatting in a cleared space before several flat wicker baskets. We become aware of a mysterious and apparently automatic lifting of the lids of the

⋆*ASIA*, January 1925. Lily Strickland Anderson (1884-1958) was a composer, writer and artist who spent ten years in India. She wrote extensively on her travels in Asia and Africa.

baskets, and suddenly we shudder at the sight of the heads of cobras, emerging as the lids fall aside. The snakes rise higher and higher, swaying rhythmically, with their spectacled hoods far distended, and their beady, opaque eyes fixed inscrutably on their masters. The lure of the music seems irresistible. Hypnotized by the plaintive tunes, the serpents begin to 'dance'.

Is there an affinity between the snake-charmer and his cobra? Have they a subtle understanding? By beholding many scenes such as this we almost come to believe in a mysterious tie between the *naga* and his vagabond master. We like to think that the snake-charmer has some inexplicable power over his serpents, that his music exercises an uncanny influence on them, as it stirs strange emotions within us, who lend ourselves to its elusive, far-away, wordless magic. But it is very easy to believe in magic in India! As a matter of fact, the snake-charmer is the only man in India who jeers at religions and cobras alike.

The chief actors in his little open-air drama are snakes, assisted sometimes by a mongoose, whom popular superstition credits with a knowledge of snake-bite antidote. The Nat himself, a vagrant of low caste, is only the managing director, the *maestro.* It is fair to say that most of the cobras that we see dancing to the seductive tunes of the gourd flute have already had their poison-glands drawn. So we cannot vouch for the statement about the mongoose. We have seen this quick little animal engage with snakes in a brief and unsportsmanlike battle to the death, staged for the benefit of tourists, in which the snakes, predestined to sacrifice and having had their chief weapons taken away from them, had no chance against their highly specialized assailant.

The snake-charmer follows a hereditary calling; he is a nomad, of Gypsy origin, who wanders from place to place over the broad plains of India. He comes in the dawn and goes out with the sunset, and no man knows his genesis or exodus. He is a strange creature, enwrapped in mystery and romance, invested with the traditions of an incredibly remote past.

It is believed by the Hindus that they are cursed by the gods and one god in particular. The legend runs thus. Once upon a time, long ago, a Nat, of the tribe of snake-charmers, played upon his *punji* in such a beguiling manner that he called forth all the snakes from their haunts and forced them to dance before him. It happened that Vishnu, who had temporarily assumed the guise of a thousand-headed cobra, felt impelled to respond to the mesmeric music. Indignant at having been forced to obey his 'snake nature' and engage in the dance along with the common reptiles, he cursed all the tribe of snake-charmers and doomed them to wander as vagabonds forevermore—homeless, restless, impermanent as the wind. To this day all snake-charmers are nomads, and nomads they will ever be. They are found at fairs and festivals in the country villages or they may be seen wandering along the city thoroughfares with their snake-baskets slung over their shoulders, playing, as they go, fragmentary melodies as strange and wild as the traditions back of them.

There is a legend that all Gipsies came originally from India and from the caste of Nats. From this same caste came also wandering minstrels, players, jugglers, conjurers, animal-trainers and itinerant dancers. They belong to the same group, very low in the social scale, and are, one and all, vagabonds. They believe that one soul pervades and dominates nature and they ignore the ramifications of Hindu theology. They are intemperate in the use of liquor and *bhang,* a narcotic made from Indian hemp, and are generally dissipated. They live today and take no thought for tomorrow. In government the Nats recognize only a nominal leader, a sort of Gipsy king, but each man is really a law unto himself, a feckless wastrel, a quack, a charlatan, or what you will—but a picturesque and attractive fellow, in spite of all that, and past master of his art.

It is characteristically Indian that, although he is a low-caste fellow, he is the companion of the cobra, symbol of Vishnu, and therefore is to be feared and respected. He himself is not concerned with his social status. Independent of criticism, defiant and superior, lie delights in the poverty of his estate and the freedom of his mind. He pretends to be the snake's master and to be able to call wild snakes from the jungle to do his bidding, and he enjoys being summoned to rid the people's huts of the snakes that live in the palm-thatched roofs.

INDIAN SNAKE-CHARMES

He always carries with him a number of trained snakes that answer the call of his flute. These he surreptitiously places in the house supposed to be snake-infested. When he begins his familiar tunes, they come crawling out straight into his waiting basket. It is an invariable rule that he shall take away alive all the snakes that he charms; in this way, he keeps his tamed assistants for another day's work. The amazed natives cannot see the fraud, but only the wonderful 'magic'. '*A waugh,* Brother! Of a truth is the Nat a great magician, in the confidence of Vishnu himself!' 'Did we not see the miracle with our own eyes?' By the time the people discover that the original snakes are still in the house, the snake-charmer has departed to pastures new, with his fee in his pocket and his tongue in his cheek!

The Nat combines elementary jugglery with snake-charming and sometimes augments his meagre show with feats of legerdemain and a few acrobatic stunts, staged *al fresco* wherever there is a gathering of people. His usual procedure is literally to 'drum up' a crowd with his 'monkey drum' (the hour-glass drum called *damru* and to excite their interest in his 'basket of tricks.' He begins his first act with a seductive theme on the gourd flute. When he has caught the attention of his audience and tuned them up to the right pitch, he stops and 'passes the hat', saying that the show will go on, provided he gets enough money. He rarely fails to collect the required funds, because Indians are among the most inquisitive people in the world.

The snake-charmer plays on an instrument that has been his traditionally for thousands of years. The flute is a gourd, with a bit of the hollowed-out stem at the small end serving as mouthpiece. Two reeds are inserted in its base: one, pierced with several fine holes, gives the melody; and the other, with a single stop, acts as a drone in the same manner as the Indian bagpipe. There are in the Calcutta Museum several examples of old gourd flutes that have as many as nine reeds. The most striking quality of the pipe is that the gourd serves as a sound chamber and the pipe produces the drone effect, which is sustained throughout the playing of the melody. The tonic note, thus constantly sounded, is accompaniment and bass combined; a fundamental harmony, or as near harmony as any Indian music ever attains. In northern India, the same instrument under the name of *tomri,* is used by the Nats. It is decorated with bright pigment and bits of glass, which when shining in the sunlight, catch and hold the attention of the snakes.

The tone of the punji is piercing, nasal and plaintive quality like that of the oboe, though of deeper timbre. It has the same effect upon the hearer as a muted French horn which always conveys a faraway feeling of indescribable poignancy. Even after living four years in India and seeing endless processions of snake-charmers, I still am vainly endeavouring to capture some of those vague and elusive tunes that are never put down in notation but simply memorized from generation to generation. The old tune is still there for me. I can never become deaf to the music of the punji nor blasé about the snake-charmer and his art. There is an elemental, primitive quality in music, a thin, reedy tone that might have come from some old pipe of Pan in an enchanted forest of Arcady. The snake-charmer may be a vagabond and a rogue, but he is master of his art.

That there is a mesmeric quality in music has long been an admitted fact, particularly in the wild and nameless melodies of the jungle-bred snake-charmer. His caste, secretive and nomadic by nature and habit, knows no laws but whim and fancy. Unkempt and undaunted, the Nat wanders free and content, an undeniably arresting figure, in rags of the colour of the heart of the sacred lotus. Small wonder that the serpent-folk are lured to follow the call of the saffron-clad piper of India! He has been born and bred close to the wild heart of Nature and is in tune with her mysteries; he has captured the melodies of the forest and jungle, the songs of the hidden streams, the brooding of secret pools, the sighing of the winds in the palms, the stealthy rustling of jungle undergrowth, the murmurings of the nocturnal life of bird and beast, the rhythm of moonlight and starshine, the crescendo of dawn and the cadences of purple night.

The snake-cult has strangely manifested itself at one time or another among nearly all peoples of the world—among the ancient Egyptians, the Chinese, the American Indians, the Aztecs. As a symbol of evil, the snake is not unknown to Christendom. It is said of him in the Scriptures, 'Now the serpent was more subtile than any beast of the field which the Lord God had made.' As evil incarnate, he tempted man to his first sin in the Garden of Eden. His name is the epitome of wickedness, of unholy wisdom and vice, and he is bound up in a thousand legends and allegories, not only in India, but throughout the world.

The snake-cult has exercised and still exercises a strong fascination upon the people of India. It dates back to pre-Aryan times but enters, in some aspect, into all forms of Hinduism. Celestial serpents, looked upon as demigods of great wisdom and power, were associated with Surya, the Vedic Sun-god. Ruined temples to the Sun and Serpent may still be found in jungle and on hill, mute but eloquent monuments of ancient faiths the origin of which is lost in the mists of antiquity. Later, the Nag, or chief snake, under the name of Sesha, was more definitely accepted as the symbol of Vishnu, the second person of the Hindu Trinity, who is depicted as resting on its body, protected by a canopy formed by its multiple hooded heads. With its tail in its mouth, the cobra, known as Ananta, symbolizes the cycle of eternity. The legend of Kaliya, the great river-snake overcome by Krishna, most widely worshiped of Hindu gods, is another remnant of the snake-cult. Vasuki and Manasa are also serpents of supernatural origin, whose names are held in great reverence.

Belief in the actual divinity of the 'serpent-folk' still persists in various parts of the country, and here are many temples dedicated to the worship of nagas, or snakes. In south India, several large snake temples are maintained, with their guardians or priests, solely by the voluntary contributions of the naga-worshippers. In north India, nagas are looked upon by some primitive tribes as half-human creatures with supernatural powers. The Naga tribes of Assam have traditions to the effect that they are actually the descendants of a mythical Nag, which came out of the water at the creation of the world. They are nature- and ancestor-worshippers, who practise incantations, witchcraft and magic and put great faith in dreams, portents and charms. On certain occasions they eat the flesh of snakes, which they look upon as spirits, and thus absorb their 'divine' wisdom. Throughout India, snake symbols, rudely carved stones depicting the coiled cobra, are frequently found under large trees. At the time of snake-festivals, these stones are decorated with flower-garlands as an indirect offering to the great Nag.

The *Naga Panchami* (Snakes' Fifth) is a day in August specially set apart for the worship and propitiation of reptiles. Offerings of milk and grain are poured into snake holes or presented at snake temples, and *puja* (worship) is held in honour of the cobra. At the beginning of the day, the families of snake-devotees bring out clay images, wooden models or coloured pictures of sacred snakes, before which are performed the religious ceremonies prescribed for the occasion. These rites usually consist of gifts of flowers, milk and grain, the reciting of *mantras* and music and feasting. It is considered an act of merit to release all imprisoned snakes, and, in some districts, the outcast jungle-dwellers bring in large baskets of assorted serpents to sell to the snake-devotees who buy them and set them free again.

Besides having religious and legendary importance the cobra is a very vital menace in the life of the people. Among the peasants, it is the appointed guardian of the cattle, an unwise choice, since thousands of cows, and other domesticated animals are killed yearly by snakes. It has been estimated that twenty thousand Indians die from snake-bite every year. Nevertheless, it is very difficult to find an orthodox Hindu who is willing to kill a snake. The only people not afraid to kill reptiles and collect a possible bounty are the outcast *jangli-wala* (jungle dwellers), *Sudras* (low-caste Hindus) and Nats, the snake-charmers.

In certain *mofussal* (country) districts, the people believe that any one bitten by a snake becomes possessed of a devil, an evil spirit. The local magician, or witch-doctor, is hurriedly called in to exorcise the devil. At his direction, the family stamp upon the wretched body of the bitten relative until he has passed and the poor creature is cured, not only of snake-bite, but of all other earthly ills that the devil can inflict upon mortals.

It is not easy to eradicate the roots of superstition planted so many centuries ago in fertile and imaginative minds. John Lockwood Kipling has summed up the traditional Indian attitude toward the cobra: 'He is the necklace of the Gods, he can give gems to the poor, he is the guardian of priceless treasures, he can change himself into manifold forms, he casts his skin annually and thus has the gift of youth, he can make milk, fruit, bread and all innocent food stark death when he passes over them, he is of high caste, he is in the confidence and counsel of Gods and demons, and when the great world was made, he was already there.'

Since the snakes continue to thrive and multiply in comparative security, there does not seem much likelihood of their extermination in the near future, and just so long as there are snakes, the snake-charmer will continue to ply his trade, to the delight of his audient and to his own profit.

CHAPTER 19

Tata, Indian Industrial Genius

The Man Behind a $70,000,000 Steel Plant Developed in India by Perin, American Engineer

Hawthorne Daniel

JAMSHEDPUR STANDS WHERE THE Bengal jungle slumbered twenty-five years ago. Today one of the greatest steel mills in the British Empire, and one of a handful that are the greatest in the world, employs forty thousand Indian workers in this city, where, so recently, a tiny jungle village stood. In all of India—perhaps in all of Asia—there is no counterpart of this.

We of the West—and particularly we of America—are accustomed to new communities that appear from nowhere and straightway take their places in the great world of our business. Yet even we can show few cities that in so short a time have developed such an industry as thrives at Jamshedpur. And in the East, where change is a matter of centuries rather than days, where a great inertia has prevailed for generations, such a city as Jamshedpur is a phenomenon almost without parallel.

But, strange as is the mere existence of this city, stranger still is the story of its beginning and its progress; for the man who planned this practical western machine in its setting of Indian unpracticality was not a Briton,

**ASIA*, June 1925. Hawthorne Daniel (1890-1981) was a prolific writer and editor of some magazines. An expert on international affairs he authored 41 books.

familiar with the smoke and noise of Middlesbrough and Sheffield. He was a native of India, a Parsi, a worshipper of fire—Jamsetji Nusservanji Tata—merchant and textile manufacturer of Bombay, who unfortunately died twenty-one years ago, before the great work for which he was responsible had taken final shape. It is to the glory of India that one of its own sons had the initiative to found the greatest of modern industries in the land. It remained for an American to play the other leading role in the building of Jamshedpur; for Charles Page Perin, American metallurgical engineer, was chosen by Jamsetji Tata as his executive builder and operator in what has come to be, not merely the greatest iron and steel works of India, but one of the greatest in the world—an industry, too, entirely owned by Indians.

The alliance came about thus. A stranger in a long coat that buttoned up to his chin and with a curious, brimless hat upon his head modestly entered the offices of Perin in New York one afternoon twenty-three years ago. He was of medium height and heavy-set. Slightly stooped and well along in years, he nevertheless looked virile. The swarthiness of his complexion contrasted sharply with his beard and hair. His piercing black eyes gave to his otherwise quiet face an expression of intensity and self-confidence. Obviously he was not an American. Just as obviously, he was not a European. His garb was of that curious type that suggests European influence without actually being European. He paused a moment, in the absence of the girl at the information desk, and then, seeing Perin's name on the half-open door of a private office, unhesitatingly entered.

'I was busy at my desk,' explained Perin, in relating the incident, 'and, as I glanced out of the corner of my eye and caught a glimpse of this strange-looking person who had entered unannounced, I wondered how he could have got past the outer barrier into my private office. Yet his foreign appearance made me curious as to what manner of man he was. I didn't look directly at him at first but continued, or pretended to continue, the work before me. He approached my desk and rested the tips of his fingers upon it. I watched them, fascinated; for, as he put more weight on his hand, his fingers bent farther and farther until my imagination suggested that they were about to touch the back of his hand. And then he spoke—in perfect English.

'You are Mr. Perin?' he asked.

I looked up and nodded, interested but somewhat puzzled.

He bowed slightly. 'I have a letter of introduction to you from Lord Avesbury,' he announced, handing me an envelope.

'Now, Lord Avesbury is a man I greatly admire and, knowing him, I knew that he would not give letters of introduction indiscriminately. So I perceived that my visitor must be a person of importance. The letter he presented established that fact in no uncertain terms. And that is how I first

PRACTICAL BUT IDEALISTIC, JAMSETJI TATA ENDOWED THE INDIAN INSTITUTE OF SCIENCE, AT BANGALORE, INTRODUCED JAPANESE METHODS OF SILK CULTURE INTO INDIA AND FOUNDED THE TATA IRON AND STEEL COMPANY, AT JAMSHEDPUR, WEST OF CALCUTTA

met Jamsetji Nusservanji Tata, perhaps the ablest commercial genius India has ever produced.'

In a land of teeming millions of poverty-stricken people, where wealth has for centuries been almost entirely in the hands of those to whom it came because of birth and inheritance—where the rajas live in unlimited luxury and the masses periodically face starvation—Tata, a commoner, had been able to build up a fortune that grew to millions. What is more, he had been able to retain an outlook that resulted in many patriotic and philanthropic activities. It was his desire to be of still greater service to India and its people that brought him half round the world to Perin's office. For thirty years he had been thinking of India's need for steel. He knew that the strength of the West was built upon iron and steel. He had been in Japan, had watched its rise to power and had seen the limitations imposed by its lack of iron and steel. In India there was iron ore, though how much was

STRIKING SIMILARITIES BETWEEN THE EUROPEAN AND THE INDIAN COUNTENANCE ARE SHOWN IN THIS OLD PICTURE OF THE TATA FAMILY OF BOMBAY. JAMSETJI TATA FOUNDER OF THE $70,000,000 TATA IRON AND STEEL COMPANY, IS SEATED SECOND FROM THE LEFT. SEATED THIRD FROM THE RIGHT IS HIS WIFE. HIS SON DORABJI, PRESENT HEAD OF THE FAMILY, STANDS AT THE RIGHT; HIS NEPHEWS, S.D. SAKLATVALA, NOW M.P., AND P.D. SAKLATVALA, NOW PRESIDENT OF THE MIDDLE STATES OIL COMPANY, OF NEW YORK, SIT LEFT TO RIGHT ON THE FLOOR. AT THE LEFT OF JAMSETJI TATA IS SEATED ONE OF HIS SISTERS; TWO MORE SIT AT HIS WIFE'S LEFT; A FOURTH STANDS NEAR THE PILLAR. IN FRONT OF IT STANDS THE URBANED S.C. TATA, AN UNCLE.

then unknown, and labour was there in vast supply. Yet steel had to be shipped into India. Why should it not be produced there?

This, then, was the meaning of that meeting in New York. Old India had come to young America for assistance. Tata, with his massive head bent earnestly forward and his black eyes lighted by a vision that would benefit three hundred million people, quietly told Perin of his plan. He wished to inoculate India with the material progress of the West. He wanted the people of India to have some other source of livelihood than the land, on which the crops often withered under a scorching sun that brought starvation. He asked Perin to help him build an Indian iron and steel industry.

And Perin—the man to whom he had come—was of the type that has made America. Young, broad-shouldered and powerful physically, keenly alert and energetic, he had within him the very qualities that were requisite for the success of Tata's enterprise. The two men were representative of the best their races produce—the one with a vision of the future, and the other with the ability to bring it to fruition.

Tata already had a large achievement behind him. In forty years he had come up almost from bankruptcy to great success in the manufacture of cotton goods in India, where he had built and operated cotton mills in which he employed only native labour and directors. He seemed to have the magic touch that turned all things to gold. His wealth was already great. In initiating his plan for an iron and steel industry, he was well aware of the failure of previous undertakings in that field. He had been advised against it and opposed by British officials and Indian laws. He had been told by heads of geological surveys that no ore deposits worthy of modern installations of machinery existed in India. But still he would not be discouraged. And finally, on a visit to England, he broached the subject to the Secretary of State for India, Lord George Hamilton, and was encouraged.

'Why don't you go in for it?' responded Lord Hamilton. 'The world is indebted to India for steel. The first steel known was the old Indian *wootz*. For centuries India has produced iron. The steel in the swords of Damascus was made of Indian iron. Why don't you build up a steel industry in India? I shall do what I can to help you, and the government will, too.'

As a result the laws that discouraged prospecting and the taking up of ore-lands were amended, and that hurdle was cleared. With the way open for prospecting, the ideas of 30 years began to take form. Two years after Tata talked with Perin, an iron-ore deposit of over a million tons was found in India—greater and richer than the iron deposits of Great Britain or of Germany or of France. The ore was taken by Tata on a concession from the government, and now a \$70,000,000 steel plant, employing 40,000 Indians, is successfully operating where 25 years ago a jungle grew. This, then, was the outcome of Tata's idea, and the task of initiating the enterprise was one for which he was brilliantly equipped.

In the first place he belonged to a distinctly commercial people—who are Zoroastrians, worshippers of fire—the Parsis. A few of these people, driven out of Mussulman Persia more than a thousand years ago, found their way to India. Having all the native Persian shrewdness in trading and being so small a group, they determined to refrain from both political and religious controversies. So, as was their tendency anyway, they turned their attention to trading and in the thousand years that followed grew wealthy and increased in numbers until there are in India today about one hundred thousand of them. It was into this atmosphere of business that Jamsetji Tata was born at Navsari in 1839. Education at the place of his birth was a simple process; he was sent to Bombay when he was thirteen and was graduated from Elphinstone College six years later.

His father was a trader in opium, as were many leading English and American merchants of that time, and carried on a considerable and remunerative trade with China. The son obtained some experience in the next three years in his father's office and in Hongkong. Then the American Civil War broke out. When the blockade happend the South created a shortage of cotton in England, the owners of the cotton mills there, in looking for supplies, turned in part to India. Bombay quickly became a partner of the trade, and young Tata and his father engaged in it. For four years they prospered, but at the end of the Civil War they were overextended and, when the inevitable crash came, very nearly went under, they managed to hold on, however, and then obtained a government contract that put them once more on their feet.

Jamsetji Tata, with the clear-sightedness that served him so well later in his plans for the steel mill and with the initiative and knowledge of the world that came to be his particular strength, was not frightened away from cotton merely because he and his father had lost heavily. Instead, he determined to build in India a cotton mill to compete with the British mills that had entered the Bombay market. He went to England, studied British mills and, having learned their methods, returned to India and built the Empress Mills, at Nagpur. These were opened in 1877, and in the succeeding 36 years they paid back thirteen times their original capital.

The fighting-spirit that was one of Tata's chief characteristics, though it is not usually thought of as an Indian quality, was most clearly illustrated in a freight-rate war into which his interest in the Empress Mills led him. Much of the output of his and other mills was shipped to China. Only one steamship-line, however, was in the trade, and this line, the famous British P&O—the Peninsular and Oriental—held a practical monopoly. It had increased the freight-rates gradually, until they had become oppressive. Requests for lower rates brought no results; so Tata went to Janan, interested a Japanese line in the trade, personally guaranteed certain shipments at certain rates for two years and returned to Bombay. He then persuaded the other mill-owners to agree to stand by him and also ship in Japanese bottoms. Immediately the P&O cut its rates from Rs. 19 to Rs. 2 a ton. The mill-owners who had signed the agreement with Tata fell away one by one and he was left alone to hold the bag. He lost heavily on the deal. But the monopoly was broken, and rates, after a time, settled down to proper sums. Tata accepted his loss with the satisfaction that, though he personally had not profited, India had.

All his life he was a hunter of facts. Here again, one meets the unexpected; for the inquisitive, experiment-loving mind is not ordinarily found in Orientals. Of Tata it made an untiring traveller, always questioning and learning. He was seldom in India for two successive years. Often he was gone for long periods, during which even his family seldom knew his exact whereabouts. His office knew where messages could be sent, but not frequently was it possible to reach him directly. Even when he returned, he said little about his journeys. Often in some casual conversation his associates learned that he had visited places they had never dreamed of his having included in his itineraries. All the time he travelled, he was eagerly observant. When on a train he never read, but sat with his eyes on the passing scene. His interest was forever being fired by applied science. As early as 1900 he had purchased a motion-picture machine for his home. Almost as soon as wireless telegraphy was invented, he installed sending and receiving sets at his Bombay residence. He had his own and his wife's rooms ventilated with air cooled by refrigeration long before anybody had done such a thing in America.

The patriotism and public-spiritedness that stimulated him in his last days to build the iron and steel works had prompted him in earlier life to erect in Bombay a hotel of majestic proportions, the Taj Mahal, one of the largest hotels in the Orient in its time. He was urged by his sons and his business associates not to undertake it; for they were sure it would lose money. 'Perhaps it will,' he admitted, 'but that makes no difference. Bombay needs a dignified and comfortable hotel in which to entertain her guests. If it loses money, that will be a bit unfortunate, but I believe it will pay.' As a matter of fact, it did pay, but to Tata that was secondary.

It was this same public-minded point of view that influenced him, not only to bring Japanese to India to teach better methods of sericulture, but also to plant in flooded Indian river valleys seeds of the products most successfully raised in the land of the pyramids. He maintained a garden—superior in many respects to the government botanical gardens—in which were planted trees, shrubs and flowers that he himself had collected in all parts of the world.

The reason for the faith that was in him in regard to the doing of useful public service was set forth to me recently by his nephew, P.D. Saklatvala, president of the Middle States Oil Company, of New York.

'Just after I finished school,' said Mr. Saklatvala, 'I was employed in Mr. Tata's Bombay office and lived with him in his beautiful home, which was filled to overflowing with *objets d'art.* My training in business came from him. About this time he was showing a great deal of interest in an enterprise that seemed to me unlikely to be profitable, although it called for a considerable outlay of money and a lot of work. At dinner one day I asked him why he was so eager to push the scheme under these conditions. He listened patiently.

'My son,' he said presently, 'you enjoy the many works of art I have in this house, and you like to visit museums in order to see other rare and beautiful things, do you not?'

'I admitted that I did.'

'You enjoy these things,' he went on, 'without regard to who owns them, and they are as beautiful to you when they belong to the public as if they belonged to you. Now, suppose, in passing through a museum, you saw a rare and beautiful vase, sitting, let us say, on the edge of its pedestal so that it might fall off and be broken. What should you do?'

'I should put it back safely in place,' I said, 'or tell some caretaker to.'

'Exactly,' he agreed. 'Yet the vase would not be yours. You would lose no money if it fell off and broke and you would gain none by seeing it made safe. Nevertheless, you would have a selfish interest in preventing its fall. Were it broken, you could not come back and see it again. You could no longer enjoy it. I have a similarly selfish motive in this enterprise you say will make no money. Probably it will not, but I do not care. It is important to India; yet it is in danger on its pedestal and may fall off and be broken. I am going to push it back where it belongs, and then I can come and see it any time I wish. I can enjoy it, and my enjoyment of it will be heightened by the realization that I have prevented its destruction.'

The wish to serve his people roused Tata to one particularly fine achievement in addition to the founding of the iron and steel industry. In Bombay he saw a city great in its possibilities but dirty with belching smokestacks and handicapped by the cost of power for manufactures and transportation. He saw also the remedy. Rising abruptly from the coastal plain within a very few miles of the city is a range of mountains called the Western Ghats. As the south-west monsoon blows over this high land, the moisture is condensed and rain falls in floods. More than 40 ft. of rainfall has been measured in some places in a single year, and most of this comes between early June and early November. Until Tata's scheme was developed, the water from this vast precipitation had not been utilized but had rushed in unresisted course through the valleys. Tata saw how all this water could be used and, after years of study, determined to have three great dams built across three of these otherwise worthless valleys. The dams were built, and, during the operation of the system in the past fourteen years, the district around Bombay has been benefited by cheap electric power as well as by the virtual elimination of dirt and smoke. The artificial lakes, over two thousand feet above sea-level, which fill the former valleys, furnish water for turbines capable of developing 100,000 horsepower in a hydroelectric plant 1,740 feet below them. Power is transmitted to Bombay, forty-two miles distant.

Tata made another valuable gift to India. Realizing the dependence of the modern world upon science and conscious of the inadequacy of the facilities available to India for scientific investigation and education, he founded, at Bangalore, the Indian Institute of Science, endowing it with about one million dollars gold. In this institute Indians are being trained in science, in order that their country may more readily take its place in the modern world.

To crown the vision, initiative and energy and the public spirit expressed in these accomplishments, there was the dogged determination usually considered by the Westerner to be his own almost exclusive possession. For thirty years Tata had pondered the problem of iron and steel. For thirty years he had questioned and investigated and thought. For thirty years he had refused to be discouraged—and ultimately he met Perin.

Tata first requested that Perin himself should go to India. But since the known ore resources were wholly inadequate for a steel plant of modern proportions, the necessary raw materials—ore, coal, limestone—had to be located. Perin thought that younger men should do this work at less preliminary cost; then he would go out to make plans and estimates for the mill. At that time, Tata had in mind a steel plant that was a modest affair. Perin saw that it was too small to be practical. But neither of them had an idea of the magnificent size the plant was to attain.

The result of their conferences was that C.M. Weld of Perin's office was sent to India, where, with a prospecting party he there made up, he searched the jungle for many months for iron. Disappointment followed disappointment. First, Sir Thomas Holland, head of the Indian Geological Survey, announced that the work being done was not likely to prove of any value, since up to that time no deposits worthy of modern machinery had been discovered. Then the deposits of the Chanda District were examined. No such high-grade ore exists in the West, except perhaps a little in Brazil. It is seventy-per-cent-pure metallic iron. The deposits were reputed to contain hundreds of millions of tons. But the Weld party found less than a million. Other deposits were located and rejected for the same reason. Weld and his assistants studied geological data in government offices. They travelled up and down India by railroad, on elephants, in bullock-carts and on foot. But they found no ore worthy of a modern American-plan steel industry. Finally, in June 1903, Weld and his party located what has come to be called the Dhullee-Rajhara Concession. Here in the jungle they found a series of deposits containing between three and four million tons of remarkably high-grade ore. With that find in hand, Tata invited Perin to visit India.

In the meantime, Perin was getting an interesting glimpse of Indian character and of Tata methods through his contact with B.J. Padshah, one of Tata's assistants, to whom had been given the task of investigating Perin. Now, Tata had a way of picking men that was all his own. Often, when he saw a man who struck him as having particular ability, he would, in effect, say, 'Follow me'—and he was usually followed. In this fashion he took into his organization a Parsi whom he had met in a railroad eating-house. This man became a successful head of the Empress Mills and handed on the work to his son, who has been equally successful. Padshah, also a Parsi, was a university man and had studied in England and in Germany. When Tata met him, he was a teacher of political economy in the University of Karachi. Tata became interested in him and induced him to give up his professorship for the post of secretary. For years he seaved in this capacity and then finally became a member of the firm with which he had been so long associated.

'The negotiations extended through several months,' Perin told me in referring to the stage of the enterprise at which he was asked to go to India. 'The consideration which I demanded was thought by the Tatas much too high. But they finally consented, and Padshah was sent to New York to accompany me. He is a student of metallurgy, a man the depth of whose knowledge I never quite knew. He has a wonderful gift of languages and can speak with discrimination and eloquence. He would be a striking person in any community. He was the Warwick of the Tata throne. But I must confess that, as we walked and walked the deck, he cross-questioned me to the point where I almost wanted to throw him overboard, just out of sheer exasperation.'

By the time Perin and Padshah reached Aden, Weld had gone farther afield to look for some iron deposits of which he had obtained an inkling from seeing a specimen of the ore in a Calcutta museum. Perin desired to join him, and Tata, being most anxious to utilize every minute of Perin's time, for which he was paying so handsomely, determined to limit Perin's stay in Bombay and expedite his examination of the ore-field.

'When I reached Aden,' Perin told me, in recounting the events of his first visit to the Tatas, 'I received a cablegram asking me whether I could ride a bicycle. I was surprised and mystified, but, despite the fact that I had not ridden one for years, I answered by cable that I could. When I arrived, I found that a part of the journey to the place where Weld was working was over twenty-four miles of villainous road and that I was expected to do it on the bicycle they had ready for me. Furthermore, I was to leave Bombay on the day I arrived. I took the train and the next day alighted to continue the journey on my bicycle. I started bravely enough along the rutty road, but time and again I was forced to use all my strength in twisting the handle-bars this way and that. Now, a bicycle is a light machine, and I always had a great deal of strength in my arms. The result was that, before I had gone many miles in this fashion, I had twisted the handle-bars completely off my bicycle. The situation was not entirely lacking in humour. There I stood in the middle of a very bad jungle road, supporting the bicycle with one hand and holding the handle-bars in the other. Luckily, the appearance of a bullock-cart going in my direction solved my problem. I dumped the broken wheel in, climbed in after it and never again took to bicycling.'

A few days later Perin and Weld located in Mayurbhanja the vast iron deposits of Guru-maishini, where more than a billion tons—perhaps three billion—lay easily accessible, but forty-five miles from the main line of the Bengal and Nagpur Railway and only a hundred forty-five miles from the Jherria coal-fields, supplying the other chief essential for a steel industry. In this one deposit India has more iron ore than is left in all of Great Britain. From this one mine more ore can be taken than from all the mines of any European country, save possibly Russia. America, it is true, has perhaps from thirty to fifty times as much, but American ore is being used at a very rapid rate.

Even before a careful estimate revealed the great size of the newly found ore deposit, Perin recognized its value and began to lay his plans for the development of the Tata iron and steel works. The railroad agreed to build the necessary branch line; then a site for the mill had to be chosen. But before detailed reports had been made, Jamsetji Nusservanji Tata, the originator of the project, died in Germany, in May 1904.

For 65 years this grand old man had worked at his self-appointed tasks. Never an opponent of the British, neither was he an advocate. Offers of official honours and dignities and titles he refused each time they were made; for he realized that, should he accept, motives would be imputed to him that could not be were he to refuse. So he lived and died a commoner.

Great was the blow dealt by Tata's death; but his son, the present Sir Dorabji Tata, now head of the house, and Padshah were most desirous of carrying out his plans. Perin and Weld therefore went ahead.

In the choice of a site for the plant, Calcutta, which was only about one hundred and fifty miles distant, was automatically eliminated, since the location had to be such as to make possible the assembly of great quantities of ore, coal and limestone at the least possible cost for freight. Moreover, Calcutta is situated in the delta of the Ganges, where borings a thousand feet deep had failed to strike anything sufficiently solid to permit the erection of the huge, vibrating plant that was planned. Should such a mill as that of the Tata Iron and Steel Company be erected at Calcutta, it slowly would bury itself in the great accumulation of the silt of the delta. A spot in the jungle was chosen, therefore, for the plant—a spot in Chota Nagpur, where only a few natives lived but where the confluence of the Subarnarekha and Karkai rivers assured an adequate supply of water. The first plan was to erect two furnaces, each capable of making one 150 tons of pig iron a day. Around this nucleus the plant was to be enlarged. So the little cart-road through the jungle to the new site, which was then called Sakchi, was widened and macadamized, strings of bullock-carts creaked to and fro and lines of half-naked workers in turbans were brought to construct the town that was to be. A weir was thrown across the river, and 600,000,000 gallons of water was impounded. Later another weir impounded 2,000,000 gallons.

Perin talked steel with a peppery Englishman, a power on one of the Indian railroads, a possible buyer. 'Why, sir!' said he, pounding the table before him as he leaned over and looked Perin straight in the eye, 'I'll eat all the rails you will ever be able to make to Indian government specifications!' And one could fairly hear his teeth snapping over the curious titbit. Years later, it happened that Perin met the same old gentleman. The railroad of which he was a director had used many thousands of tons of Tata rails. Perin reminded him of his promise. 'Why, nothing of the sort, sir!' he replied just as positively as he had when he pounded the table years before.

The two blast-furnaces were ready for operation by 1907, and the output of pig iron for the first year was sold at a profit sufficiently great to pay the entire cost of the furnaces. The government inspector assigned to the mill was Dr. McWilliam of Sheffield, who, in Perin's opinion, was responsible for the excellence of the product that the mill turned out from the first. The steel mill, however, lost as much as the blast-furnaces made, and the directors and advisers of the plant were faced with the necessity of finding a successful method of making steel in the tropics.

'Imagine a country,' said Perin in describing the difficulty created by the climate, 'in which, from the middle of March to the middle of June, hot, dry siroccos blow; a country in which, during that portion of the year, the temperature gradually advances until by May the thermometer often registers over 125 degrees in the shade, and at night the temperature often stays as high as 95 degrees and sometimes well over 100. Imagine such a land, growing hotter and hotter, with heat-waves that make the landscape quiver as if with ague. And then imagine a sudden great downpour of rain about the middle of June—when for days and weeks the skies are overcast, the ground soaked, the eaves pouring—and through it all extreme variations of temperature exaggerated by the high humidity. Imagine the rice-fed natives—men of little stamina, standing in such weather before the furnaces, with the blinding glare of white-hot metal in their eyes and the terrific heat sapping their strength. What wonder is there that the Indians do not do the work that men are capable of in milder climes? What wonder that Westerners, unaccustomed to the glare, the heat, the fiercely shining sun, the pouring rains, break down, not merely physically, but mentally and morally as well?'

Complicate this problem of climate with that of handling thousands of employees—men and women, people of numerous religions, castes and prejudices, all suspicious of the great machine they have helped to build and operate. A Hindu hates the thought of beef and leather; for cattle are sacred beasts to him. A Mahommedan despises the grease of the machines; for to him all grease is suggestive of the pig, which is anathema. A Jain will brush off the ground on which he rests, lest, inadvertently, he crush an insect and so snuff out a life. A Hindu may be threatened with sudden death: a higher-caste Hindu could prevent it; yet he cannot touch his fellow creature, lest he himself should pay a religious penalty. And thousands of the women—many of them grandmothers at twenty-three or four—must tend their smaller children while they work. Others must have shielded places where they may live in *purdah,* ever hidden.

Yet India has vast wealth, hardly heard of in this country, which may become a power behind industrial development. 'There are millions in India awaiting investment if the people can be sure that the money will pay dividends without danger of loss,' Sir Dorabji Tata has said. 'I do not know that you have heard of India's buried wealth, but it is enormous. I have seen estimates that gold to the amount of $3,000,000,000 is buried under the ground. There are millions which are hoarded in the shape of jewelry and a great amount is hidden away in small sums. We want to get this money into circulation and we hope to do so some day. At the same time, we have many rich men.'

Sir Dorabji is conservative in his idea of the future of India's industrial development. 'Our home market,' he has said, 'will take all that we or any native institution can make for generations to come.' That is probably the practical view of the case. But one has only to use his imagination slightly in order to conceive of an India with an industrial machine that may at some time reach out for foreign markets for its products. If that day should come, what will be the effect upon the industry of the United States, Great Britain and Europe? It is in contemplation of some such prospect that the significance of the Tata enterprise becomes apparent.

But whether or not the Orient ever enters the Western market with manufactures, the outlook before the West in relation to the East is serious so far as iron and steel are concerned. South America, Australia, Africa, the polar regions, have not, it is true, been carefully searched for iron, and in the next half-century great deposits may be found. But at the present time the future of iron lies at least partly in Asia, with India playing an important role. It may be that 70 years hence the Orient, through its ore reserves, will swing the balance of iron-and-steel control from the West to itself.

The Tata steel-plant inspires two visions of the future. The first is of a relentless conflict between two civilizations. The second is of a union of East and West in a cooperation producing a satisfactory resultant differing from both. The one-hundred-per-cent machine-like efficiency of the West may be lacking, but as compensation there may be a large enough admixture of the Eastern sense of leisure and permanency to make existence more tolerable than Western industrialism seems to be making Western life at the present time. And my reason for so believing is that this very union—India with America, in the persons of Jamsetji Tata and Charles Page Perin—is responsible for this huge, successful steel-plant in India.

I can hear those who doubt Indian capacity for initiative and persistence in purpose and effort assert that Jamsetji Tata is a shining exception, or that, had his peculiar genius not chanced to be combined with Perin's, the outcome would not have been the same. I am prepared to admit that Tata was a genius, that there have been few like him and that the combination with Perin was exceedingly happy. But I hold that, if India could produce one Tata at the threshold of its entrance upon an industrial age, it will be able to produce many another as it advances beyond the threshold. And therein lies one of the great possibilities for a rebirth of the East.

CHAPTER 20

Gandhi's Spinning-Wheel and the Steel Plow

J.S. Parker

STREAMING THROUGH A NINE-storied gateway modelled after the *gopuram* of the famous Hampi temple, known of old as Vijayanagar, thousands of Indians force their way toward the tent where the sessions of the Thirty-ninth Indian National Congress are being held. Within a huge white *pandal,* or dome, made entirely of the hand-spun and hand-woven cloth called *khaddar,* are gathered twenty thousand delegates and visitors. They sit cross-legged on the ground. Around the outer fringe of the crowd other delegates occupy tiers of benches resembling American circus seats. Directly opposite the entrance is a raised dais, where distinguished delegates and visitors sit under a canopy. In the middle a speakers' stand or platform rises about eighteen feet above the ground. Seated on a chair is Mahatma Gandhi, presiding at his first Congress since his release from prison. On the dais are the Moslem Ali brothers, Pundit Motilal Nehru, C.R. Das, leader of the Swaraj Party and mayor of Calcutta, Mrs. Naidu, Dr. Annie Besant, president of the Theosophical Society, Lala Lajpat Rai and other Nationalists. In the hearts of all these persons, thus gathered at Belgaum, in Christmas week of 1924, to consider the problems of India, present and future, burns the fire of patriotism, expressed in speech and in resolution.

**ASIA*, July 1925. J.S. Parker was an academician engaged in teaching at Missionary Schools in Bombay Presidency.

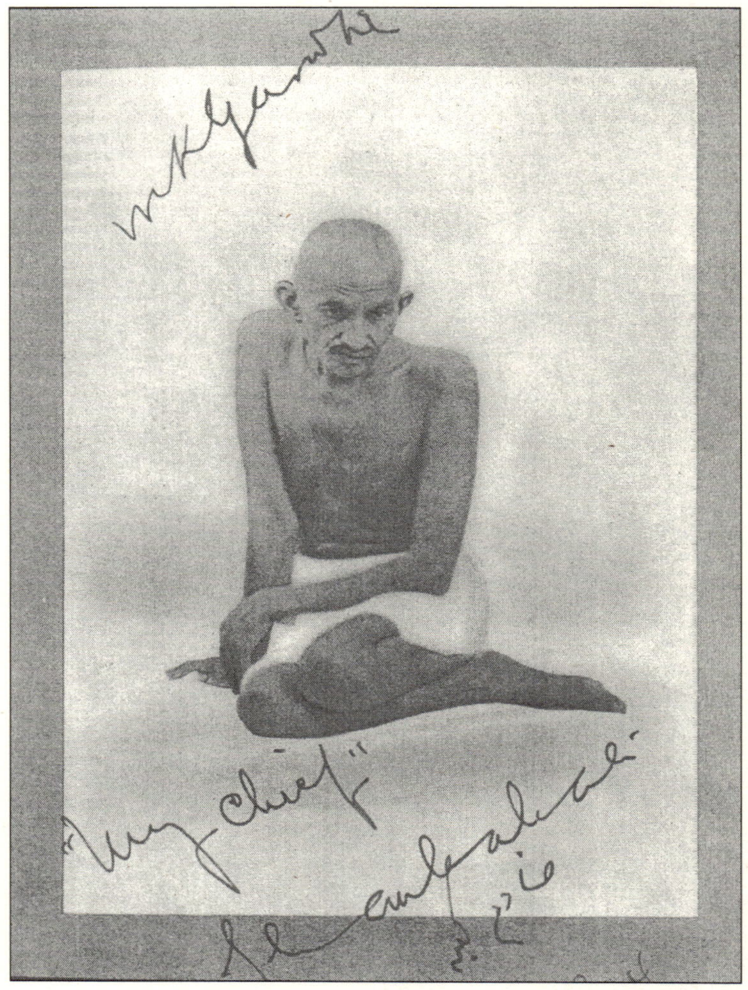

THIS AUTOGRAPHED PICTURE OF MAHATMA GANDHI, SIGNED 'MY CHIEF' BY SHAUKAT ALI, ONE OF TWO BROTHERS WHO HAVE LED MOSLEM AGITATION IN INDIA, IS A RECORD OF HINDU-MOSLEM UNITY AT THE BELGAUM CONGRESS

The scene changes to an obscure corner outside the main Congress camp. A quick walk of five minutes has brought us to an industrial exhibition held in an enclosure walled with canvas. In the section given over to machinery is a small booth. Within it are three native iron plows; also, on a table, are placed some booklets; standing in the doorway is a representative of the firm of Kirloskar Brothers, Limited, manufacturers of the best iron plows made in India. There is no throng outside the doors of this exhibition. Few persons enter the gate. Fewer still stop for even a glance at the booth of Kirloskar Brothers, as they hasten to the shops displaying hand-spun and hand-woven cloth.

Yet that obscure booth and those three iron plows stand for patriotism, too. In the hearts of the Kirloskar brothers burns a love for Hindustan just as zealous as that which fires the souls of Gandhi and his fellow politicians. But it is expressed in a different way. And this diversity in the choice of practical methods for improving India accounts for much of the political puzzle in that land.

The crowded Congress tent and the neglected industrial booth are emblematic of Indian thinking among the extremists. This thinking lies at the root of the opposition typified by the throwing out of budgets in the legislative councils. Even for their platform the extremists offer as the main plank only, 'Back to the spinning-wheel.' Constructive improvement of India, through application of the principles of efficiency, to industry and especially to agriculture, means little to them.

To understand the importance of plows as an expression of patriotism, one must realize how primitive are the conditions under which most Indian farmers work. Some of them only scratch the surface of the ground with a sharp stick. Many of them scratch it a little more deeply with a wooden plow. A very few use steel plows imported from America. A constantly increasing number are using Indian-made steel plows. These latter are able to turn the ground completely over, thus insuring better crops, as they themselves have proved again and again.

Gandhi, of course, realizes the importance of agriculture to India. More than 90 per cent of the people of India are either engaged in farming or dependent on it. But they cannot work in the fields during the blazing heat of the summer, and Gandhi proposes that they supplement the tilling of the soil by the cottage industry of hand-spinning. Thus they will raise their economic level. It was for this reason that Gandhi pushed through this Congress an amendment to its constitution, making membership dependent upon the presentation of twenty-four thousand yards of home-spun yarn of good grade each year. Even the fiery Swaraj leaders, C.R. Das and Pundit Motilal Nehru, who, with their aristocratic organizing ability, balk at the actual work of spinning, have been brought within the terms of the franchise; for there is a provision permitting persons unable or unwilling to spin to bring yarn spun by a substitute.

To me, an American used to large-scale production, this cottage-industry movement seemed to be a backward step. In a short interview near midnight, after a long session of the subjects committee of the Congress, Mahatma Gandhi himself answered my question about the probable value of the spinning-wheel in future generations when the industrial day now dawning in India will have reached its noon-tide. He said that he believed in improved agricultural tools, provided the purpose was to help the farmer get better crops and not to exploit him for the profit of the manufacturer. He said he believed in improving the spinning-wheel as far as possible. 'But

I do not believe,' he added, 'in your mills with their hundreds of spindles, all run by electricity.' When I pointed out to him that steel plows, which improved the lot of the farmer, were made possible by electricity, he replied, 'But there you get into a labyrinth'—which was his way of intimating that he was tired, that it was late, that he did not care to discuss the subject any further! A minute before he had said: 'India's new industrial age will not come in your generation or in mine. Like a practical man I am going to take what I can with the spinning-wheel.'

The Indian National Congress, founded in 1885, was planned to give Indians of all political or religious persuasions a chance to voice an opinion on matters affecting India. Since the Congress had no official status, it had to content itself with passing resolutions. With the inauguration in 1920 of the Indian Legislative Assembly, the Congress apparently lost its reason for existence, but Indian opposition to the reform measures, under which the Assembly itself began to function, gave to the Congress, now captured by the Nationalists under Gandhi, a new lease of life. The policy of non-cooperation with the government was set up. This specifically involved a boycott of the forthcoming elections to provincial and national legislative bodies. After Gandhi's arrest in 1922, C.R. Das, his successor, favoured participation by Indians in the government, in order to prove by a policy of obstruction that the reform measure of a responsibility divided between Indian legislators and British executives with absolute vetoing power was unworkable. The newly founded Swaraj Party, under the astute leadership of Das, gained many seats in the 1924 elections and has carried on, from within, a warfare against the government. Gandhi has now had to give way on non-cooperation. Meanwhile Das and the Swarajists are in active control of the political trend. It is significant that, at a time when the Indianization of government is rapidly advancing, both Gandhi and Das have recently pronounced themselves in favour of a self-governing India that shall remain a part of the British Empire.

But benefiting the peasants is not Gandhi's only purpose. He firmly believes that India's best chance to get home rule is to pinch the British people where they are weak—in the pocketbook! For some years he has been trying to boycott all foreign goods, which of course would include all British goods. Whether he honestly believes in his own heart that only Indian-made things ought to be used is hard to say; my guess is that he does not know himself. He has an idea that, when British interests lose their trade with the Indians, they will demand that home rule shall be given to India, in the interest of renewed commercial intercourse. Here in a nutshell is his political strategy. Here are the real reasons for his boycott campaigns, although he may have cloaked them underneath appeals for a return to 'India's Golden Age.' The coup that he performed at the Belgaum Congress is good politics—on paper, anyhow! He has intensified the boycott by limiting it to mill-made cloth; he is going to hit the Britisher in a single industry—which is his greatest—the Lancashire mills. If he succeeds in gaining a large membership for the Congress under the terms of the new franchise, he will surely launch a thunderbolt of khaddar at the Lancashire mill-owners, who have influence, to say the least, in Downing Street.

But Gandhi is primarily a spiritual leader; he derives his power to influence chiefly from the integrity of his own character. During the busy days of the Congress sessions, when, as its president, he had to attend numerous meetings in addition to writing articles and letters and receiving visitors, he sat down at his spinning-wheel every day to spin his own quota of yarn. His schedule for the day at the Congress was that of an extremely busy man. He rose at four in the morning and spent a short period at prayer. Then he began work and often laboured until midnight with a short walk as his only intermission. Every evening at half past seven he had another prayer service, which was very impressive. On Mondays he observed absolute silence, speaking not a word to any one, but writing notes.

He was clothed in the conventional *dhoti,* a garment reaching from the waist to the knees. Sometimes he wore a sort of shawl, partly or entirely covering his breast; but at the opening session of the Congress he discarded this. On Mondays he scribbled on a pad with long, strong fingers strangely out of harmony with the frail appearance of his lean, ascetic body. He has a picturesque look but is far from striking or handsome. His full lips and meagre facial contour are positively ugly. His black hair, closely cropped except for a wisp at the back, is graying with age, and his black mustache also is slightly gray. His voice, though he speaks fluently, is sharp and almost harsh at times; it utterly lacks musical tone.

As a speaker Gandhi cannot be called an orator. His appeal is primarily to the intellect and not to the emotions. In his delivery he shows the influence of English training; he is quiet, reserved. But every syllable is distinctly enunciated, almost clipped short. His voice, not naturally powerful, carried to every part of the huge circus tent in which the Congress meetings were held. He is an exceedingly able chairman; he conducted in a masterly way the meetings of the subjects committee. His smile was ready to break into laughter at any joke; his goodnature was always to the fore. Once, when an excited speaker used the words 'hypocrite and liar', Gandhi stopped him at once and warned him to use more parliamentary language. Humility is one of the characteristics that endear Gandhi to the people and give him his power. At the opening meeting he declared: 'I have repeatedly admitted that I am a fallible being. I am just as good or just as bad a mortal as you are, and therefore I want you to dismiss my personality from the equation.' Although he is still a force to be reckoned with in India, he is no longer, I think, blindly worshipped. Just how potent his influence is, will be decided by the popular reaction to his spinning-franchise. Partly as a result of it, membership in the Congress, which had been 123,000 in 1923, dropped in January, February and early March to 9,124.

A single thread unites the various strands complexly interwoven in the Congress; namely, an intense desire for self-government. This desire is reinforced by an unpractical idealism, which shows itself with peculiar clarity in the cases of two Bengali gentlemen whom I met during the Congress. Both are trained chemists; one possesses the degree of doctor of philosophy from Calcutta University. This man, S.C. Bose (not the famous Indian scientist of the same name), has done important research in coal-tar dyes and once held a high position in the government mint, Calcutta. The other man is S.C. Chatterjee, Dacca, Bengal, a fanatical Swarajist. In fact, he was once a member of the anarchical party of Bengal (the cause of the recent Bengal Ordinance authorizing the irregular arrest and trial of suspects) but, according to his story, was converted to non-violence by Mahatma Gandhi. Here are two men with specialized training in the field of chemistry who have given up important work to induce farmers to spin and to weave on handlooms!

They see nothing incongruous in abandoning constructive research at a time when India needs above all else the application of science to every phase of industry and agriculture. Indians do not take technical courses in large numbers, and trained scientists are scarce. These men, instead of recognizing that they must develop industrial life as a prerequisite to self-government, think that, if they once get self-government, they can develop industry.

One hundred years hence Indian historians will record the deeds of the Thirty-ninth Indian National Congress. But they will also record the improvement brought about in the course of the century in the lot of the peasants and will credit it in part to the manufacture of steel plows. In general, Gandhi's objections to the evils of Western industrialism are valid. But the Kirloskar brothers also are alive to these evils. In Kirloskarwadi they have built up a model factory town. They are to western India what Henry Ford is to Detroit. They do welfare-work, physical and social, in their factory on a scale unknown in other plants. Most of their employees live with their families in clean, well-lighted, sanitary homes, which contrast strikingly with the wretched *chals,* or lodging-houses, in which workers of Bombay and Sholapur mills drag out existence. The Kirloskar brothers are proving that machines in themselves are valuable and that the good in Western industrialism can be separated from the bad. Doubtless their very practical patriotism will do more to hasten the day of *swaraj*, or self-government, for Hindustan than will the activities of the National Congress.

CHAPTER 21

Nautch-Girls and Old Rhythms of India

Lily Strickland Anderson

TO ME SHE WILL ALWAYS REMAIN THE ideal nautch-girl. I call her Jasmina; for the name fits her well. Never again have I seen one so petite, so sylphlike, so eloquent of the romance of those legendary nautch-girls, the Apsarases, who were the celestial dancers of Hindu mythology.

As we sat there, in an open marble courtyard in Bombay, steeped in moonlight, mesmerized by music, she made her entrance with the dramatic effect of sheer simplicity and lack of self-consciousness. Costumed in shimmering silk and tinsel, she took the centre of the stage and fell into the attitude that preluded her first dance. She was a small and graceful creature, with skin the colour of old ivory. Her oval face was crowned with luxuriant masses of blue-black hair; the size of her eyes was enhanced with *kohl,* and her hands and feet were tinted with henna.

What pleasanter setting for a real nautch than a moonlit night of April! Our host, the Raja of a very wealthy Native State in India, whom we had met on our first voyage from Marseilles to Bombay, had arranged the party for us at the home of a rich Indian friend of his. During the passage he had displayed the greatest pleasure because of our interest in India and our excited expectancy over its wonders and mysteries. And now, among other entertainments, we were to be treated to a nautch-party, one of the accustomed phases of hospitality in the country. That this was a special nautch-party I knew at once; for the dancer chosen for our pleasure was

**ASIA*, August 1925.

quite, in an oriental way, the prettiest girl I had ever seen. The Raja told us with characteristic Indian frankness that he had secured her services for the evening for Rs. 200, that she was sixteen and that, chaperoned by her mother and father, she had come from Delhi.

We were given chairs, as a concession to our race, while, with the exception of the Raja and his party, the remainder of the guests sat or lolled on cushions and bolsters in true eastern style. At intervals cool sherbets were handed around by silent-footed, white-clad servants, and we were offered sweetmeats, cardamom-seeds and paan a combination of betel, areca-nut and lime for chewing. To add to the bizarre effect of the scene, a gaily dressed dwarf kept the air moving over our heads with an enormous peacock-feather fan. It was like the setting for an Arabian night's entertainment.

At one side squatted the musicians, two drummers, a flutist and a player on the *sitar,* a popular stringed instrument of India. The pulsing drums set the rhythm of the music, the plaintive flute began the elusive strain, and the sitar carried the melody in soft tones. The persistent beat of the drum worked us up to a high pitch of expectation as the music rose and fell. In prolonged cadences the melody swelled and then died away on some unfamiliar subdominant note that seemed to leave the theme in mid-air, waiting to be completed. We had not known that it was the custom for nautch-girls to combine dancing with singing; so we were greatly surprised when Jasmina opened wide her red lips and burst into shrill and raucous tones. As she began her song, she turned directly toward my husband, who, as male guest of honour, was singled out for personal attention. She sang literally at him, to the growing amusement and delight of the Indian audience. After this compliment had been drawn out for about a half-hour, I asked the Raja what Jasinina was singing about, and he answered with attempted nonchalance and evident embarrassment, 'Oh, she is singing about the gods, Krishna and Rama, you know.' We did not know then, since that was in the early days of our adventuring; but we afterwards learned that the songs of the nautch-girls deal entirely with amorous episodes in the lives of the gods. A favourite is the story of Krishna's having multiplied himself into sixteen thousand forms so that he could tread 'the primrose path of dalliance' with the sixteen thousand *gopis,* or heavenly milkmaids, in the fields of Brindaban.

The music went on in waves of tumultuous sound, the drummers more and more under the hypnotic influence of their instruments as they cried out an occasional 'Well done!' by way of encouragement to the dancer. Whirling and swaying, Jasinina wove her spell on twinkling feet, her arms and hands fluent with the eloquence of her theme. Her dance began at the finger-tips, each digit moving with deliberate meaning. Then the whole hand took up the rhythm, which gradually extended to the arms and on through the body until her entire form was one with the music. Her muscular control and coordination were admirable, as she worked herself up to the climax of her dance and then drooped gracefully to the floor salaaming at the conclusion of her first number.

In the intervals between the dances, she withdrew to one side to rest and change her costume, with the assistance of her maid. For refreshment, she drew from her girdle a small silver box and extracted from it a triangle of pan, which she inserted in her mouth and chewed with a bovine, impersonal expression, as if she were alone and remote from mankind.

Her next number was the traditional peacock-dance, one of the most popular in the repertoire of the nautch-girl. She was garbed in iridescent sequins and veils, beautiful in colour and design, and, for all the world like a proud and royal bird of India, she strutted, preened and postured through the more stilted measures of her piece. She sang again, and this time I did not ask for a translation of her song but thought her voice quite appropriate to the name of the dance!

THE NAUTCH-GIRL, IN HER LONG, VOLUMINOUS SKIRT, NEVER HEARD OF THE 'LAMP-SHADE' BALLET-DRESSES OR BACCHANAL COSTUMES OF THE FOLICS-BERGÈRE OR THE ZIEGFELD FOLLIES. THE THREADS OF GOLD AND SILVER GLEAM AS SHE WHIRLS RAPIDLY ROUND, DANCING TO THE ACCOMPANIMENT OF THE 'TABLA', A PAIR OF DRUMS, WHICH SETS THE RHYTHM OF THE MUSIC, AND THE 'SITAR', WHICH CARRIES THE PLAINTIVE MELODY.

At the conclusion of the entertainment we were invited to inspect Jasmina's wardrobe, which more than justified all that has been said of the gorgeousness of Indian costumes. Instead of *saris,* she wore diaphanous trousers and voluminous skirts and little short-sleeved jackets of embroidered satin. In most of her dances she used veils of pastel tulle. Her skirts were loaded down with gold and silver thread and ornamented with jewels and tiny mirrors that flashed in the light as if a thousand fireflies had settled on her. We also duly admired her collection of jewellery, which included many bracelets, rings, earrings, necklaces, pendants and bandeaux for the hair.

In the course of our residence in India, and on the opposite side of the country from Bombay, I later saw many nautches, but never another Jasmina, never such cameo-like features as hers, such large and slumberous eyes and so dainty a form. One group of dancers stands out in especially bold contrast with her. The occasion was a private nautch-party given in honour of a distinguished visitor, at the Maidan Theatre, in Calcutta. It was an attempt to present a nautch ensemble, and it undoubtedly gave any strangers present a very bad impression of nautches and of Indian music in general.

The artificiality of the stage was accentuated by its profuse decorations of abnormal palms, variegated marble pillars and garish cushions. The impossible back drop showed an indigo river, distant temple and lurid sky, in which hung an immense yellow moon, as heavy and opaque-looking as a fat cheese. The orchestra had been assembled with a view to quantity rather than quality of instruments. There was an array of drums and sitars and that device of modern European manufacture called the harmonium, something of a cross bet between an accordion and a parlour-organ. A collection of cymbal-players added to the hubbub, and all the musicians struggled valiantly to play in unison. There were some who never caught up with the theme. The drums rose in a loud crescendo, and the cymbals clashed at hysterical intervals during the prelude for the nautch.

The well-meaning manager had evidently gathered in his dancers, 'not wisely, but too well', from the four corners of Bengal. The nautch-girls ('girls' is euphemistic), lumbering about the stage like a stray herd of buffaloes, looked awkwardly self-conscious and bewildered. They evidently had not rehearsed and had no idea what they were supposed to do, but they made gallant though non-unified attempts at posturing, gesticulating and singing in the composite harsh voice of nautch-girls!

The crude stage-setting, the raucous music, the obese Bengali dancers, who looked as if they had absorbed a too steady diet of rice, curry, *ghee* and sweetmeats, gave the effect of a caricature. The bovine caperings of that particular nautch-party reminded me of a verse in *The Lays of Ind,* where, also, seductive naughtiness was vainly expected of the dancing-girls:

The Reverend McPherson believed that the Nautch
Was a most diabolical sort of debauch;
He thought that that dance's voluptuous mazes
Would turn a man's brain and allure him to blazes!—
That almond-eyed girls,
Dressed in bangles and pearls,
And other scant jims
Disclosing their limbs,
With movements suggestive
And harmony festive,
With fire in their eyes, and love on their lips,
And passion in each of their elegant skips,
As beauteous as angels, as wicked as devils,
Performed at these highly indelicate revels

No nautch can be seen at its best in a setting so artificial as the Maidan Theatre. Where self-consciousness enters, inspiration ends; and the real nautch-girl strikes an entirely anachronistic note in a modern theatre. Most nautch-girls lack all the subtlety of sensuous appeal that one looks for in the East. They are rarely young, as Indians judge age; they are usually fat and overdressed and have acquired a hard and calculating expression as if their thoughts were on *pice* rather than the fine points of the dance.

It is the dream of every nautch-girl not bound to temple service to be given a permanent position on some raja's estate, where she can reap an independent harvest and collect jewels and fine clothes. It is said that many nautch-girls, having amassed a fortune, have in their virtuous old age bequeathed all their property to Hindu temples. As a whole they may be divided into two main classes, the temple dancers and the freelances. There are others, like Jasmina, who travel under the guardianship of their parents and who charge a good fee from any one desiring their services, but this type is in the minority.

The freelances have entered their profession voluntarily and go about from village to village, staging impromptu performances in the hope of gathering a few pice. The grossest of the sisterhood are the common girls of the marketplace, predatory harpies without brains or ambition or even the grace of clean garments. The freelances usually travel in company with a musician, preferably a drummer, who plays their accompaniment. If they have an orchestra, it comprises a player on a *tabla,* or pair of drums, a sitar-player and a flutist; thus, with percussion, wood-wind and string, they have at their command the essentials in the Indian trio of musical instruments. They are not bound to any temple management, but wander as they like, conferring their favours as it pleases their fancy. For a hundred rupees, one can purchase the services of a small band of ordinary nautch-girls and musicians who will come early and stay late, prepared to draw out the night's entertainment with an endless repertoire. They sing and dance tirelessly for hours. It is usual to hear and see them at a private Indian *tamasha*—procession, dinner, garden-party or any other type of festivity where they supposedly will amuse the guests.

The temple-dancers are the typical nautch-girls in south India, especially. To many temples are attached bands of trained nautch-girls called devadasis, or 'servants of the gods', who take part in the ceremonies several times a day. They perform at public religious festivals and they may also be engaged for minor duties, such as weddings, the installation of a new household god and public tamashas. Since they lend a note of colour to any fete, they are encouraged and patronized by rajas and lesser social lights. They are paid at so much a performance, the proceeds to be divided among the dancers with a percentage for the priests. Any private *bakshish* or any gift of jewels they may keep as their own.

The Abbé J.A. Dubois, an unimpeachable authority on Indian customs, was very harsh in his criticism of the morals and manners of the temple-dancers of south India. But in some sense morals, like manners, are a matter of geography. To the Hindu masses it is not strange that the devadasis are courtesans. These dancers, who are trained from childhood, form a dancing-girls caste, recruited by new births and by adoptions. Little girls are both purchased and received as gifts; for, notwithstanding the duties involved, it is not considered disgraceful for a mother to dedicate her child to service in a temple. But once a girl enters the temple, she becomes a slave as well as a servant or bride of the gods, or, more accurately, of the priests, who are the mouthpieces of the gods. If she fails to save any money during the years of her usefulness to priests and worshippers, she is maintained on a sort of pension, part of the temple funds reserved for that purpose. Although ordained to serve the gods, she is, paradoxically, beyond the pale of respectability. She is debarred from marriage and tabooed socially by the elect. A few Indians devoted to social progress now feel this ethical contradiction so strongly that they are supporting a programme for the reform of the dancing-girls' caste. These men and women successfully used their influence to prevent the appearance of nautch-girls at the Empire Exhibition in London last, year, but in India of course they must combat racial temper and the lethargy of custom.

The Indian nautch-girls claim a very high and ancient lineage. According to tradition they are descended from the divine Apsarases, the celestial dancers who wove rhythmical magic in the court of Indra, the Hindu god of the firmament. The Apsarases, or heavenly nymphs, and the Gandharvas, or heavenly singers, were the makers of music in this court on the Hindu Mount Parnassus, or Mount Meru, somewhere in the northern Himalaya. Rembha and two other nymphs among the Apsarases are taken as the ideal types of bodily loveliness and perfected accomplishments. Rembha, whom legend called the Indian Venus, rose from the foam at the churning of the waters when the gods searched for the elixir of immortality. She was also the first classical dancer and imparted her art to mortals. The other Apsarases were her companions on her journeys, and they were all under the patronage of Chandra, the god of the moon, and Kama, the god of love.

The Gandharvas, or celestial singers, sixty million in number, 'who were born imbibing melody', were supposed to be the sons of Brahma. These musicians made matrimonial alliances with the Apsarases, their descendants in turn with demigods and the children of the latter with mortals, until the nautch-girl came into being. From these forebears, she is said to have inherited her love for music and dancing. However little credence may be given to this version of her lineage, it is a fact that the nautch-girl plays a most important part in the life of India. Aside from all the fantastic legends surrounding her, she is worthy of study for her own sake.

She follows custom, not only in regard to music and dancing, but in her toilet, and even in cosmetics and styles of hair-dressing and bathing. Her toilet begins with the ceremonial bath, a rite attended by prayers and *mantras,* or invocations to the gods. After the bath she is thoroughly massaged with scented oils made from coco-palms, olives, mustard or sandalwood. An oil-rub is considered very beneficial to the skin, as well as necessary to render the limbs and muscles more pliant and supple. This same oil is spread on the hair and combed into it to give the gloss greatly desired by Indian women. Finger-tips, palms of the hands, toes and soles of the feet are stained a deeper red, and the eyelids and brows are darkened with kohl. The effect of kohl, though artificial is pleasing, as it serves to accentuate the size of the eyes and gives them a lustrous appearance. Powdered saffron is used to add a golden tint to the skin, much the same as a toned powder is used by a Western woman. As a final touch, a little mark, in red or yellow pigment, is placed in the centre of the forehead; whatever its religious significance, it serves as a sort of beauty-spot and is certainly a sophisticated adjunct to the toilet. Heavy perfumes of jasmine, frangipani, attar of roses, sandalwood, musk and ambergris are much in favour; for the nautch-girl delights in strong scents.

Bathed, anointed in oil, perfumed, with her hair adorned and shining, she wraps about her body her sari, if that is her chosen garb, bestowing the six yards of material with a deft touch that would be the despair of a modern modiste; for the draping of the sari is an instinctive process, an inheritance from ages past. I know of no more graceful and lovely dress, except the flowing robes of the Periclean period in Greece. The nautch costumes, as well as the music, vary somewhat, however. Some girls wear trousers and boleros; others, full skirts or saris. They may be completely swathed in saris or clad scantily above the waist, according to whether they are Bengalis or Punjabis. All dancers of any importance possess handsome wardrobes of brocades, embroidered silks and satins. The voluminousness of the full, plaited skirts, adorned with gold and silver thread or small mirrors, is apparent as the dancers whirl rapidly round. Sometimes the skirts stand out stiffly like own umbrellas, revealing trousers of thin material beneath.

If I had any criticism to offer concerning the costumes, it would be that the nautch-girls are overdressed and weighed down with heavy garments. But it is custom, and that ends it. No doubt these votaries of an ancient craft would be horribly shocked if they could see a performance of the Ziegfeld Follies or visit the Folies-Bergere or other extravaganzas in vogue in the West. The real nautch-girl never heard of a 'lamp-shade' ballet-dress or the bacchanal leopard-skin-autumnal-grape costume. The seminude modern classical dancer or the rhythm-intoxicated jazz enthusiast, whirling through the syncopated measures of some barbaric fox-trot, has no place in her imagination.

The Indian nautch-girl is dignified, deliberate and serious. Though she knows nothing about 'artistic restraint', she nevertheless has the natural restraint of the primitive—an elemental graveness and placidity. She is, above all, leisurely and takes no account of time. Her dance begins with almost imperceptible movements, gradually gathering momentum with the crescendo of the music. Her slow, undulating postures are graceful sedate and instinct with charm. When she achieves a climax, it is genuine, because she works up to it naturally and in accordance with the development of her dance. Then she gives and gives freely, with the spontaneity of a wild bird's song.

She is mistress of the art of motion, though for the other form of rhythm that she uses I cannot say much by way of praise, since nature has given her the voice of the peacock rather than of the bulbul. The whole body of the dancer, even to flexible fingers and feet, responds to the decrescendo or crescendo of the tempo. She moves sinuously, *en rapport* with the minor cadences of the music, which continues in waves of unbroken sound. There is undoubtedly something hypnotic about it all, especially in the right setting—out-of-doors on a moonlit Indian night. The picture is sensuous and pagan if you like, but none the less natural, harmonious and satisfying.

One must attend a nautch, not in the spirit of criticism or of drawing unfavourable comparisons, but with one's mind made up beforehand to endure endless monotony and repetition, without having one's senses dulled to new impressions. With unqualified reserve one must give oneself to the time-annihilating spell of the music. A nautch today in India is an echo from a thousand years ago. Therein lies the charm of both music and dancing. They were handed down by the gods direct! The Indian audiences are keenly in sympathy with the dance. They feel and understand the music; its rhythm, its nuances have been bred in them for countless generations. Yes, there is a decided affinity between the Indian audience and the performer. Nor is it difficult for the outsider to submit himself to the mesmerism of the drum-beat and gradually to absorb some understanding of the essence of the music and the coordination of the dancer with it. He begins to experience, through flowing melody, a primordial response to the throbbing rhythm.

Occidental impressions of oriental dancing may delight the eye and enchant the mind, as do all art-forms fashioned by the imagination of idealistic exponents of beauty and rhythm combined. The stage-setting may be splendid, the music sensuous and the dancers themselves lovely, but the one essential is lacking, and that is reality. We are, after all, seeing 'impressions' of Eastern dancing, shaped and modified to meet the understanding of the Western mind—a very different thing from an actual nautch in India. The 'impressions' may be more harmoniously conceived, more esthetically pleasing, but the stage-setting is artificial and the music, built on the Western scale, is created with the help of instruments and tones never dreamed of in India. All Indian music is melodic rather than harmonic. There is much to be said in favour of the single-melody line; unhampered by the chords and contrapuntal harmonies that sometimes distract the ear, it registers more keenly upon the mind. A symphony orchestra cannot possibly be so effective for a nautch as one or two drums in the hands of inspired players in a natural, simple setting in India. The real nautch-girl needs nothing more.

The enchanted moonlight filters down through the palm-trees and discovers the dancer; the air is filled with the heavy scent of jasmine; the stage is the hard-baked earth of old Ind; the audience, of the people, frankly demonstrative and voluble in appreciation. Even an outsider, beholding a nautch for the first time on a warm, perfumed night on the edge of the jungle, must feel a tug at his heartstrings, an answer to some awakening chord of memory, a 'far, familiar note' like an echo from immemorial years. To me there is great charm in the dances of India, a charm that can never be captured or reproduced by any Westerner. The nautch springs from the heart of the land. It is a rhythmic picture moving against the screen of time, a tapestry woven, out of the primitive emotions of an ancient race. It is the lifting of a misty veil behind which we may descry down lengthening aisles the secretive, the romantic, the mysterious past of an incredibly remote old India.

CHAPTER 22

India's 'Soul-Power'

The Hindu Secret of Bearing the Burden of Life Without the Gospel of Getting On

Jane Alden

I WAS FEELING VERY MUCH DASHED and depressed, in the appalling hotel room I was temporarily occupying in Madras—an apartment familiarly known as 'The Kennel', for its lack of light and air. On arriving in Madras from Ceylon, I had found that the teacher from whom I intended asking instruction—a brother of my Hindu friend at home—was away on a protracted vacation; also that the retreat-house for women, where I had hoped to stay, had burned down, that its matron had been killed and that there was no place or opening for me anywhere! Here in the hotel, along with my rather staggering disappointment and the first of the heavy fall rains, I wondered dismally why on earth I had ever started on this wild-goose chase half-way round the world—why I had ever left home to come to India.

But of course I knew very well why. And the all-importance of the journey to me made momentary disappointments and obstacles trifling. So I jumped up, shook the dank, dark dreariness of 'The Kennel' from my skirts and out to seek what I could find, then and there, that resting.

**ASIA*, October 1925. Jane Alden lived in India during 1920s to study Indian philosophy, mythology and folklore.

I had not far to go. No farther than Adyar—the headquarters of my theosophists again!—and that grand and picturesque personage, their President, Annie Besant.

Be whatever you may think of Besant's agitations or of the religious and psychic reputation of the Theosophical Society, come into the presence of the gallant figure that at seventy-eight has weathered the storm, from her early days of free-thinking and communication to the violent and now seemingly vicious fight for Indian home rule; see her there in the amazing dignity of the pillared hall at Adyar, the old amber lamps lighting up the forceful countenance with its crown of white hair, the white robes with touches of Indian gold; watch her standing in the midest of the rapt circle of her students of all nations—of Brahmans, businesslike Americans, French Germans, Persians, Japanese; gaze at that multilifted faces and imagine behind them the far spread multitude of the adoring masses of India, to whom she has been mother, guide, protector, friend and behold Annie Besant, if you can, what a thrill!

This was my first picture of her, when I was privileged to hear her address the theosophical lodge at Adyar on 'Expansion of Consciousness in the Individual' and understood why Bernard Shaw calls her the most brilliant speaker he ever knew.

The second picture—a striking contrast, but no more striking than the mystical inner doctrine of theosophy and its very practical outer works—I saw in her busy office in the native quarter, where she runs a newspaper. No esoteric refinements here; but through the swarming bazars of the workaday Indian masses to the workaday gray door of *New India,* up worn rows of steps through crowded rooms of native typesetters, past the outer portcullis marked 'Staff Only' and thus to the editorial sanctum. There, before a big, piled-up desk, surrounded by papers, clippings, office paraphernalia of all sorts, I found Annie Besant the statesman and publicist, counsellor of viceroys and ministers, the woman of affairs.

She heard my plight, looked me over with those penetrating eyes of hers and said, 'Should you like to come and stay at Adyar for a while?'

I thanked her but explained that I was not a theosophist.

'Why not? You seem to know many of our people.'

'Yes, and they've been most awfully kind to me. But I'm not a bit of an occultist, and frankly it's all too complicated and confusing for me.'

She regarded me, not at all displeased by this candor. 'I like honesty. It's rare from lone women in India, who generally jump at the chance of cheap and comfortable quarters at Adyar and accommodate their spiritual views accordingly. I'm sorry you're not a theosophist. But here's a suggestion that comes to me: while you're waiting for your *swami,* why not go along up to Mrs. Rawlins at our Hill College? She'll show you more of India in a week than you'll see in these cities in a year.'

'I'd love it—but what about Mrs. Rawlins? She might be bored with me or too busy.'

'Bored—too busy? You don't know Mabel Rawlins! Great woman—pupil of Leschetizky and a brilliant musician, wife of a first-rate novelist and lecturer. He's the president of our college, and they both joined our Order of Service and gave up enticing careers to come out here and work for nothing at Indian education. Certainly she'll have you—I'll write to her.'

I was met at the Hill College station by a boy with the most beautiful face I had ever seen. He said his name was Krishna and that he had brought a bullock-cart to convey me the eight miles to the college. In this—the 'covered wagon' of India—we now set forth: a seraph in a white toga and a sinner in a beige travelling-frock, pursued by other violently interested bullock-carts, full of shouting Indian ladies and gentlemen.

For breaking the ice there is nothing like a bullock-cart. By the time Krishna and I had been bounced and jolted and hurtled over the long stretch of hilly brown country and had discussed several international matters important to ourselves, we were friends.

'I think you must have had a very strong motive to leave your home and come so great a distance to India,' he said as we neared the end of our ride. 'Why, if you please?'

'I came to learn.'

'From India?' he asked incredulously.

'Certainly. I met some of your people in America, and, from what I saw of them, I was convinced that your country had a great deal to teach me.'

'Most Westerners do not think that,' said Krishna, with all the warmth of resentment perpetually seething. 'They call us barbarians and hold themselves very superior to us.'

'Excuse me, but do you not call them by the very same word—and hold yourselves superior to them to the extent of keeping the whole of the ocean as taboo between you?'

Krishna laughed good-naturedly. 'But you see we are the conquered race; we have a natural right to feel aloof and bitter.'

'You were aloof before you were conquered. In fact, that was the reason you were conquered, wasn't it?—your persistent aloofness from one another, your lack of cooperation for defence. I can't let you, with your caste-mark between your eyes this minute, score up one on the West for snobbery!'

The boy flushed deeply.

Lightly, then, I held my hand to him to help me down—ignoring caste to that extent, anyhow—and he smiled again.

And there we were at the white-domed college buildings, and in the gateway, waving a welcoming hand, was Rawlins.

I liked her at once—such a sturdy, almost virile figure, with her strong face and short, iron-gray hair, in the midst of her group of sensitive-featured

Indian boys. Her husband was away at a convention, and she was in charge. She looked capable to me of being in charge of anything. 'Well, you are sporting, coming away up here to visit an unknown hill-tribe,' was her generous greeting as we shook hands.

We went up to her sitting-room and had coffee; and there began the steady stream of student boy visitors, who came and continued coming, in perpetual pilgrimage, every hour of the day while I was there.

Krishna, as proud first acquaintance, brought his two intimates—Ali, a Mahommedan, very dark and tall and fiercely good-looking, and a Mr. Ram Prasad—'Mr.' because older than the others and distinguished in having spent two years at a university in America. An arresting creature, this Ram Prasad, with his burning eyes and prematurely white locks atop his dark face—extraordinarily unquiet for a Hindu.

These three constituted themselves my bodyguard; and many were the walks, talks and testings of East-West friendship we were to know together.

First they took me, not to a ball-game or the campus or the swimming-pool, but, characteristically, to chapel. They seemed so eager about this that I was moved to ask, on the way across the field to the auditorium, 'Is your chapel compulsory?'

They looked a little puzzled.

'Of course everybody goes,' said Krishna.

He led the way into the big bare room where the entire college of eighty or ninety boys was assembled: the little boys of the preparatory school in front; then the intermediates; the dignified seniors and professors in the rear.

I knew they came from every corner of the vast country; I knew they represented every caste and creed and type. And, as they gazed up at me with such eager interest, such cordial smiles—little and big, light and dark, it seemed that here at last was my welcome to India and that, in some strange way, instead of visiting a foreign people in a foreign country, I had come home.

When asked to speak to the hoys, I said just that, adding: 'You of India wear your caste-mark between your eyes. So really does every man of every country. And I in my travels round the earth have learned to look for that invisible but unmistakable sign—the something of character, sympathy, congeniality or lack of it that every person, of whatever civilization, flashes to one from between his eyes. For the eyes are the windows of the soul; and from them the soul looks out and hails its own, in America, India, Europe or China—throughout every nook and corner of the globe.'

Then the regular chapel exercises began.

First they all together recited with intensity, almost with passion, some of Tagore's *Gitanjali* verses:

Where the mind is without fear and the head is held high;
Where knowledge is free;
Where the world has not been broken up into fragments by narrow domestic walls;
Where words come out from the depths of truth;
Where tireless striving stretches its arms towards perfection;
Where the clear stream of reason has not lost its way into the dreary desert sand of dead habit;
Where the mind is led forward by thee into ever-widening thought and action—
Into that heaven of freedom, my Father, let my country awake!

Then Krishna, who was head boy of the school, chanted a Hindu prayer in Sanskrit. After him, a Buddhist boy chanted a Buddhist prayer; then a Moslem, a Mahommedan prayer—the entire assembly remaining concentrated in absolute stillness and reverence during each one of these rituals.

'And is it just the same every day?' I asked Mrs. Rawlins.

'Every day in the year. In fact, I think the boys have come to the point where they can worship just as truly in the prayer of their neighbour as in their own. The only thing they couldn't stand would be not to worship at all.'

The separate prayers for the different religious sections at the Hill College were followed by the collective national Scout song; for Mrs. Besant has been wisely fostering the Boy Scout movement in India. It did your heart good to hear the lusty vigour of the young Indian throats in the still all too frail Indian bodies.

Never have I known chapel exercises like those, where each boy obviously enjoyed every minute, to the depths of him, or whence I myself went forth with any such sense of real and abiding inspiration.

When Krishna came that afternoon to take me for a walk, I was waiting for him, with more than one question. 'Tell me something,' I began as we strolled along the hill-path. 'Indian boys really like religion, don't they?'

'Like religion?' The Hindu boy looked at me in amazement. 'Why should they not like religion? It is the whole of life!'

'Where did you learn that?' I asked. 'What religion do your people teach you when you are little?'

'They do not teach us any religion—the way you mean teaching. Nobody can teach it, though it may be communicated or absorbed, sometimes, through other people.'

'From whom do you absorb it, then?' I questioned.

'From those who already have it,' came the prompt reply. 'From the *gurus*, the religious men, like the great *rishis,* our old philosophers of the forest colonies, who would refuse to teach, counting themselves always students, though other seekers for truth might come and live and study with them.

'But you do have these gurus, or religious men, to help you—even now in modern times? What do they do?'

'Oh, yes. The guru is a sacred friend and helper because he already has that Light we seek. All the guru does, outwardly, is to give certain breathings, exercises in concentrating the mind and a line or two of prayer: "I meditate on Him who is the Creator of this universe; may He enlighten my mind." That way the mind is made open and receptive. All each needs to do, all each can do, is just to make himself a clear medium through which the Infinite Spirit can grow and flower by its own nature. All the teacher can do is to create an atmosphere by being that atmosphere himself.'

'And the parents, the other relatives and the friends of the child, don't they try to mold him or teach him anything, either?'

Krishna shook his head. 'The best way to teach is to be,' he persisted.

'I'm afraid your system would never suit the domineering West, Krishna,' I said. 'There, from the moment a child is born, he must do what we tell him to do, be what we've decided it's best for him to be—whether "we" happens to be the family, the church, the school board or the social community. It rarely occurs to us that there may be something in him to unfold that we don't know about, something finer, perhaps, than the thing we're bending every effort to make him become.'

'Is it so?' Krishna pondered this wonderingly. 'What is your ideal, then, that you teach a child in America? Material success—getting on in this world—is that all?'

'Well, I shouldn't call it just material success. That's only its outer clothing. Rather, I should call our ideal social responsibility.'

'But, if a man has obtained no understanding of truth, what good will the society he has served do him when it comes time to die?'

'Perhaps we do not think so much about that as of what good he can do to society. You see him as a spiritual being, in his relation to infinite and eternal life; we see him as a human being, in his relation to other human beings and every-day life. Really he is both.'

Fixing his great eyes on me, somberly, this son of the ancient philosophers demanded in reply: 'No matter how powerful or fine a society you may have, how much good you may do or what rewards you may receive, without spiritual wisdom, constant spiritual inspiration, how can you bear life?'

How indeed! Is not that what the West is beginning to wonder?

But I answered Krishna: 'Perhaps my people would ask you how you Hindus have been able to bear life all these years with no relief for your wretched millions in poverty, no money nor scientific knowledge to prevent your awful famines, no organized force to keep the invader from consuming your resources and your lives. In other words, we would ask you, how can you bear life without practical power?'

We had come to the end of the path. We stood there, exchanging a long look, almost like the naked spirits of East and West, searching, inquiring of one another.

Finally Krishna said, unmasking all his pain to me, 'We bear it very hardly!'

'So do we,' I said then, showing him mine.

There was a moment of feeling so intense that I very femininely feared I was going to cry. But Krishna, a true Oriental, brushed aside the instant of emotion, saying: 'I was wondering whether you would like to go with me to see one of these gurus we were speaking of. My brother's guru is not far from here—the other side of the market merely.'

So we turned back toward the town, a pleasant huddle of brown buildings and terraced Indian roofs, past the perpetual panorama of Indian pictures—an old man in a violet toga, leading a white donkey; a woman in dull blue and gold, carrying a brass jar on her sleek, dark head; and then the market-place, where brisk trading was going on among the golden grains and red chillies. The cherished bullocks lay about, luxurious and benevolent, on the outskirts, like spoiled children—the most important members of the family.

'Once a year we have a festival for them,' Krishna said, smiling. 'Then they are hung with garlands, anklets, tassels, bells, and given the best of everything, to thank them for their work. Finally they are led outside the town and must run through a fire—for purification. We think God is in animals also, as in everything. And bullocks are the Indian man's best friends. But I suppose you find these customs very primitive?'

'They seem to me very charming, Krishna, on the contrary,' I said with casual matter-of-factness.

He was as quick to beam as he had been to shrink. 'You really like these things? Then I will tell you much, everything I know about India!' he promised joyously.

The first thing he told me was apropos of Hari's guru. Hari, he said, was 'living all the time beside *Guruji,* and serving him, in the old style that many Indian fathers and mothers wish to see revived. But if Hari had not convinced him of his earnestness and great desire for truth, Guruji would never have accepted him. Of course, knowledge is the most sacred and precious thing in life, not to be given away lightly. We have a saying, "Wonderful must be the teacher and wonderful the taught." One ancient teacher kept a king's son waiting outside for three days, while he tested him by menial tasks and this ignoring'.

I had visions of a teacher at home keeping a royal young American son three days outside! Came the American mother's voice, demanding of her Jack or Tommy anxiously, 'Do you think you're going to like your teacher, dear?' and knowing only too well that, if he does not, for a year at least all is lost!

Then, with Krishna, I arrived at the temple where the Indian guru lived. First of all, on entering the courtyard, we saw the young Hari—a boy of twelve or thirteen, sitting cross-legged before the shrine—eyes closed, face uplifted, in motionless and profound meditation.

When he became aware of us, however, he rose and saluted us happily and without a trace of embarrassment or self-consciousness at being interrupted in his devotions. 'I was reading and meditating upon *Gita*,' he explained as naturally as a boy at home would have told you he was reading *Robinson Crusoe.*

Krishna regarded him affectionately. 'He studies all the time *Gita*, this one. I think he is going to be a *sadhu*, or holy man. Well, old fellow, I have brought a western lady guest to see our Guruji. Please give him this offering'—he produced some sweetmeats and fruit we had got in the market—'and ask if he will kindly receive us'.

In a few minutes the child returned, moving with a lovely rhythm through the cloistered passages, and conducted us to the master.

He was that, one knew the moment one saw the commanding profile of the proud old eagle, spare, small-boned, with the frame of the ascetic and the features of the aristocrat. His shaved head threw into startling relief the high and very narrow forehead. In the white robe of the *brahmacharin,* or religious student, with the ever-beautiful Hindu hands folded upon his balanced knees, he sat upon his plain wooden platform, the picture of repose and poised intelligence, the personification indeed of the old Aryan ideal.

Nothing in the bare, whitewashed cell but a couple of brass utensils and a few books; there was about it all a fierce, almost an aggressive, purity. Krishna was right: the guru was an atmosphere in himself; and none who came within his radius could fail to be affected by that frosty clearness.

Krishna presented me, and Hari presented Krishna's offering, which was received with no thanks but with a quiet gesture of acceptance. It seemed that the guru spoke excellent English, having the degree of master of arts from the University of Calcutta—a fact of which, as the conversation proceeded, he appeared to be rather ashamed than proud.

'Krishna has been telling me something of your Hindu teaching traditions,' I said by way of introduction. 'I feel that I am very fortunate to meet you.'

The guru made a deprecating sound. 'I am glad,' he said, 'to have you meet some Hindu boys uncontaminated by the bureaucracy or the

THE LARGE MULTITUDES OF THEOSOPHISTS IN INDIA, ANNIE BESANT, THEIR PRESIDENT, IS MOTHER, GUIDE, DELIVERER. SINCE HER EARLY DAYS OF FREE-THINKING AND EXCOMMUNICATION SHE HAS WEATHERED EVERY STORM AND IS NOW, AT SEVENTY-EIGHT, A PICTURESQUE AND GALLANT FIGURE. UNWEARIED CHAMPION OF 'SWARAJ', SHE WENT TO ENGLAND LAST JULY IN BEHALF OF THE COMMONWEALTH OF INDIA BILL.

missionaries. Yes, these theosophists are very good—a prey to psychism, perhaps, but at least they appreciate the superiority of the Indian culture.'

I said they seemed to.

'Outside of India,' he continued calmly, 'the whole world is fixed on just one purpose, enjoyment of the physical senses.'

'Have you lived much in the countries outside of India?'

'No, but one need only read their literature. England, France, America—the whole ideal before these nations is to live the brute in a polished way.'

Now, I had come to the East acknowledging its spiritual superiority. But to be met by the East itself with this satisfied assertion of superiority and to be told that our American fathers and mothers, striving and sacrificing so that their children might have a little better chance, were attempting 'to live the brute in a polished way' was a trifle startling.

'All people are instinctively good to their own,' said the guru when I objected to his criticism. 'That in the main is egoism, however, since what is good and successful in the child reflects back to the credit of the father. But in India, I am happy to say, we have long ago outgrown this materialism.'

'Oh, I have not found India entirely without materialism,' I protested. 'Here, and during the weeks I spent in Ceylon, I have heard quite as much talk of money as ever I heard in America. And the people seem quite as much concerned over *tamashas* and wedding-parties and *saris* and jewels and academic degrees and posts as *vakils* or sub-commissioners as the average run of humankind with its human baubles anywhere.'

'Well, we will not quarrel over that,' said the guru indulgently. 'Anyhow Krishna tells me you are here to study Hindu philosophy; so evidently you have love for higher things. And you have read our *Upanishads,* then. Are they not gloriously inspiring? As Max Müller has said, "the very height and apex of human expression, reaching out after the divine."'

THROUGH MEDITATION, ON THE BANKS OF THE HOLY GANGES, THE YOUNG HINDU ATTAINS SPIRITUAL STRENGTH AND WISDOM. FROM THE DREARY VALLEY OF EVERYDAY LIFE HE ASCENDS THROUGH THOUGHT TO GLORIOUS HEIGHTS. FOR HIM RELIGION IS THE WHOLE OF LIFE; IT IS COMMUNICATED TO HIM BY THE 'GURUS', OR RELIGIOUS MEN, SEEKERS AFTER TRUTH WHO KNOW THAT THE BEST WAY TO TEACH IS TO BE.

He closed his eyes and straightened his spine. His whole body seemed to expand and be emancipated as he rolled out the sonorous lines: 'Thou art our father. Thou art our mother. Thou art our beloved friend. Thou art He that beareth the burdens of the universe: help me to bear the little burden of this life!'

Verse after verse of the majestic Sanskrit stanzas filled the little room. In the midst of those three motionless and transcendent figures—for the two boys were, like the guru, transported beyond time and space—one felt again the almost overwhelming force of this strenuous ascetic and of the whole Indian ideal.

Returning to ordinary consciousness, he rather spoiled it by saying: 'Back to the *dharma,* the old ideal of Aryavarta! Let us regain the heritage of our ancient rishis, and then the proud West shall bow the knee. Back to the greatness of old India!'

'I am with you, sir!' said Krishna, heartily.

'I, too,' said Hari. 'Guruji believes we shall conquer the world by India's soul-power.'

'But I thought that India's soul was in realizing the Infinite, not in conquering the world. And how can you go back?' I suggested. 'Today you are living in an entirely different world from the old India.'

'Thanks to the foreign bureaucracy, yes,' said the Hindu teacher bitterly. 'But we shall lead our future generations back to the old ideas.'

'Has your English education, all that it has opened up to you, been of no use or satisfaction to you, then? And could Krishna and these other boys today earn their living and support their mothers and brothers with the help only of the Hindu classics?'

'Not under the bureaucracy. But in the future—'

'But you are apt to remain partially under the bureaucracy for many years—at least until these young men are trained in that very organized knowledge and fitness to rule that you seem to despise. And when they are, they will rule not as the isolated Indians of other days but as modern, cosmopolitan men and women.'

'You Western ladies have very vigorous ideas,' said the guru, smiling constrainedly.

'Our Eastern ladies do not go about or express themselves so freely.'

'When they have conquered the world and seen more of it they will,' I said, smiling back.

Then, repenting, I steered him to his own topic, the Hindu classics. He launched into a great disquisition on Schopenhauer's admiration of the *Upanishads* and on Schopenhauer and the Vedantists on free will, and for a half-hour he talked brilliantly and interestingly.

I went back from my visit to the guru to meet his special objects of detestation, the Christian missionaries of the vicinity, at tea. Mrs. Rawlins was on very good terms with these European colleagues. I found them in her little western sitting-room, discussing their great common interest, Indian women.

'Another baby for the Raos,' announced Dr. Brown. 'That makes the fifth, and his third wife before he's twenty-eight! This present girl is just thirteen and will probably die of fever like the others. How long are the Indians going to keep it up—this sacrifice of women?' Looking utterly spent, she dropped down on the couch and gulped Mrs. Rawlins' cup of hot tea. But she seemed unable to eat. 'An old storeroom where the grains are kept,' she went on incoherently; 'old stoves, old rags, rats! Unclean, are they—not to be allowed in the house to have their children? Well, then, why aren't they too unclean to have them at all? It makes my blood boil! This is the fourth talk I've had with Rao, and I've talked with the headman of the village as well.'

'Does she really mean all that?' I asked Mrs. Rawlins. 'Is it all true?'

'Only too true,' my hostess replied tersely. 'Same old story—every house, every woman, in the town. Always promises, when you talk to the men—going to change things, going to reform. And next time the same thing over.'

Yet they had festivals for bullocks! 'And do Krishna and the other boys know about this?' I asked. 'And Krishna's brother's guru, who is so superior about Indian civilization?'

'To them it's so much a matter of course that they never even think of it, my dear.' The scorn in her voice more than matched Guruji's scorn for the brutal West!

Miss Steele meanwhile was telling one of her every-day experiences: 'I caught her just as she was about to sell the child to the sweeper for a handful of *pan* to chew. I hadn't any pan, but the mother said, "Oh, take her for two *annas* then." Think of it—four cents! So the little thing's home at the mission this minute. Probably she'll become as great a treasure as Miss Farnum's right-hand helper, Radha. She was sold to a brothel and then brought to our hospital when she was twelve. We bought her outright for twenty-five *rupees,* and she's really the finest girl we have.'

Miss Farnuin said: 'Yes, and I've another for you, Mildred. You remember that Bengali woman who's been intent on offering her baby to the god? Well, I've been going to see the mother and telling her about Jesus, and she's going to let us have the child instead. They're awfully poor, and she can't afford to keep her, but she says she'd rather give the little girl to a god who thinks just the same of Brahmans and pariahs.'

CHAPTER 23

Are Gandhi and Ford on the Same Road?

Drew Pearson

IF YOU WERE TO SEARCH THE FOUR corners of the world, you would not find two men superficially more unlike than Mahatma Gandhi and Henry Ford. Gandhi is a small, frail man, brown-skinned and naked to the waist. He sits cross-legged on a straw mat, serene and unflustered by what goes on around him. Ford is a tall, angular dynamo of energy, who cannot sit still a minute. While talking to you, he leans back in his swivel-chair, sits forward, crosses his legs, uncrosses them. Gandhi is visionary; Ford is practical. But both men are idealists, and it is in their ideals, their desire for human welfare, that they are strangely close together.

Mahatma Gandhi lives on the cool-running Sabarmati River at a point where it drops down from the Aravalli Hills and spreads out upon the plain of Ahmedabad. Henry Ford lives beside the river Rouge, muddier perhaps than the Sabarmati, but meandering down through the hills of Michigan to the lake plain near Detroit in the same lazy fashion. A dam across the Rouge generates electricity to do Ford's cooking and grind his corn; but from up behind Gandhi's house the steady thump-thump of a wooden mallet pounding corn in a hollowed stone is evidence that nothing more than sleepy, grunting buffaloes or shadowy forms stealing down to bathe at the dusk of dawn disturbs the Sabarmati.

**ASIA*, December 1926. Drew Pearson (1897-1969) was a well known journalist and commentator at N.B.C. Radio.

HENRY FORD, INDUSTRIAL IDEALIST

Ford lives at the end of a vistaed driveway in a palace that the stranger is barely allowed to glimpse before a guard challenges him. Across the street from Ford's estate is his Dearborn office, down at the mouth of the river the blast-furnaces of the Rouge plant loom black against the sky, and the modern machinery at Highland Park, Detroit, covers two hundred and seventy-eight busy acres. Within a radius of four miles, one hundred and forty thousand men toil for Ford—so many that the closing of their shifts must be carefully timed lest their exodus choke the streets.

Gandhi dwells within walls of mud and straw, with red-tiled roof and stone floor. The family sleep on straw mats spread upon the floor or upon the ground outside. So I found them when first I stumbled into their compound at ten one night. I was a stranger and from a strange land, but they took me in. Gandhi's home forms the nucleus of another industrial centre. It is called the *Ashram,* which means a cooperative settlement, and is made up of his nephews and cousins and grandchildren and nationalist students from every corner of India, who live in whitewashed cottages and toil at plow or loom. I heard their melodious chanting of Hindu prayers at four in the morning as I lay dozing on my mat beside the Sabarmati, and I knew their day's work was about to begin. Before breakfast they bathed in the river, ground the day's corn, cleaned their cottages. At seven the Ashram began to resound with the click-clack of the shuttle and the whir-whir of the spinning-wheel. No whistles, no smoke nor dust, no endless chains carrying four-cylinder motors past lines of men, each with a screw to tighten, a bolt to place. Just the zip-zip-zip of the cotton-carder from a room where a Bengali student squatted upon the floor, and outside the droning of the Indian summer.

IN A HOUSE OF MUD AND STRAW, ON THE SABARMATI RIVER, IN INDIA, MAHATMA GANDHI WORKS, DENOUNCING MACHINERY AND ILLS ATTENDING ITS USE. SPEED, TOO, IS ANATHEMA. 'GOOD TRAVELS AT SNAIL'S PACE', SAYS THIS HINDU SAINT.

Ford is fond of children; so is Gandhi. Ford has three grandsons in whom he is trying to arouse an interest in mechanics with every toy that money will buy. The latest is a miniature threshing-machine with an eight-horse-power steam-engine, which I saw efficiently sorting grain from chaff, to the great glee of its small owners. Gandhi's six-year-old granddaughter, lacking such elaborate toys, seized upon my toothpaste and managed to decorate her pet dog with streaks of white from ear to tail before he could make a chagrined exit. Then, quite carried away with the way of exploring a gentleman's travelling-kit she pounced upon my razor and was about to slash off one dainty eyebrow when I intervened and nearly broke up our friendship. Both Ford and Gandhi are early risers and are abstemious. Ford is up at six and on his farm. He seldom bothers about breakfast. Gandhi also eats but two meals, at sunrise and sunset. His diet consists of goat's milk and fruit and is limited to two kinds of food a day. If, for instance, he uses salt and pepper in his soup, he considers these two ingredients, together with the soup as three kinds of food, and eats only once more during the remainder of the day. Gandhi is no poseur and does not mean to be a fanatic. He adopted this ration many years ago because he felt that mankind in general ate a too much. When he was a popular young lawyer, he was invited to so many banquets that he sickened of the sight of men stuffing themselves and resolved that he would not eat after sunset. He uses no knife and fork but eats in the orthodox Hindu fashion, with the thumb and first two fingers of the right hand and without letting the left hand touch the food.

Gandhi has fought the machine age as valiantly as Ford has championed it. Henry Ford is not just a railroad-owner but a speed-demon. One day he told me that he had just driven from Grand Rapids to Dearborn—one hundred and seventy miles—in four hours. On this subject of locomotion, which Ford has known more than any other one man to make cheap and easy Gandhi remarks, 'Nature requires man to restrict movements as far as his hands and feet will take him.' For Gandhi both speed and railroads are anathema. 'Good travels at snail's pace,' he says. 'It can, there-fore have little to do with the railways. Those who want to do good are not in a hurry; they know that to impregnate people with good requires a long time. But good has wings. To build a house takes time. Its construction takes time. Furthermore, the railways have spread plague. Best physicians will tell you that where means of electrical locomotion have increased, the health of the people has suffered.' Yet these two men, differing widely—for Ford's mode of life would jar the lives of Gandhi and Gandhi's would drive Ford crazy with inactivity—these two, though seven thousand miles apart, have concluded, by separate processes of thought, that the greatest problem confronting their countries—India and the United States—is the big city. And, while pursuing the problem, each in his own peculiar and individualistic way, they have arrived at the same solution.

The remedy, Henry Ford has figured out, while experimenting with his Dearborn farm and factories, is the removal of industry to the village, where it can be combined with farming. 'The farm has its dull season,' he points out, 'when the farmer can come into the village factory. The factory also has its dull season. That is the time for the workman to go out on the land to help produce food.'

And Mahatma Gandhi, sitting cross-legged upon his mat in the Sabarmati Ashram, declares: 'What the Indian peasant needs is not a revolution in agriculture, but a supplementary industry. India has almost seven hundred fifty thousand villages scattered over its vast area. The great majority of the people face a hand-to-mouth existence. Because of the rainy monsoon seasons and the droughts between, millions are living in enforced idleness at least four months of the year. The most natural solution is the spinning-wheel, which was an essential in every home a century ago, but was driven out by deliberate economic pressure. Its restoration solves India's economic problem at one stroke. It saves millions of Indian homes from economic distress and is a most effective insurance against famine.

Moreover, in weaning thousands of women away from factory life and the prostitution of the cities, the spinning-wheel is also a moral instrument.'

Gandhi is a doer as well as a theorizer. He has worked out his theories under a few open sheds at his Ashram. Under one of them a half-dozen carpenters with a set of clumsy hand-tools are making spinning-wheels. Crude and inefficient affairs they appear to be, but in a demonstration given by Gandhi's able nieces, they turned out an incredible amount of cotton-thread. The spinning-wheels are stacked up inside the shed and have overflowed to great piles outside, from which they are sent to every corner of the land, until the spinning-wheel on a background of red, white and green has become the national emblem of India. But Gandhi has not stopped there. Across the road from the Ashram a white school building of rather imposing proportions houses a hundred students sent from the various provinces of India to learn the ancient arts of carding, spinning and weaving and then to return and spread their knowledge among the farmers.

Gandhi's logic seems sound. Raw cotton is India's chief money crop. Why should it be packed up in bales, to be shipped four thousand five hundred miles to England, turned into cotton cloth in the mills of Lancashire, packed up and sent four thousand five hundred miles back again? Let each *ryot,* Gandhi says, make cotton homespun on his own farm. Furthermore, let him do it during the slack season.

Ford uses similar logic. He asks why men should be herded into street-cars to hang by straps for an hour twice a day to and from the city, instead of staying in the country and having the materials shipped to them. Furthermore, what objection is there to employment of the farmer during his slack season?

When I questioned him regarding the success of his village industries, he said: 'Go out and see for yourself. Have a good look around. Talk to the foremen and see how they like our experiment. Then come back and I'll talk to you.'

Accordingly, I went up the river Rouge, once harnessed by a half-dozen mud and timber dams with overhead water-wheels and old-fashioned mills, which ground the grist of the countryside. Today, reharnessed by new concrete dams, supplying power to modern turbines in clean white factories, the river Rouge is grinding out carbureter valves and generator cut-outs and magneto parts for Ford cars the world over. The first of these, located at Nankin, a metropolis of fourteen houses, employed eleven men—incidentally a substantial majority of the male population—in making a hundred and three thousand, five hundred vibrator-cushion-spring-spacer-rivets per day. The Rouge at this point gave only fifteen horsepower, but a few miles farther up, at Plymouth, a larger dam supplied a hundred horsepower and employed thirty-three men. Phoenix, with a hundred and fifty girls, and Northville, with three hundred and eighty men, complete Ford's village industries on the Rouge. At each, workers and foremen told the same story.

CHAPTER 24

Machines and Gods in a Bombay Mill

Hindu Festivals and Caste Practices that Enliven Factory Routine

Henry R. Band

THE STARTING UP OF A WORKS OR factory in India is by no means the matter-of-fact business it is in the West. The fitters, the carpenters and the masons may have finished their tasks, but the engine must not make its first revolution until the masters, be they Hindu, Mahommedan or Parsi, have consulted the astrologers and an auspicious day has been appointed for the opening ceremony. Apart from the formal turning of a wheel by a privileged official, an inauguration rite must be carried out, and this is the more important observance of the two. Thus, at the outset, one runs against a fundamental difference between East and West in the interweaving of the spiritual with the material; of religion and its rites with work.

I had come out from England to organize and run a modern bleach- and dye-works for its Parsi owners in Bombay. Now I had reached the stage when the works was practically complete and the doorways were being made gay with streamers and garlands of flowers in preparation for the opening ceremony. Parsis quickly assimilate Western customs and mannerisms; they adopt articles of Western attire and Western business methods, attend European theaters and concerts and mix in European society. Yet at heart

**ASIA*, December 1926. Henry R. Band was the British manager of Bombay Dyeing Mills.

they have not changed much; their ritual at the Fire Temple is the same they brought from Persia centuries ago; their marriage ceremonial still includes the long-drawn-out recital of blessings in a language understood by few; they still expose their dead to the vultures in the towers of silence and retain their almost fanatical reverence for the four sacred elements.

Cowasji, my assistant, I took to be a typical modern Parsi—clever and intelligent. What impressed me at first was his Western outlook on matters relating to the works. I might have been discussing the subject with another European. He viewed rather indulgently the superstitions of the Hindu workmen and was almost apologetic when telling me of certain caste rules that must be observed. But I struck the eastern note when he began to explain the Parsi invocation ceremony, which would take place before the formal opening of the works. 'No person who is not a Parsi must witness the proceedings,' he said; and I gathered that the beneficial effect of the ceremony would be destroyed if its privacy were violated by one of alien faith.

Four Parsi priests arrived at the works very early in the morning and commenced their prayers. 'It will take them two hours to go through the ceremony,' Cowasji told me.

'Do you understand the nature of the ritual?' I inquired.

'No, the priests recite the prayers in Sanskrit. Very few Parsis who are not priests understand this language; the language used by Parsis in Bombay is Gujarati.'

Meantime Mahadeo, my Mahratta *mukaddam*, or foreman, had informed me that his men—who were, like him, not Parsis but Hindus—wanted to make *puja* before the engine started. Cowasji said this puja, or worship, was most important; if it were not carried out, the men would have no faith in the machinery, and any future accident would be set down to the omission. So I told Mahadeo to get on with the ceremony. The men took a coconut, broke it over the fly-wheel of the engine, sprinkled red powder over the moving parts and on certain machines in the department, cheered vigorously and clapped their hands. Coconut and sugar were next distributed, and the men daubed their foreheads with red powder.

All was now ready for the official opening. The chief director of the company, turned on the compressed air, and the diesel engine made its first revolution. In a speech that followed, the works was declared open. My friend who had erected the engine submitted, like myself, to being garlanded and received a bouquet of flowers. Garlanding of officials in this fashion, was the custom on all ceremonial occasions.

The engaging of hands for the new works was an occupation fraught with perplexity; for it meant delving into an involved social order of which the West knows nothing. All the castes and subcastes seemed alike to me at first, and my common sense told me to be guided by custom and precedent rather than my own judgement. Seated at the office table, with Cowasji on one side and Mahadeo on the other, I interviewed the applicants. Most of them came provided with *chits,* which correspond to 'characters' or letters of recommendation. These chits were essential, but it was fortunate for some of the workmen who presented themselves that they did not understand English; otherwise their chits would not have had so long a life. One chit would state that the bearer was a scoundrel. He would hand it to me with a smile; I would read it and return it to him, making him none the wiser. Many were written by professional letter-writers, who recorded their clients' qualifications in flowery language and supplied date, signature and all for a few *annas.*

'Are they all Mahrattas, Mahadeo?' I asked at last, after we had engaged a large number of hands and registered their thumb-prints.

'Almost,' interrupted Cowasji. 'They must be all of one caste to work with water in the bleaching department.' Afterward, upon analysing the work-hands engaged, I found I had 90 per cent Mahratta coolies and 7 per cent Hindu subcastes, such as Vanis, Kumbhars and Kulvadis. My Mahrattas would work with these particular subcastes but observed distinctions in eating and drinking.

The term 'Mahratta' is confusing since it refers both to a tribe and to a particular caste. Tribally Mahrattas are of various castes, but such as we had to do with were Sudras, according to the old fourfold classification in Manu's Law of Caste. They are an agricultural people of the southern Mahratta country, or Maharashtra, which lies to the south and east of Bombay adjacent to the Western Ghats. Such of these Mahrattas as can be spared from their farms come up to Bombay to work in the mills, and there they make plenty of money. They constitute the backbone of the industrial classes of the city, a sturdy, independent, hardworking community adhering rigidly to caste rules. But when the season for sowing the crops comes round, first one and then another Mahratta workman will bring a telegram to say that his wife's mother or his uncle is on the point of death, or there is a dispute over the land and he must return at once. It is just as well to examine the dates of the wires; for they may have been used on previous occasions. The mill-workers like to go to their native country for wedding and funeral ceremonies; and, if a wife is pregnant, her husband endeavours to take her to her native village among her own folk until the birth of her child. In the planting season a fourth of the employees, or even more, are likely to be away at times. The best attendance is during the monsoon, when the boat service across the harbour is discontinued on account of rough seas; for most of the Mahrattas must sail to the mainland to get to their homes.

In addition to these Mahrattas and a few workmen of the subcastes with which they would work, I engaged a Mochi, or belt piecener; a Mali, or gardener, a Mahommedan coolie, a Portuguese and a Parsi fitter and two Mahars. All these castes and subcastes and the outcasts caused some confusion in my mind at the beginning of my Bombay career, but among themselves my mill-workers knew their exact position in the social order—with whom to eat and with whom not to eat; with whom to work and with whom not to work. The low caste and outcast workmen were necessary for certain jobs that the other men refused to do. The Hindu Mochi, or belt piecener, for example, was of low caste; his occupation was to handle leather, which is really the skin of a dead animal and, according to Hindu teaching, would pollute my Mahratta workmen. Modern conditions have modified the prohibition against leather; for educated Hindus wear leather shoes, and in a works where leather belts are employed on the machine the Hindu machine-men cannot avoid handling them from time to time. Although workers from the villages do so most reluctantly, they fall in with the practice on seeing workmen of their own caste set the example.

To handle the tallow used in the finishing department the Mahommedan was engaged. A Hindu would have lost his employment rather than touch it.

It happened once, however, that some cloth which came from the weaving department to be bleached, smelt of rancid tallow. 'Do you recognize the smell, Cowasji?' I asked.

'The tallow used in the sizing department was bad, sir.'

'Has it occurred to you that the Mahrattas will raise no objection to bleaching this cloth?'

'No, why should they raise any?'

'Why do we employ the Mahommedan oiler and greaser?'

'To put tallow on the calender bearings.'

'But a Hindu will not do it.'

'Oh, no. He would go home first.'

'Well, look here, there is tallow in that cloth, and the men do not object to handling it. You see how a caste rule has been broken unconsciously by factory usage. But do not make the men any the wiser.'

Although a Mahommedan would handle tallow, there were some things he would not do. So we had two Mahars, whose duties were to clean out the drains and perform other scavenger work at which both Hindus and Mahommedans draw the line. Mahars are not allowed to enter Hindu temples and by caste Hindus are regarded as outcasts, or pariahs. Nevertheless, they are indispensable and are tolerated by all classes of Indians. Throughout Bombay they are employed as municipal sweepers, navvies and masons. Their condition lies lightly on them; they give the impression of being happy and contented. They exercise reasonable intelligence and accept their low-born estate, eating and drinking apart from the rest of the workers and avoiding too close contact with them.

A very important person in my Indian factory was the barber. Like the Mochi a Hindu barber is of low caste; he has to handle the hair and skin of all castes, both high and low. I allowed a member of this fraternity to erect his shanty in the works compound; for, according to established custom, the men may receive the attentions of the barber during working hours. Each workman contributed a few *annas* monthly. In the intervals of work the shed became a resting and gossiping place where the men surreptitiously drew a few whiffs from a native cigarette as they awaited their turn. Occasionally the shed became full to overflowing, but a stroll in that direction would send the men scattering.

Another person much in evidence about the works was the Mali, or member of the gardener caste. His official occupation was watering the plants about the factory grounds during the dry season and weeding during the monsoon, but actually he spent most of his time in running errands; a Mali is a general factotum. The only real gardening ours did was to grow a few vegetables for his own use in a secluded spot near the well.

The distinctions between these various castes were at first bewildering and I made mistakes—but with mistakes came enlightenment. My Hindu bearer one day requested me to find employment for his brother, an intelligent and good-looking young man. On my return to the works I called Mahadeo and asked if there was a vacancy that this man could fill.

He shook his head. 'Mahrattas will not work with him,' said he; 'his caste is not good.'

I called Cowasji, since Mahadeo, although a good workman and organizer, was illiterate and could seldom give a reason for the caste rules to which he and his men held so rigidly. 'My bearer,' I explained, 'is a caste Hindu and worships the Hindu gods. He is a Sudra as a Mahratta is; yet he is of a lower caste. Why is it?'

'There are many divisions of Sudras,' answered Cowasji. 'These Mahrattas are among the highest; the caste to which your servant belongs is of the lowest. Your Mahratta mill-worker will not become a personal servant of a European since he would have to handle his master's food and clothing. He would consider himself polluted, and his caste fellows would impose punishment upon him. You will notice that the Mahratta workmen will not eat with the Mochi and the barber; they are Sudras also, but of lower castes.'

'This all seems very stupid, Cowasji.'

'It is their caste law, and, even if they were willing to do certain things, the caste to which they belong would not allow it. A high-caste man dare not touch the food or water of one of lower caste or that of an outcast.'

'Who are the outcasts then?'

'Mahommedans, Mahars, Europeans, Parsis—'

'Do they class us on the same level as the sweepers then?'

'Oh, no. They look upon Mahars as pariahs.

Mahars, on the other hand, consider themselves polluted they have to associate with Mangs and similar tribes. Infact a Mahar will be alienated from his own group if he carries one of a higher caste.'

'So this caste idea exists even in outcast tribes.'

'Do not Europeans practise it? They will look upon an Englishwoman who marries one of Indian blood as an outcast.'

Since we were treading on dangerous ground, I hastily changed the subject. On another occasion an even more subtle distinction of caste came to my notice. I found one of my higher end Hindus from the bleaching department washing a towel that had been used by a Parsi assistant. 'Send that man back to his work, mahadeo,' I said, 'and get a coolie to do this job.' He ordered the man away but did not put a coolie in his place. I guessed by his hesitating manner that some caste rule was involved.

When I had a few minutes to spare, I asked Cowasji for an explanation.

'The man who was washing my towel was not a Mahratta but a Pardeshi from Central India. He is like the Dhobi, or washerman caste. The Dhobi who washes your clothes is of the same caste. He is a caste Hindu, not of so high a caste as your Mahratta coolies; the difference is so slight that they will work with him in the bleaching department. But a coolie such as you inducted Mahadeo to send would not touch the towel belonging to me, because I had used it for my body and in their eyes I am an outcast.'

'I thought all the Mahrattas employed in the bleaching department were of the Dhobi caste by virtue of their work.'

'In a way you are right; that is, they will wash and bleach cloth that has come direct from the loom, but, when it has been used by one who is not of their caste, it would mean pollution to wash it.'

'How many Pardeshis of this caste have we working in the bleaching department?'

'One only.'

'I see you have made provision to get your bits of washing done.'

He laughed but did not deny it. It was the custom, since the works was owned by Parsis, to allow the few Parsi employees a certain amount of time off to say their prayers. A small room was set apart for the purpose. I was not supposed to enter it, but I believe a bath and other conveniences had been installed there; for a large number of towels gave occupation to the Pardeshi Dhobi.

Water is a divider of castes, and, wherever it is used, as in the bleaching and dyeing departments, there is a greater risk of caste contamination. In

Hindu-owned mills where Brahman clerks are employed a separate source of water may be provided for them; if a well is available, so much the better. But generally speaking all castes will now use piped water, content to rinse the tap and allow a little to run before using it. In the handling of water, however, there is no compromise. If a non-Hindu, or a Hindu of lower caste, puts his hands into water where a Mahratta coolie is working, there will be trouble. This was why my men insisted that only one caste should be employed to work in the bleaching department. Though I tried often to reason with Mahadeo about this matter, he had no explanation to give; it was a caste rule that must be obeyed.

The fastidiousness of caste Hindus extended to eating and the ritual purification preceding it. In some respects their practices promoted better health. My Mahrattas were extravagant with water. I had several taps in the compound, and they were needed. Before meals the workers washed out their mouths and bathed their hands and feet, and they repeated the same operations afterward. They were careful to clean the brass vessels which contained their food and from which they drank, using for this purpose, however, the mud of the road, regardless of its filth. Curry with rice was the principal food of the mill-workers, though the Ghaties, a hill caste of Mahrattas, often brought *chapatis,* a kind of flat cakes baked on a hot stone.

I have many times been asked whether it is true that, if the shadow of a European or any outcast crosses the food of a Hindu while he is eating, he will throw his food away. My men generally took their food where a shadow could not pass or reach them—in a shed, beneath a high wall or in some corner. On odd occasions, however, their position was not so secure.

'Sir,' said Cowasji to me one day, 'Rama, the calender man, has thrown his food away—your shadow crossed it as he was eating.'

'Are you sure?' I asked in surprise.

'Mahadeo says so,' answered Cowasji diplomatically. I sent for Mahadeo. 'What is this I hear about my shadow crossing Rama's food?' I inquired.

It does not matter. Sahib did not know. It was Rama's fault; he should have had his food with the other men.'

'And has he thrown his food away?'

'Yes, sahib.'

'And he will have nothing to eat until night?'

'The men gave him something.'

'Where bad feeling prevails, an incident like this can create a disturbance, but it is excused where there is certainty that no offense is meant.

My Hindu workmen send their wives, sisters and mothers to toil in the works; I had more than hundred women there. All but a few pardeshis and two old Mommedans were Mahrattas. These soft-eyed, barefoot women impressed me at first as being too frail for hard manual labour. Shrinking

GANPATI, THE ELEPHANT-HEADED GOD, HERE AWAITS THE FESTIVAL PROCESSION THAT WILL CARRY HIM, WITH THOUSANDS OF OTHER SMALL GANPATIS, TO BE GLORIOUSLY CAST INTO THE SEA.

creatures they seemed, pressing their eyes and faces to the ground as I passed them. They were employed principally in folding towels; for I had a huge towel department. To keep the women in order and to regulate thier work, it was necessary for me to appoint a woman; so for some time I watched them at thier tasks and finally I made choice of a Mahratta widow named Dhundi, who appeared to be an intelligent worker and manifested considerable spirit. I was amazed to see how speedily she had her department in control; for arranging the work for more than a hundred girls was no light task. One of my many duties was to examine each girl as she left at the end of the day's work. At first I was a little reluctant to adopt this custom, which is universal in the works in Bombay, but I quickly saw the need of it, since a great deal of cloth may find its way outside beneath an innocent-looking *sari.*

Some managers claim that they have nothing but trouble with woman workers, an understandable state affairs in works where the hands number thousands. Much of the mischief arises from the jealousy and intrigue that are ever present in an Indian works. My forewoman's greatest difficulty arose from jealousy. A foreman in the warehouse lorded it over her and for a time secretly got control of a number of the women, taking advantage of its being in a Hindu woman's nature to obey a man rather than a woman. The settling of disputes of this sort is one of the most difficult tasks the European has to face. The intriguing employee may have such a following that he can defy the manager, particularly when labour happens to be scarce.

In the rare instances when my workwomen had to be reprimanded I left the task with Dhundi. There were times when a languor in the department made it necessary to stir the women into activity. All I needed to do was to say sarcastically to Dhundi, '*Asty, asty jao*'—'Go slowly.' She understood my meaning, and in a short time they would all be in full swing. On such occasions I suspected fast-days, and I was generally right. After working the greater portion of a day without touching food, the women grew weary.

About small matters they were very excitable and talkative. Disturbances often would occur among them, usually when I had gone off to my bungalow for tea or luncheon. Once on my return from tiffin I experienced something of a shock to find all the women standing in the works compound, gesticulating and making no end of a noise.

'What's to do, Dhundi?' I asked; for she was among them and looked as incensed as the rest. I felt sure something serious had happened.

'So-and-so'—one of my assistants—'has beaten Sita and broken one of her gold earrings,' she almost shrieked. 'Sahib does not beat us, and *he* must not beat us. We will all go home unless sahib punishes him.'

The women were in high dudgeon. However, settling disputes comes in a day's work; the matter was finally smoothed over, so that they went back to their tasks.

'Look, sahib!' Dhundi cried, on another occasion, dragging a woman forward out of an excited group and pointing to a red betel-nut stain on her sari. 'Lukshman has spit on her. Does he think he can defile us?'

'All of you set back to work, and I will see about the matter,' I said.

'Nay, sahib. Lukshman must be sent home. Are we to be treated like pariahs? Have we no caste?'

'Come to my office and let us hear what he has to say.'

They followed me, and Lukshman was brought forward, looking very crestfallen amid the shrill execrations of the women. They all talked at once in the way Mahrattas do when anything excites them.

'Silence!' I cried. 'What have you to say for yourself, Lukshman?'

'I was going upstairs, sahib, and spit over the banister. The spittle accidentally fell on Radha, who was passing.'

'Have you no eyes?' shouted one girl.

'I did not do this thing purposely. Am I not of their caste? Do I not know it means defilement?'

Gradually quieting down, the women finally agreed that, since it was an accident, they would go to work again if Lukshman apologized. There was a caste principle involved in this act; the touch of saliva renders anything impure in the eyes of Hindus.

My workwomen were a valuable help to me in my study of Mahratta customs. Their many ceremonies constituted the only break in their monotonous existence. Whenever a group of them appeared at work wearing all their jewellery and their silk saris, I knew something was afoot—a caste tea, perhaps, a feast to the dead or the celebration of some event in family life, such as a betrothal or a daughter's arrival at womanhood. Dhundi might bring them down to my office later and say, 'Sahib, all the married women want two hours' leave to go to the temple to pray for their husbands,' or, 'All the widows want to go to offer puja to their dead husbands.' Some of the women once went to offer sacrifice to the seven sages, or *rishis,* for forgiveness of sins they had committed. They did not tell me so, but I found out. One could not keep account of the many ceremonies demanding the absence of certain sections of the women.

There are times when these numerous and complicated caste practices make one wonder if mill life has effected any change in the Hindu mill workers. Brief consideration, and the decision will be that it has. One recognizes that their traditional beliefs have changed little, but efforts have been made to adjust these strange old philosophies to conditions obtaining in modern factory life. When performing factory duties, the Hindu quickly falls into the routine of things and masters practical details with a clear and rational understanding of what he is about. But the mysterious movements of the machinery raise a formidable barrier. Every Hindu workman worships his means of livelihood—a weaver his loom; a writer his pen; a tailor his needle and scissors; a farmer his tools. A barber touches his forehead with the back of his razor as an act of worship each time he shaves a man. Surely, a works with its strange devices must also be under the influence of a presiding deity.

Practical evidence of animistic belief was seen every morning when the work-people touched the steps with their fingers and then touched their foreheads as they entered the factory. Moreover, they felt certain that malevolent spirits had their abode in the individual machines. They solved the problem of propitiating the deities and spirits that, so they believed, controlled the destinies of the factory by an imposing annual festival, known as the Surya-Narayan-puja. It is celebrated at all factories in Bombay where Hindus are employed.

CHAPTER 25

What GI's Learned in India

Norman Kiell

WHILE SERVING IN INDIA I WAS prompted by a growing concern for the mutual ignorance that exists between Indians and Americans, to embark upon an inquiry of how American personnel there felt about India and how much they had absorbed of the country.

A few months after I had arrived in the country, it became evident to me that Americans stationed there were almost unanimously indifferent to India and her problems.

It was also true that Indians rarely went out of their way to develop American friendships. Not unless the soldier sought such contact and pursued it, did understanding jell. Indian hospitality seldom found its way to Americans for a variety of reasons, of course. Now 250,000 Americans are carrying home a tale of a sordid, illiterate, depressed country without having the opportunity to tell a different story. Each of these men has at least ten friends to whom he is going to relate, if he hasn't already done so, a dreadful story of India. Thus, two and a half million Americans are going to have or already have, a vastly distorted picture of India, given them by 'authoritative' eyewitnesses, whose words and opinions their equally impressionable friends and relatives have no reason to doubt.

⋆*ASIA AND THE AMERICAS*, May 1946. Norman Kiell was Public Relations specialist with the US Air Force in India during the World War II.

One of the questions I asked was, 'Have you met any Indians other than those with whom you worked?' Americans generally met only four types of Indians: the coolies, the merchants, the Anglo-Indian stenographers and the beggars. It is significant to note that nearly two-thirds of the Americans had never met any Indians socially.

For this poll, I interviewed 100 men and women at random, out of a possible 15,000 who were waiting for ships to take them back to their homes. These interviews occurred between February 14 and 24—in other words, from a few days to two weeks after the riots occurred in Calcutta. Unfortunately, at the height of the mob violence, a truck convoy carrying 3,000 homeward-bound American troops to the *S.S. Marine Angel* was attacked and stoned by irresponsible elements of the Indian community. Several GI's were wounded, one seriously enough to be taken to the hospital. The reaction of the soldiers was immediate and ominous. Feelings ran dangerously high. The GI's could not understand why Americans should be attacked.

Thus many interviewees answered 'No' when I asked them if India should have her freedom, because they insisted there were no responsible leadership and the only law would be mob law.

Of the 100 people interviewed, 87 were enlisted men of all ranks, 9 were officers, and 4 were Red Cross women. The group included 9 Negroes, 1 Mexican-American, 1 Japanese-American. All branches of the service were interviewed, from infantry to cavalry, but the Air Force largely predominated.

The typical man of this poll is, then, a buck sergeant, a member of the AAF, had a fairly responsible job in civilian life and has completed his high school education. He is about 28 years old, has had approximately a year and a half in India. With this background in mind, let us see what he thinks and how he feels and what he knows about India.

Question I

The language most commonly spoken is Hindustani. Yet when our typical buck sergeant, who had been in India for eighteen months, was asked, 'About how many words of Hindustani do you speak?' he was only able to reply, 'A dozen, more or less.'

The language barrier was so great that it never was overcome. Even if a foreigner wanted to study Hindustani seriously, he would be handicapped by the lack of an adequate textbook.

Question II

HOW DO YOU TELL THE DIFFERENCE BETWEEN A HINDU AND A MOHAMMEDAN?

By the hair	59
By dress	19
By headdress	13
By food	13
By manner of address	5
By amulets	6
By religious manifestations	6
By racial differences	6
Don't know	27

Question III

DO YOU BELIEVE THAT INDIA SHOULD HAVE HER FREEDOM?

Yes	49
No	24
Eventually, not now	14
Don't know	7
Undecided	5
Don't care	1

'Yes' comments:

Natural right of every nation to be free. . . . While England has control, there will always be trouble. . . . India will never be content unless it is free. They must work for themselves. . . . The argument that India isn't ready is foolish. Every country goes through such a period. Britain has never shown the ability to govern the Indians properly. . . . I don't like to see India pushed around the way the British are doing. There are enough smart Indians to run the country. . . . The British have no right to be in India. . . . India should be allowed to govern her own destiny but she should remain within the British Commonwealth of Nations, like Australia or Canada. . . . Nobody should live like the Indians do. . . . With freedom, the Indians would be more ambitious and do things for themselves. . . .

'No' comments:

India would not know what to do with freedom. . . . The political leaders have no control over the mobs. India is not fit to rule. . . . Indians are not educated enough to maintain a government. . . . Better off under British rule. . . . Not dependable. . . .

India does not want freedom. . . . The Indians need some one to run them. . . . Too much religious strife. . . .

'Eventually, not now' comments:

Must rid herself first of the caste system. . . . India should be put on a probationary period, like the Philippines. . . . Too much internal dissension. . . . They lack unity. If they had freedom now, the unrest would be greater than ever. . . . Too much sectionalism. . . . Needs more education. . . . Right now, they'd run wild. Not ready for it.

'Undecided' comments:

Before I came to India, I'd say yes. Now I don't know. . . . Yes, in order to get rid of the British; no, because they can't band together.

Question IV

DO YOU THINK THE HINDUS AND MUSLIMS CAN WORK TOGETHER AMICABLY?

Yes	49
No	35
Don't know	16

'Yes' comments:

In time, yes. Under the present leadership, no. Gandhi and Jinnah are too extreme in their demands. . . . With right leadership, yes. . . . After a period of turmoil. . . . I foresee a period of civil strife necessary to make possible a national movement. . . . It will take time. Like our Civil War, I believe there will be civil war in India. . . . The US did it. . . . They do now. 'Problems' are largely theoretical. . . . My coolies worked together. . . . Yes, if they were free of England (Opinion of 4). . . . Yes. I have seen it in Calcutta. The British are the troublemakers. . . . If they do away with the caste system. . . . There must be a way, if they tried. . . . They joined forces in the February riots. If it's for a common cause, they will work together. . . .

'No' comments:

Too many castes. . . . They could, but I don't think they will. . . . Religious differences are too dominant. . . . They say themselves they want to be divided. . . . Jinnah says no; and Indians will follow the leaders because they have no initiative. . . . They are at each other's throats. They hate each other more than they do the British. . . . The intellectuals can; the average Indian cannot. . . . Each wants more than the other will give. . . . Each religious group is out to do the other. . . . Too fanatical; they do not trust one another. . . . Not from what I've read in the newspapers. . . . Too much communal conflict, as evidenced in religious processions of either faiths being attacked. . . .

Question V

WHAT DO YOU FEEL IS INDIA'S GREATEST PROBLEM?

Lack of education	25
Religious differences	21
Caste system	10
National disunity	10
Overpopulation	9
Poverty	5
Independence	5
Famine	3
Miscellaneous	8
Don't know	4

Comments:

Mass education needed so that the people can run the country instead of being led by a few religious leaders. . . . Lack of cooperation among themselves. . . . Emotional immaturity. They react very childishly to all problems. . . . A lethargy of national spirit due to years of oppression plus lack of educational system plus serfdom rule under the yoke of British and Raja states.

Question VI

CAN YOU NAME FIVE OF INDIA'S LEADING POLITICAL. FIGURES?

4 were able to name more than 5; 5 were able to name 5; 8 were able to name 4; 18 were able to name 3; 24 were able to name 2; 29 were able to name 1; 12 were unable to name any.

This is the number of votes the leaders polled:

Gandhi	88
Nehru	42
Sarat Chandra Bose	29
Jinnah	24
Mrs. Vijayalakshmi Pandit	7
Lord Wavell	7
Maulana Azad	5

Comments:

Is Nehru leader of the Muslims?

Azad is a Hindu officer, one of Bose's (Subhas) lieutenants.

I think there's a man by the name of Jinnah.

That woman who made a trip to the US, whatever her name is. . . . There's a woman who went to the States for a loan.

Lots of names I can't pronounce.

Is there a person, N-e-h-r-u?

Wavell—He's British, I believe, appointed by the King of England.

Question VII

DO YOU FEEL THAT YOU HAVE HAD AMPLE OPPORTUNITY TO FAMILIARIZE YOURSELF FAIRLY WITH INDIAN PROBLEMS?

Yes	23
Yes, but I did not take advantage of it	12
No	65

Comments:

As much as I wanted. . . . I've discussed them with representatives of all religions who worked under me. . . . It did not take long. . . . Yes, but I had no interest at all in them. . . . Yes, I supervised 55 coolies. . . . I didn't try. . . . No opportunity for access to literature. . . . I've not been able to associate enough with Indians. . . . Just the coolies. . . . I've stayed away from them entirely. . . . Army personnel do not have the opportunity to meet Indians or establish close relations with them. . . . No, because of army restrictions. . . . Nobody in the army can unless he's inquisitive enough to look for it. . . . We were in India for a different purpose. We met only the lower classes. . . . Army life is not conducive to learning a true picture of India. . . . The language barrier was too great. . . . There's so much to India; I've just seen Calcutta. . . . I have not talked with the farmers. . . . Too much control by the British. . . . All I know is from reading biased English newspapers. . . . Didn't have the chance to visit with Indians and get information. . . . None of my business. . . . Can't learn from the people; they don't know; they are concerned primarily with getting enough to eat and clothe themselves. . . .

Question VIII

HAVE YOU MET ANY INDIANS SOCIALLY—OTHER THAN THOSE WITH WHOM YOU WORKED AND OTHER THAN MERCHANTS?

Yes	38
No	62

QUESTION IX

IF INDIA WERE TO GET HER FREEDOM, WHO DO YOU THINK SHOULD GUIDE HER DESTINY?

A representative government, similar to the US	36

Comments:

A party system, based on political reasons, not religious faiths. . . . A coalition group of representative individuals. . . . Nehru should be the first president. . . . Representatives from each class of peoples. . . . Free elections. . . . Democratic government, naturally. . . . People of different religious faiths should have fair representation. . . .

Mahatma Gandhi	2
The Muslims	1
The Hindus	2
The United Nations	4
Jawaharlal Nehru	2
Sarat Chandra Bose	1
Pakistan	2

Pakistan led by Jinnah and Hindustan led by Gandhi.

Dominion Status	1
The United States	2
A Socialist Government	2
A King or a President	1
The Indians themselves have to decide that	3
England should continue to guide her	2
Anglo-Indians	1
Don't care	1
Don't know	36

Question X

DO YOU APPROVE GENERALLY OF BRITISH RULE IN INDIA?

Yes	24
Yes and no	7
No	66

'Yes' comments:

They have given the Indians electricity, sewerage; the Indians have benefited by world trade. The British have vastly improved the country by roads, schools, waterworks, sanitation. . . . The discontent is all because of the Indians themselves. . . . The British have done the best they can but they do not treat the Indians right. . . . The British cannot do any more without the Indians helping them. Politically, Britain has not gone as far as she can. . . . It appears to be a bad case of misrule but it is better than the absence of rule. . . . Britain has made a number of attempts to give India more freedom. Wavell is doing the best he can to find a common meeting ground for Indian political leaders. But the masses are illiterate. . . . The Indians' welfare is the Britishers' welfare. I have not seen the British do anything outlandishly cruel to the Indians. . . . The British are doing as well as any other nation similarly situated. . . . Good rule. . . . Better than the US could do. . . . Yes, because of the caste system. . . . Yes, because the Indians cannot get together. . . . The people are uneducated and hard to get along with. . . . The English keep order in India. . . . If it were not for the British there would be civil war. . . . If it were not for British industrialization, India would never be what it is today. . . .

'No' comments:

The British are milking India dry. . . . They have taken everything out, put little in. . . . Britain is bleeding India to death. . . . The British have enslaved the Indians. They've taken the raw materials out, sent them to England or Australia for manufacture, then returned them to India to be sold. . . . England is interested only in Indians who have capital, not with the people as a whole. . . . England is smart enough to sustain religious animosities and so control the country. . . . The British don't even treat the Indians as human beings. . . . I believe in no country ruling another. . . . No, but the Indians could not have done any better. . . . If the country is any reflection of British rule—no! . . . Similar to the Jews under the Nazis. . . . The British have everything, the Indians nothing. . . . Too domineering and overbearing. . . . Too much repression, cause for riots, hatred. . . . The British policy of abetting the Princes and vice versa is reprehensible. . . . The only thing Britain has done for India is to educate the higher class people. . . . It is obvious that British traditional policy is not to develop the country economically or physically. . . . Education has been repressed. . . .

Don't know:	3

Index